PITT LATIN AMERICAN SERIES

The Origins of the
Peruvian Labor Movement

The Origins of the Peruvian Labor Movement, 1883–1919

PETER BLANCHARD

UNIVERSITY OF PITTSBURGH PRESS

Published by the University of Pittsburgh Press, Pittsburgh, PA 15260
Copyright © 1982, University of Pittsburgh Press
All rights reserved
Feffer and Simons, Inc., London
Manufactured in the United States of America

Library of Congress Cataloging in Publication Data

Blanchard, Peter, 1946–
    The origins of the Peruvian labor movement, 1883-1919.

    (Pitt Latin American series)
    Bibliography: p. 195
    Includes index.
    1. Trade-unions—Peru—History. 2. Strikes and lockouts—Peru—History. I. Title.
II. Series.
HD6642.B55   331.88'0985   81-23102
ISBN 0-8229-3455-8   AACR2

This book has been published with the help of a grant from the Social Science Federation of Canada using funds provided by the Social Sciences and Humanities Research Council of Canada.

To my parents

Contents

	List of Tables **xiii**
	Preface **xv**
	Acknowledgments **xix**
1	The Setting, 1883–1919 **3**
2	The Early Mobilization, 1858–1895 **15**
3	Political Involvement, 1895–1912 **29**
4	The Influence of Anarchism, 1895–1912 **47**
5	The Intensification of Industrial Action, 1895–1912 **65**
6	The Impact of Guillermo Billinghurst, 1912–1914 **84**
7	The First World War **102**
8	Rural Workers in the Labor Movement **120**
9	The Eight-Hour Day, January 1919 **148**
10	And After **160**
	Notes **175**
	Bibliography **195**
	Index **205**

Tables

1 Production of Copper, Sugar, Petroleum, and Cotton, 1900–1920 **6**
2 Value of Principal Exports, 1900–1919 **6**
3 Percentage Share of Peruvian Exports, 1901–1920 **7**
4 Factories in Lima and Callao **9**
5 Employees in the Textile Industry, 1902–1920 **12**
6 Rural Workers in Peru, 1905–1920 **13**
7 Increases in the Cost of Food in Lima, 1897–1906 **50**
8 Wages of Lima and Callao Workers, 1895–1911 **52**
9 Wages in Lima, 1911 **53**
10 Strikes in Callao, August 1895-April 1912 **68**
11 Strikes in Lima, August 1895-April 1912 **74**
12 Daily Wages in Lima and Callao, 1912–1918 **104**
13 Increases in the Cost of Living, 1913–1920 **105**
14 Average Hours of Work and Wages in the Sugar Industry, 1912–1919 **131**
15 Mining Wages in the Department of Junín, 1908–1918 **137**
16 Petroleum Workers' Wages, 1917–1919 **146**

Preface

Between October 1883 and January 1919 the bases of the modern labor movement in Peru were laid. From the Treaty of Ancón which terminated four years of warfare between Peru and Chile, to the government decree establishing the eight-hour work day, Peru's workers developed into an active and influential sector of Peruvian society. By forming organizations, participating in the nation's political life, and engaging in industrial agitation, they revealed a growing class consciousness and an ability to compel both employers and governments to respond to their demands.

This was a notable accomplishment for the workers of a nation not known for the militancy of its laboring population; traditionally, Peru has been viewed as a country dominated by a small oligarchy running affairs in its own interest with little local interference. It was a rural country with a labor force composed mainly of Indian peasants whose influence was considered minimal because of the strict control exercised by employers and isolation from the mainstream of labor developments. Yet, the Peruvian workers were one of the first groups in all Latin America to win the eight-hour day, and they won it before the workers in many industrialized nations with more advanced labor movements. Their success can be seen as a result of Peru's relative political stability and economic growth after 1883 and of the example and influence of workers' movements elsewhere. But the ultimate cause was the Peruvian workers' own struggle, their commitment to change, and their willingness to adopt whatever means were necessary to achieve change.

The time span chosen for this study is somewhat arbitrary, for obviously the roots of the labor movement go much deeper than 1883 and extend at least to the formation of the first mutual aid societies in the 1850s and, perhaps, to the first craft guilds of the colonial period. There is, nevertheless, justification for the later date: the real surge of organization and agitation began after the War of the Pacific, and the movement as such did not become evident until that time.

In the same way, the year 1919 cannot really be said to mark the definitive closing date of the formative period. Most of the patterns that appeared during this period continued unchanged for many years, while other characteristics that might be considered "formative" did not appear until after 1919; yet it was something of a turning point. During that year the Peruvian workers achieved one of their greatest successes, marking the culmination of thirty years of struggle and unquestionably establishing themselves as a force to be reckoned with. Subsequently Peru began to experience a number of new and distinct pressures related to the eleven-year dictatorship of President Augusto Leguía. Historians have described this period beginning in July 1919 as "a new era in the republican history of Peru" and "a major turning point in Peruvian history."[1] It can be set apart from what had gone before by both economic and political factors: American capital now flowed into the country in unprecedented amounts, and the old landed elite had to share more and more power with an emerging urban bourgeoisie; new political parties, particularly the Alianza Popular Revolucionaria Americana (APRA) party of Víctor Raúl Haya de la Torre and, to a lesser extent, the Peruvian Communist party, began to influence national life. All these elements had a profound impact on the lives of the workers and the direction of their movement.

This examination of the Peruvian labor movement does not cover every element of the work force. It concentrates on the workers in the capital, Lima, and its port, Callao, with some space devoted to the workers on the sugar and cotton estates, in the mines and petroleum fields. This focus reflects the importance of these groups, both in terms of their activities in their respective areas and their impact on the general movement. At a more prosaic level, it also reflects the material available. I have ignored workers in other urban centers like Arequipa, Trujillo, and Cuzco, and large sections of the rural population. Where the former are concerned, the available information indicates that their experiences were similar to the Lima trends, but their history remains largely unwritten as does the history of most of the rural workers; when their story becomes known it is conceivable that some of the arguments presented here will have to be revised.

Just as the movements in the provincial centers reflected what was happening in Lima, the movement in Lima reflected what was happening in much of the rest of Latin America. In the late nineteenth and early twentieth centuries the various Latin American countries were experiencing many of the same political, economic, social, and intellectual pressures, and their general development followed much the same pattern. This similarity was true also of the respective labor movements that grew in response to these pressures. Thus, the patterns emerging in Peru were similar to those in Argentina, Brazil, Chile, Mexico, and elsewhere. There were some differences in terms of the timing of developments, which sectors of the work force were most active, the importance of outside pressures, and the impact of European ideologies, but the general trends and experiences bore a striking resemblance.[2]

This is a study of what happened in Peru. It examines the growth of one particular movement and seeks to explain the successes and failures of that movement, with the ultimate aim of clarifying why Peru has had such great difficulty in casting off the restrictive cloak of its past. Specific components of the labor force are examined in terms of their importance to the movement as a whole. Before detailing the growth of a particular group like the railway workers or the textile workers or the careers of particular labor leaders, an understanding of the context in which these groups and individuals were operating was necessary. This remained my primary concern, but with the hope that it might lead to further studies of a more specific nature.

One last point: there will undoubtedly be some disagreement with my use of the term "working class." I realize that all the groups described do not fall into the commonly accepted definition of the term, the most obvious "offenders" being urban artisans who owned shops and employed workers, and certain rural groups who possessed land from which they made a living while simultaneously working for others. However, these groups considered themselves to be part of the working class and were accepted by other workers as part of that class; since this is their story, they should be the ones to decide who comprised their ranks. Moreover, they conform to a definition of class that has emerged from a study of another working class. E. P. Thompson, in his book on the English working class, has written that the members of a class "share the same congeries of interests, social experiences, traditions and value-systems, . . . [and] have a *disposition* to *behave* as a class, to define themselves in their actions and in their consciousness in relation to other groups of people in class ways."[3] This seems to describe rather well the situation in Peru in the late nineteenth and early twentieth centuries.

Acknowledgments

I wish to thank a number of people and institutions without whose assistance I would never have completed this book. Its merits are largely a result of their efforts; the faults that remain are mine alone. The manuscript first took shape as a doctoral thesis under the supervision of Professor John Lynch, now director of the Institute of Latin American Studies, London. He has continued to follow its progress with interest and has frequently provided much appreciated advice. Bill Albert and Rory Miller, two fellow students of Peruvian history, read an early draft of the manuscript and made many useful suggestions for improvements.

No historian can be successful without the assistance of the staffs of libraries and archives. Although my relationship with some of them became a bit strained at times, I owe a debt to those of the Biblioteca Nacional, Archivo del Fuero Agrario, Archivo del Congreso, Cámara de Comercio, ENAFER-Perú, and Pontificia Universidad Católica del Perú in Lima; the municipal library in Arequipa; *La Industria* in Trujillo; the International Institute of Social History in Amsterdam; the Public Record Office, British Museum, University of London Senate House Library, Institute of Historical Research, University College London libraries, Canning House, Guildhall Library, and Balfour Williamson & Co. Ltd. in London; and the University of Toronto libraries in Toronto.

I owe special thanks to Dr. Félix Denegri Luna who allowed me to use his magnificent library in Lima, and to three individuals who provided me with their personal insights into Peruvian developments: Dr. Jorge Basadre, Ronald Gordon, and Víctor Raúl Haya de la Torre.

At different stages I received financial assistance from the Central Research Fund of the University of London, the Bellot Trust Fund of the History Department, University College London, the Canada Council, and the Humanities and Social Sciences Committee of the Research Board of the University of Toronto.

On a more personal level I wish to thank my parents to whom I have dedicated this book. At several times when serious obstacles forced me to consider whether I was making the right decision in pursuing an academic career they supplied much-needed encouragement and support, although they must have had reservations about my chosen field and my particular subject of interest. They did everything in their power to assist me in my goal and I shall always be grateful.

I also want to thank Kenny and Inghild Tejada and two québecoises, Louise Blouin and Solange Lambert, whose generosity, hospitality, and friendship made my visits to Lima, a city that does not rank among my favorites, bearable and often very pleasant.

Finally, I wish to acknowledge the very deep debt that I owe to my wife, Joanna. She has painstakingly read through the manuscript, making a variety of suggestions for improvements in both content and style. More importantly, she has maintained her sense of humor in the face of enormous odds and thereby eased my task immeasurably.

The Origins of the
Peruvian Labor Movement

1 The Setting, 1883–1919

The years between 1883 and 1919, which saw the emergence of the Peruvian labor movement, were a period of change for much of the country. Although the traditional structures remained largely intact, many elements came under attack and were transformed as Peruvians sought to duplicate the developments then being experienced by the wealthier, industrializing nations. Modernization affected all aspects of life—political, social, economic, and cultural—and while it was welcomed by its beneficiaries, it simultaneously produced widespread uncertainties, distress, dislocations, and confrontations. These modernizing trends, both positive and negative, provide the background to the appearance and development of the labor movement.

The post-1883 developments contrasted sharply with what had prevailed during the sixty-two years since independence. Peru's first decades as a republic had been marked by anarchy and chaos as a series of self-seeking military caudillos competed for control of the country. The instability lasted until the 1840s when a mestizo general, Ramón Castilla, assumed the presidency. He managed to establish a degree of order that lasted off and on until his death in 1862. One of the factors assisting Castilla was a growth in exports based on the exploitation of guano. Peru possessed large deposits of this natural fertilizer on the islands off its coast, and the industrializing countries, with their agricultural production expanding to feed growing numbers of factory workers, provided a ready market.

Although the guano boom made little physical impression upon Peru—a few railways were built into the interior, financed by the guano returns—it created a new capitalist class. In the past, the country's elite had been mainly coastal plantation owners and sierra *hacendados* (landowners); now there was a new group of wealthy men, many of whom bought estates along the coast to share in the profits from the expanding sugar and cotton industries. More progressive than the old elite, these

4 The Origins of the Peruvian Labor Movement

nouveaux riches pushed to modernize the country. Their economic interests also drew them into politics, for they wanted to be able to protect their new enterprises. In 1871 a group of these businessmen, who wanted more control over the guano industry and objected to the continuing military domination of the country, formed a political party, the Civilista party. The following year they managed to elect their leader, Manuel Pardo, as Peru's first civilian president.

Unfortunately for Pardo and the Civilistas, the fortunes of the country declined sharply following his election. The returns from guano fell as supplies ran out, and the exploitation of nitrates, guano's successor, led the country to disaster. The nitrates were located in Peru's southern province of Tarapacá and in the neighboring regions of Bolivia. In 1879 a dispute between Chile and Bolivia over the nitrate fields involved Peru as Bolivia's ally and war ensued. At first the Peruvian forces had some success, but gradually the momentum shifted and they suffered a series of humiliating defeats. The country was invaded, Lima was occupied, control of the guano islands was lost for a time, and Tarapacá and the nitrate fields were ceded to Chile forever by the Treaty of Ancón of 1883.[1]

It was in the aftermath of this disaster that Peru began to take on a new appearance. In the political field, military leaders regained control of the country for a time, but they proved ineffective in solving Peru's multitudinous problems and were driven out of power in 1895 by a coalition of civilian forces. This was followed by an unprecented period of "democratic" rule for Peru. Between 1895 and 1919 the ballot box had greater influence than the gun in choosing Peru's leaders. The executive and the two legislative chambers, the Senate and the Chamber of Deputies, were elected more or less according to the constitution, and during those years only one president was removed from office by force.

With the constitution apparently working for the first time, party politics developed. The Civilista party was the most important, and from 1900 it controlled both the executive and the legislative chambers. Opposing the Civilistas was the Democratic party, formed in 1884 by the popular demagogue Nicolás de Piérola. Piérola's reputation was based on his almost legendary attempts to win control of the government by force and his escapes from disaster. His party differed little in ideology from the Civilistas, but because it was the opposition party and because of Piérola's reputation, it tended to attract the support of the masses and even of those with socialist leanings, giving it a more progressive appearance. Allied with the Democrats was the Liberal party, founded in 1901 by another caudillo figure, Augusto Durand. Most of the Liberals' pressure was exerted through the pages of the influential Lima daily, *La Prensa*. The military, too, had their party, rather inappropriately called the Constitutional party, which was founded in 1884 and was the political vehicle of the war hero General Andrés A. Cáceres.

The founding of the parties and the holding of regular elections did not mean that the Peruvian people as a whole were making political decisions. The elite continued to dominate the nation's political life by limiting the suffrage and controlling the electoral mechanisms. The number of voters was small, constituting less than 5 percent of the population, so that elections were easily manipulated. Altering the composition of the Congress was almost impossible since the Congress itself confirmed congressional election results, and the majority party ensured that its members retained their majority.[2] In this situation the influence of the masses was limited. However, because the electoral system seemed to be operating, the various parties sought the support of the masses and offered benefits to win them over. In addition, it appeared that a worker could be elected to office and this, too, attracted the lower classes into participating in the political process.

Following the war with Chile, the economic situation of Peru changed. The loss of the nitrate fields forced the country to establish its economy along different lines. Gone was the dependence on a single export; instead, there was diversification as sugar, cotton, copper, petroleum, wool, and rubber were exploited, mainly for export. Sugar was the primary export during the period before 1920, but copper and cotton came close behind, especially during the years of the First World War when the demand for raw materials rose to unprecedented levels (see tables 1, 2, and 3).

The main beneficiaries of this expansion in the primary producing sector of the economy were a number of Peruvian and foreign entrepreneurs. Both Peruvians and foreigners were involved in the production of almost every commodity, but in general Peruvians tended to concentrate in the area of agricultural production, while foreign firms were more evident in the mining and petroleum industries.[3]

Peru's economy was not entirely export oriented. Beginning in the 1890s and lasting approximately a decade, something of a boom occurred in the industrial sector. Previously the number of factories had been small. Most of the country's manufactures had been produced in small artisan shops, a few factories specializing in goods like pasta, cottonseed oil, beer, cocaine, chocolate, and textiles, and rural sugar and rice mills. This situation changed in the 1890s as the number of public utilities,

Table 1: Production of Copper, Sugar, Petroleum, and Cotton, 1900–1920

	Copper (tons)	Sugar (000 tons)	Petroleum (000 barrels)	Cotton (tons)
1900	9,865	140	289	—
1901	11,414	135	295	9,611
1902	9,096	—	243	8,524
1903	9,497	153	281	9,651
1904	9,504	157	293	9,882
1905	12,213	162	376	10,765/12,061
1906	13,474	169	536	12,637
1907	20,482	141	758	14,484
1908	19,854	157	953	18,719
1909	20,068	158	1,424	23,805
1910	27,374	172	1,270	—
1911	27,735	179	1,478	—
1912	26,969	188	1,768	—
1913	27,776	179	2,070	—
1914	27,090	223	1,854	—
1915	34,727	258	2,603	—
1916	43,078	271	2,617	27,426
1917	45,176	248	2,627	27,125
1918	44,414	283	2,536	30,687
1919	39,230	282	2,639	33,558
1920	32,981	314	2,825	38,396

Sources: Flores Galindo, *Los Mineros de la Cerro de Pasco 1900–1930*, table 4, p. 35; Thorp and Bertram, *Peru 1890–1977: Growth and Policy in an Open Economy*, table 5.2, p. 76, table A.2.3, p. 340.

Table 2: Value of Principal Exports, 1900–1919 (in Peruvian pounds)

	Cotton	Sugar & Derivatives	Hides	Wool	Petroleum & Derivatives	Copper
1900	326,074	1,455,813	108,559	296,673	185	621,065
1913	1,420,230	1,412,665	193,809	516,891	910,259	2,010,618
1914	1,405,220	2,640,952	182,068	507,591	888,672	1,682,817
1915	1,260,477	2,976,605	159,954	598,392	1,143,977	3,372,187
1916	1,722,805	3,978,779	327,186	938,075	1,387,778	5,942,263
1917	2,878,515	4,111,463	322,858	1,711,734	1,182,051	6,250,738
1918	3,760,812	4,162,595	170,447	2,704,612	1,415,383	5,866,014
1919	6,635,782	8,314,321	624,466	1,631,664	2,320,319	4,920,449

Source: Basadre and Ferrero, *La Cámara de Comercio de Lima*, p. 107.
Note: 1 Peruvian pound or libra = 10 soles.

Table 3: Percentage Share of Peruvian Exports, 1901–1920

	Sugar	Cotton	Rubber	Wool	Oil	Copper
1901	24	9	—	6	—	22
1902	33	8	10	6	—	8
1903	27	8	11	11	1	7
1904	25	7	16	8	—	9
1905	32	7	16	8	—	10
1906	25	8	17	9	—	14
1907	14	8	17	7	1	31
1908	19	15	11	5	2	22
1909	18	19	17	6	2	19
1910	20	14	18	7	2	13
1911	20	14	8	5	5	22
1912	15	11	14	4	8	25
1913	15	16	9	6	10	22
1914	30	16	5	6	10	19
1915	26	11	5	5	10	29
1916	24	10	4	6	8	36
1917	22	15	3	9	6	34
1918	21	19	2	14	7	29
1919	31	25	2	6	9	18
1920	42	30	1	2	5	12

Source: Albert, *An Essay on the Peruvian Sugar Industry 1880–1920,* table 10b, p. 30a.

financial institutions, and factories in Peru, and particularly in Lima, increased. The expansion was partly a response to the country's relative political stability, especially after 1895. Also, the situation was propitious for the local investment of profits from the copper, sugar, and cotton industries, so that some of the expansion was locally financed. Moreover, Peru was once again an attractive area for foreign investment. With the signing of the Grace Contract in 1889, the country's foreign debt was canceled in return for concessions to Peru's foreign bondholders, a group subsequently incorporated into the British-based "Peruvian Corporation."[4]

The industrial expansion of the 1890s included "four cotton, two woolen, and one or two knitting mills; several sugar *centrales* [mills] and cottonseed-oil mills; mechanized tobacco factories and ice plants; machine-equipped lumber mills and furniture factories; a few big flour mills and numerous spaghetti factories, foundries and more breweries and wineries; mechanized soap and candle factories; additional shirt factories; a hat factory, a match factory, and a few cocaine factories; a modernized plant or two for pottery and tile; [and] perhaps a few bottling plants for soft drinks." At the same time, some of the existing firms were expanded. The industrial growth slowed around 1905 in response to a recession in the United States and the greater attraction of the expanding export sector to foreign and local investors. Nevertheless, the number of factories continued to grow: from 264 in 1902, to 291 in 1905, and 505 in 1918.[5]

Most of the industrial development occurred in Lima and its port of Callao. Statistics are scarce and contradictory, so there is no accurate picture of the factory growth, but there is an indication of the types of factories established and a sense of industrial expansion. Joaquín Capelo, in *Sociología de Lima*, claimed that there were 69 factories in Lima in 1890. A more limited survey in 1907 listed 56 firms in both Lima and Callao, and a 1920 survey arrived at a total of 244 industrial establishments in the province of Lima.[6] The majority of these produced nondurable consumer goods, mainly food and clothing (see table 4).

The number of factories could be supplemented by artisan shops. There were hundreds of these—in 1903, for example, there were 730 in Lima alone—and although some were being replaced by the new factories, they continued to be an important adjunct to the industrial sector.[7]

The leading manufacturing sector in Peru during this period was the textile industry. By 1920 there were fifteen major textile mills in Peru, nine of which were located in the Lima area. They included seven cotton mills: Vitarte (established in 1873), San Jacinto (1897), La Victoria (1898), El Progreso (1901), La Providencia (1902, later called El Inca), La Bellota (1913), and La Unión (1918); and two woolen mills: Santa Catalina (1889) and El Pacífico (1918). The mills were mainly a result of English, American, and Italian investment and entrepreneurship, and nationals of these countries monopolized the managerial and technical positions. There was some Peruvian involvement. Santa Catalina was financed by and later taken over by José María Peña Costa and Mariano Ignacio Prado; Prado was also one of the owners of San Jacinto. La Victoria was owned by another prominent Peruvian family, the Pardos.[8]

The changes in the economy had repercussions in the social sphere. The traditional social culture with its tiny elite and large lower class remained basically intact, but new groups were emerging and threatening the stability of this structure. Measures had to be taken to meet their demands without weakening the position of the upper class, which was already in a state of transition because of the guano boom and experienced

Table 4: Factories in Lima and Callao

	Lima[a] 1890	Lima & Callao[b] 1902	Lima & Callao[c] 1907	Province of Lima[d] 1920	Lima & Callao[d] 1920	Lima & Callao[e] 1920
Cigarettes	5	6	3	—	—	—
Furniture	17	2	2	17	—	—
Biscuits &	1	1	1	—	}14	2
chocolates	—	—	4	11		7
Lumber yards	4	4	4	5	—	—
Brooms	3	2	1	7	—	2
Spaghetti	3	6	—	6	4	6
Soap &	7	}7	}4	18	22	}12
candles	—			5	8	
Liquor	6	4	1	8	9	5
Breweries	4	3	2	2	3	4
Paper	—	1	—	1	—	1
Soda	4	—	—	—	—	1
Glass	1	1	—	1	—	2
Ice	2	—	—	4	—	1
Cottonseed oil	1	1	1	3	8	4
Gas	1	—	—	1	—	1
Electricity	1	—	—	1	—	—
Textiles	1	6	8	9	8	8
Matches	1	2	1	—	1	1
Hats	—	2	1	10	2	—
Soft drinks	—	3	1	8	16	13
Foundries	—	6	2	9	—	—
Tanneries	—	6	3	19	15	—
Bricks &	—	—	}3	}6	—	1
mosaics	—	—			—	4
Printing	—	—	6	5	—	—
Flour mills	—	10	8	5	5	2
Shirts	—	9	—	13	—	—
Shoes	—	2	—	5	6	—
Wax	—	4	—	3	—	1

Sources: a. Capelo, *Sociología de Lima*, 1:128; b. Perú, Ministerio de Fomento, *Reseña Industrial del Perú*, pp. 22–37; c. Cámara de Diputados, *Accidentes del Trabajo*, pp. xlvii–xlviii; d. Jiménez, "Estadística Industrial del Perú," pp. xxviii–xxxiv, 14 passim; e. Perú, Ministerio de Hacienda, *Resumen del Censo de las Provincias de Lima y Callao*, tables 4, 5, 6. (I have included only those factories that have been specifically listed as such.)

Note: These figures refer to different geographical regions and were collected by individuals with different definitions of "factory," so they are not really comparable.

further changes following the war with Chile. Possession of land remained a key criterion for upper-class membership, but with the expansion of the urban centers and urban-related enterprises such as banking, insurance, utilities, and manufacturing, it became common for the elite to be involved in both urban and rural activities and, in some cases, to devote themselves entirely to urban concerns. Families like the Pardos, who owned the Tumán sugar plantation and La Victoria cotton mill, and the Prados, with their textile mills, electricity company, and banking interests, were typical of this trend. Many had close ties with foreign capitalists, especially with exporting firms like Duncan Fox, W. R. Grace, and Graham Rowe, some of which, in turn, became local landholders.[9] The expanding economic interests of the elite required political protection, so control of the government by their party, the Civilista party, became a primary concern.[10]

Below the elite was a small middle group. It might best be defined in a negative way: those not able to claim membership in the upper class, but who did not see themselves as members of the lower class. Their links tended to be with the upper classes as they adopted the social, economic, and political values of those above them. They were predominantly an urban group, many of them immigrants, and their total number small. Within the urban centers they may have constituted a significant percentage of the population since membership included managers and some owners of the new industrial and financial concerns, master craftsmen, military officers, intellectuals, public employees, small businessmen, shop owners, teachers, technicians, and other professionals. It has been estimated by Capelo that in 1890, 40,000 of Lima's 108,340 inhabitants could be lumped into the middle class. However, their impact was limited, and other writers claim that it was not until the second decade of the twentieth century that the middle class emerged as a distinct social element with particular aims and interests.[11]

The mass of the population was at the bottom of the social ladder. This was not a monolithic or united group but, in general, its members supplied the labor, services and, in some cases, tribute that maintained the elite in its position of power. They toiled on the sierra haciendas, cultivated sugar and cotton on the coastal plantations, extracted copper from the sierra mines, tapped rubber trees in the *selva* (jungle), and drilled for oil on the northern coast. In the urban centers they worked in the factories, mills, and shops, on the docks, construction sites, and railways, and in various other occupations. Many individuals who owned their own little piece of land or small business belonged to this group.

Indians from the sierra and the jungle were contracted or even forced to work in the mines, on the coastal plantations, or in the rubber forests. In the towns artisans often had their own shops and aspired to middle-class status, but their style of life differed little from that of wage earners because their earnings were so low.

It is almost impossible to calculate the size of these three sectors of the population. Even for the total population we have only estimates since there was no national census between 1876 and 1940. According to the 1876 census, there were 2,699,106 people in Peru. An 1896 survey calculated that the population had reached 4,609,999 but this figure seems somewhat inflated because later estimates reckoned the population to be much smaller. According to a 1908 survey, the number had grown to 3,547,829, and another in 1920 arrived at a figure of 4,862,000. The distribution of the population remained more or less constant with two-thirds of the people living in the sierra and the rest in the coastal river valleys and scattered throughout the vast expanse of the eastern selva.[12]

Statistics for the urban population are somewhat better, but only for the most important centers of Lima and Callao. According to the 1876 census, Lima's population stood at 100,156. It increased very slowly as a result of the war, to 103,956 in 1891, but then grew more rapidly, reaching 140,884 in 1908 and 223,807 in 1920. Callao's population fell from 33,502 in 1876 to 28,932 in 1898, but then rose to 34,436 in 1905 and 52,843 in 1920. The other major urban centers of Arequipa, Cuzco, and Trujillo had much smaller populations. In 1908 they were estimated to be 35,000, 18,500 and 10,000 respectively.[13]

For the present study, it would be useful to have figures for the number of urban dwellers who were workers. Some statistics for Lima and Callao do exist but are, unfortunately, of limited value. Municipal censuses were taken in 1905, 1908, and 1920, and attempts were made to divide the population into professions. However, workers and employers seem to have been lumped together in the various categories; there was such a broad definition of factory workers that the category included most artisans as well as others, such as laundry workers and barbers; and there was a large number of people listed as unemployed or vagrants who may have been workers temporarily without jobs. Nevertheless, the figures provide a general idea of the size of the urban laboring population.

The censuses of 1876, 1905, 1908, and 1920 list most of the workers and artisans of Lima and Callao under the heading "Industries and Manual Arts." For Lima, the number grew from 9,548 in 1876 to 23,879 in 1908 and 44,327 in 1920. For Callao, the number rose from 4,111 in 1905 to 8,426 in 1920.[14] Attempts have also been made to calculate the factory labor force; Capelo estimated that Lima's factory workers totaled 6,000 in 1890, with an additional 16,000 artisans. This estimate seems somewhat high if compared with the above census figures. Other, later figures also raise questions about the reliability of Capelo's estimate. A 1907 survey of factories, mills, foundries, printing firms, sawmills, and breweries in Lima and Callao found only 4,404 workers. The 1920 municipal census listed 13,197 men, women, and children employed in the factories of Lima, although many of these "factories" would more properly be described as artisan shops. There were an additional 778 factory workers in the rest of the province of Lima and 2,183 in Callao.[15]

In the important textile industry the number of employees, including masters and workers, rose from 1,250 in 1902 to 3,835 in 1918. Table 5 gives a further breakdown of this particular sector of the work force thoughout Peru.

The figures are not precise, but they give some idea of the numbers of workers involved and their growing importance within the urban population: in Lima the proportion of workers and artisans rose from 9.5 percent of the population in 1876 to 16.9 in 1908 and 19.8 in 1920. In Callao the increase was from 11.9 percent in 1905 to 15.9 in 1920. It was in part because of their numbers that the workers of Lima and Callao became the most important element of the labor movement that emerged after 1883. Their residence in the capital meant that they had access to the centers of political power and to the leaders of the nation who could be influenced by their agitation. In the capital they were also in contact with foreigners and foreign ideas, newspapers and periodicals that reported on national and international events, and intellectuals and academics who commented on these ideas and events, all of which had an impact on the local workers.

Table 5: Employees in the Textile Industry, 1902–1920
(Lima figures in brackets)

	Cotton Mills		Woolen Mills	
1902	850	—	400	[400]
1905	1,000	—	480	[330]
1918	3,100	[2,586]	735	[370]
1920	—	[2,393]	—	[599]

Sources: Thorp and Bertram, "Industrialization in an Open Economy," table III.11, p. 71; Yepes del Castillo, *Perú 1820–1920: Un siglo de desarrollo capitalista*, p. 171; Jiménez, "Estadística Industrial del Perú," p. 13; Ministerio de Hacienda, *Resumen del Censo de las Provincias de Lima y Callao,* tables 4 & 5, pp. 266–77, 286–93.

In the rural sector the number of workers was much greater than in the cities (see table 6). They were concentrated in certain parts of the country—on the plantations, in the mines, and in the oil fields—and they, too, could be an important force if mobilized. The problem was that various obstacles hindered mobilization and thereby delayed the formation of a rural labor movement. Among these were the composition of the labor force itself, the employers' control over the workers, the support provided the employers by the government, and the isolation and distance from the more dynamic urban sectors of the labor force.

Isolation remained a constant problem and frustrated not only the creation of a national labor movement but the unity of the country as a whole. Fortunately for the workers and for Peru, the isolation was gradually being eroded by roads and railways built into the interior. In 1893 the Central Railway was completed from Lima and Callao to La Oroya, linking what was to become the primary mining region with the coast. In 1909 it was extended to the important sierra market town of Huancayo. The Southern Railway was finished in 1908, joining the port of Mollendo to Cuzco via Peru's second city, Arequipa, and the town of Puno on Lake

Table 6: Rural Workers in Peru, 1905–1920

	Mine Workers (including petroleum workers)	Sugar Workers			Cotton Workers	
		Field		Mill		
		Men	Women		Men	Women
1905	9,651	—	—	—	—	—
1906	13,361	—	—	—	—	—
1907	14,877	—	—	—	—	—
1908	15,652	—	—	—	—	—
1909	15,000	—	—	—	—	—
1910	16,500	—	—	—	—	—
1911	17,000	—	—	—	—	—
1912	18,610	19,296	649	—	—	—
1913	19,515	20,393	549	—	—	—
1914	20,335	21,154	727	—	—	—
1915	21,480	19,782	855	3,796	18,120	2,394
1916	22,759	18,576	990	3,890	19,368	2,998
1917	23,738	18,233	1,053	3,549	25,063	2,295
1918	21,310	19,437	1,229	4,415	29,139	2,908
1919	22,000	20,971	1,284	4,241	31,965	4,182
1920	22,500	22,900	1,120	4,840	—	—

Sources: Jiménez, "Estadística Minera del Perú en 1921," p. 156; Perú, Ministerio de Hacienda y Comercio, *Extracto Estadístico del Perú, 1926*, pp. 106, 113.

Titicaca. Other, smaller railways were being constructed from Peru's lesser ports along the coast to the local centers, and these ports in turn were linked to Callao by steamships running up and down the coast.

Because of the improvements in transportation and communication, goods, people, and ideas could now move about the country more easily than ever before. This is not to say that all parts of the country were linked by an effective network of roads, railways, and steamships: much of the country was still isolated and self-sufficient and has remained so to the present day. But there was now some communication between those areas producing primary and manufactured goods, and this allowed contacts between the respective workers. This communication was to play an important role in the mobilization of the rural workers and to assist in the creation of a stronger and more influential labor movement.

2 The Early Mobilization, 1858–1895

The mobilization of Peru's workers began in the late 1850s with the formation of mutual aid societies and the outbreak of labor agitation. Both were primarily a response to the economic conditions of the time. The chaos resulting from the War of the Pacific produced an added incentive to both organization and agitation, prompting the formation of larger societies with wider objectives and the occurrence of more frequent and more violent strikes. As a result, by 1895 when the military, who had ruled Peru since the war, were driven from power, significant sections of the labor force in Lima and Callao had experienced some initial mobilization and were becoming aware of their potential strength.

The mutual aid societies that appeared in Peru in the mid-nineteenth century were heirs to an older form of workers organization, the artisan guild. Guilds had been established during the colonial period, and many survived into the republic. Formed to protect the interests of the artisans, they issued rules and regulations concerning such things as quality of work and apprenticeship and occasionally got involved in politics to try to influence the level of duties on their products and cost of trade licenses. In addition, they pressed for legislation to grant freedom of trade, industry, and labor. Other forms of workers organizations—confraternities and workers brotherhoods—were also active at this time; they were church-directed groups composed of artisans and seem to have served primarily a social function.[1]

These early organizations were still in existence at mid-century when mutual aid societies began to appear. The first was the Sociedad Democrática del Callao (Democratic Society of Callao), formed in 1858.[2] Two years later a group of Lima artisans, including the master tailor Juan Antonio Zubiaga, established the capital's first mutual aid society, the Sociedad Artesanos de Auxilios Mutuos (Artisans' Mutual Aid Society). Subsequently, several societies were formed in Lima and Callao, and as the interest in mutual aid spread to the surrounding towns, societies also appeared in Cuzco and Arequipa.[3]

The establishment of the societies occurred at a time when workers throughout the world were forming organizations ranging from friendly societies, similar to Peru's mutual aid societies, to early trade unions. The reasons were often the same regardless of locale: industrialization, the emergence of an industrial proletariat, and growing concern about workers' rights. In Peru the industrial sector was expanding; by 1876 there were factories in Lima and Callao producing a variety of nondurable consumer goods, as well as a foundry, four breweries, and a textile mill.[4] They were challenging the artisans' traditional monopoly over manufacturing and causing them to join the mutual aid societies, which offered some degree of protection in addition to other benefits. The societies incorporated masters, workers, apprentices, and their families. They offered, in return for small weekly or monthly dues, financial aid to members who were sick or unable to work and, in some instances, to those who were unemployed. If a member died, they contributed to the funeral costs.[5] The societies also attracted members by promoting adult education and industrial exhibits, awarding prizes, and publishing newspapers.

After the war with Chile (1879–1883), the number of mutual aid societies grew more rapidly as the hardships produced by the war aroused increased workers' interest in their benefits. The situation was desperate. Commerce had been almost completely paralyzed during the war, cutting off imports and exports. The entirety of the coast and even parts of the interior were invaded and pillaged by the Chileans, so that in 1883 much of the country lay in ruins. The coastal sugar industry had been all but destroyed, the guano islands had fallen under Chilean control, and the Tarapacá nitrate fields were lost forever. Moreover, Peru was bankrupt, the national banks had gone into liquidation, and the internal debt had risen to alarming proportions. The money supply was increasingly problematic as specie was scarce and the paper bills printed to replace it quickly depreciated in value, reflecting the lack of popular confidence.

The political situation was equally desperate. Fighting continued after the war as General Andrés A. Cáceres, who had carried out a guerrilla campaign in the interior against the Chileans, refused to accept either the peace treaty or the Chilean-backed government of General Miguel Iglesias. Civil war resulted, lasting until December 1885 when Cáceres invaded Lima and forced Iglesias to resign. There were also many local uprisings as bandits and groups of *montoneros* (rural guerrillas) took advantage of the instability and lack of local authorities. In the sierra, Indian villagers tried to regain lands they had lost in the past by attacking hacendados and capturing remote haciendas. In some areas these attacks threatened to explode into rebellions or racial warfare.

In Lima, conditions mirrored the national catastrophe. Fierce battles had been fought in the environs of the city in 1881; the city had been occupied until 1884, parts of it looted, and the people suffered greatly. Many of the men had died in the fighting so that at war's end women outnumbered men. The economic privations of the period reduced many of the survivors to a state of penury. Few had money, and the depreciation of the paper bills reduced buying power still further. A "moral degradation" had set in with the defeat. Marriages were rare and prostitution rife.[6]

For Lima's working population the situation was particularly critical. H. M. Brent, the acting American consul in Callao, reported at the end of the war that the employment picture was bleak with jobs almost unobtainable. Few of the importing houses were hiring workers since they could not find a market for their goods; this was typical of the labor situation as a whole. With unemployment high, workers were accepting jobs where they could at wages amounting to one-half or even one-third of what they had been five years earlier. Women looking for work could find it only in private homes as domestic servants, although a few had found jobs in the Santa Clara cotton-cloth factory. Artisans, too, were suffering because of the "general stagnation of business, the lack of capital, and the disinclination of those with capital to grant credit or accommodation." The lack of money and depreciation of the paper bills meant that the laborers of the city had little for food and housing. Their diet was restricted to rice, beans, fish, and potatoes, with sometimes a little pork or beef. Housing took the form of a couple of rooms in long alleyways or *callejones,* which were inexpensive but usually unsanitary and overcrowded. Brent concluded, "At this moment in Peru, ninety-nine out of a hundred of the classes alluded to live literally from hand to mouth, and this is emphatically proven by a ramble through the streets of Lima, and the spectacle of the countless pawnbrokers' shops and places for the purchase of old furniture and household goods that have come into existence since the war, and that are crowded to the roofs by the accumulation of such objects sold at a ruinous sacrifice by the people to whom I refer."[7]

It was in response to this situation that the number of mutual aid societies grew. They ranged from the general, attracting members from all walks of life, to the specific, restricting membership to those of a particular profession like hat makers or bakery workers. Outside Lima the situation was the same, as centers like Arequipa, Trujillo, Cerro de Pasco, Tarma, and Zorritos had their mutual aid societies. In Arequipa the church played a prominent part; the most influential of the local societies there was the Circulo de Obreros Católicos (Circle of Catholic Workers), formed in 1896. Elsewhere the church's influence was less noticeable.[8]

In Lima the success of these organizations in meeting their members' needs stimulated interest in a larger, more influential body to represent not merely the artisans but the entire working class. Wider representation would ensure greater influence and supply more money for benefits. The continuing economic difficulties provided additional pressure and eventually led to the formation of the Confederación de Artesanos "Unión Universal" (Artisans' Confederation "Universal Union") in 1891.

The Confederación was not a new organization. It had been founded originally in 1871 as the Sociedad Republicana de la "Unión Universal" de Artesanos (Republican Society of the "Universal Union" of Artisans). Apparently it did not prosper for it was reorganized at least once before the war, and there were plans to reorganize it again after 1883 with a broader mandate. The reorganization was directed by a blacksmith, Manuel Gomez, assisted by a number of prominent Lima artisans including two carpenters, Manuel S. Valcarcel and Julio César, two shoemakers, Manuel Bolívar and Adrian Zubiaga, and a machinist, Juan Grieve.[9] On May 30, 1886, a group of 166 artisans met to lay the foundations for the reorganized Sociedad de Artesanos de la "Unión Universal" (Artisans' Society of the "Universal Union"), as it was then called, and Gomez was named its first president.[10]

The reorganized society was a federation of separate guilds. Existing guilds could join, as could individuals who would be organized into guilds or more general societies. Each federated group retained its separate and independent identity, had its own executive, and made its own decisions concerning its own affairs. Decisions on subjects of common interest were made by a central executive which had been elected by the executives of the federated guilds. The society's working capital came from subscriptions, donations, dues, rentals on buildings and rooms that it owned, benefits, raffles, and the sale of handicrafts. While dedicated primarily to mutualist activities, it also adopted some progressive social goals. Its general aims were to bring the working class together and make every Peruvian worker a worthy and moral individual at home, a conscientious citizen of the republic, and an effective and healthy participant in the nation's economic development. This was to be achieved by educating members and their families, assisting the unemployed, defending members' legal rights, mediating between members and their employers in disputes, and working for the moral and material well-being of the society and its members and of the working class in general. It was not to be a militant organization. Like other mutual aid societies, it was to avoid all political and religious entanglements. Individual members were free to express their own political and religious beliefs, but the executive was expressly forbidden from participating in any religious or political act, either directly or indirectly, since the society embraced "workers of different nationalities, creeds, and beliefs."[11]

The society grew rapidly. In July 1888, 3,000 members attended a dedication ceremony for a new headquarters. By 1891, when the decision about the name had finally settled on the Confederación de Artesanos "Unión Universal," there were eleven member-guilds: tailors, carpenters, shoemakers, cigarette makers, painters, mechanics and blacksmiths, masons, plumbers and gasfitters, bakery workers, millers, and typographical workers. Other groups such as jewelers, barbers, and textile workers joined or were formed subsequently. As this list indicates, although the Confederación claimed to represent the entire working class, it was from the beginning primarily an artisan organization, and artisans tended to dominate its executive.[12]

From the beginning the Confederación was also a conservative organization. During its early years this was expected, for the primary concern then was to establish a sound base. Therefore, it scrupulously avoided drawing attention to itself. It restricted its activities to organizing workers and ventured into the outside world only to display its patriotism. In 1890 it proposed that the national guard form a special corps of sappers from the Confederación's members, and in 1894 when war with Ecuador seemed likely, it agreed to contribute towards the acquisition of a warship. The refusal to get involved bore fruit: the Confederación gained a reputation for respectability, and in July 1892 the provincial council of Lima awarded it a silver medal for promoting the association of the working class. The following year its president, Julio César, was appointed to Lima's municipal board of eminent citizens which administered the city's communal lands. This was the first time an artisan had occupied such a post in the municipality.[13]

Yet, despite the conservatism of the Confederación and the other workers societies, their appearance attracted official concern, an indication perhaps of their growing influence, for their activities hardly merited such attention. Lima's authorities tried to establish control by demanding the right to approve the societies' executives. In 1884 the subprefect of Lima commented that his intention in naming the executives of the coachmakers' and carters' guilds was to put individuals in charge who were responsible to him, for he felt that groups of this sort had "to be watched constantly."[14] The prefect of Lima tried another approach. In August 1886 he introduced a decree that compelled all artisans and rural and urban workers in the department to register with the local authorities and carry identity cards. The cards were to contain all information pertinent to the individual's work and had to be presented on demand. Any worker who failed to do so or any employer who hired a worker without a card or already employed elsewhere would be subject to fines.

The decree aroused immediate worker opposition. The typographical workers protested that it infringed the constitutional guarantees of personal and industrial freedom since it compelled workers to obtain official approval for any change of job. They argued that a worker had the right to find a job wherever he wished without interference. They also objected to the identity cards because they cost twenty centavos, which they viewed as a form of taxation. And if they worked for an employer whose name was not on the card, they would be considered vagrants.

The prefect defended his decree by pointing out that there were growing numbers of unemployed, vagrants, and drunks in the city; there had been repeated protests about mistreatment and lack of compliance with obligations by both workers and employers; and there had been rumors of strikes since the beginning of the year, and recent disorders had occurred in a pasta factory. He felt he no longer could merely throw the recalcitrant in jail, but that some other method of control was necessary. This required improved information about the conditions of the workers, which could best be obtained by registration. However, his argument received little support when the dispute went to the Supreme Court of Lima. The attorney general felt that the decree would not fulfill the prefect's aims, called its restrictive elements "odious," and then vetoed it.[15]

More important to the officials' concern was a second element in the development of the labor movement that, unlike the societies' activities, posed a more obvious threat to public order: strikes had begun to occur. As the prefect noted, they were occurring with increasing frequency and involving larger numbers of workers. It is possible that the authorities saw a link between the commencement of the strikes and the appearance of the societies and thought that by controlling one, they could limit the other.

Labor agitation seems to have been something new for Peru. Details of the prewar period are scanty, and the one available source mentions only two significant confrontations during these years: in 1858 artisans in Lima and Callao rioted against a government decree permitting the importation of wooden doors, windows, and mouldings, which threatened the livelihood of local carpenters, and in 1872 men who had been hired to tear down Lima's old city walls went on strike for higher pay.[16] Other evidence suggests that labor unrest was more widespread than this. The Callao harbor workers went on strike for more pay in June 1877 and again in July 1881 during the Chilean occupation. That same year more than one hundred workers in Lima's Cohen cigarette factory went on strike for a wage increase.[17] Moreover, the outbreak of agitation at the end of the war, although largely tied to the economic conditions of the time, suggests some previous militancy and strike experience.

The main cause of popular discontent during the decade following the war was the stagnant economy and, in particular, the unstable currency. Depreciation of the paper bills increased as President Cáceres began removing them from circulation. In early 1887 the *Panama Star & Herald* reported that the police and army had not been paid because the customs revenue in Peru, from which the government derived most of its income, was almost nil. As for the people, they were "commencing to murmur. There is little or no work for them—and owing to the constant depreciation of the paper money, the main circulating medium, prices of all articles in that currency have steadily risen out of all proportion to the scanty wages paid." Commerce was suffering so that the shipping, port, and railway companies, as well as some factories, were releasing workers. Other companies had closed completely, and the number of urban unemployed grew daily.[18]

Loss of confidence accompanied the depreciation of the bills. Lima's market vendors and bakeries began insisting upon payment in silver. Subsequent discussions between the bakers and the municipal government over the price of bread was a factor in the formation of the bakery workers society, the Sociedad "Estrella del Perú" ("Star of Peru"), in April 1887. It included both bakery owners and workers and became a federated society of the Confederación de Artesanos.

Other sectors of the work force were more militant. In September 1886 some of Lima's shoemakers went on strike, demanding a wage increase and payment of their wages in silver. The following year workers in the tram repair shops declared a strike because of the deteriorated state of the bills used to pay them; the company explained that this was the only money it had. And in October 1887 most of the city's carriage drivers struck to demand a wage increase to fifty soles per month—in silver—as well as other improvements including sick pay, job guarantees, and the removal of fines. Like earlier strikers, they had little success, for the company merely hired new drivers.[19]

By the end of 1887 the financial situation was critical. The steady depreciation meant that one silver sol, which before the war had been equal in value to one paper sol, was now officially worth twenty-five paper soles and up to thirty-three in the streets. In the shops, ten-sol notes were being discounted by two and three soles. In November the value of the bills plunged still further when the government decreed that it would no longer accept them for taxes, stamps, duties, or any other official charges. This led to violent demonstrations as merchants, artisans, and workers who still held bills took to the streets of Lima on December 14 and 15 and clashed with troops. In an attempt to calm the population Cáceres agreed to meet representatives of the artisans. Instead of offering a solution, he blamed the workers for the recent disturbances and insisted that the societies convince their members to accept the bills since this was the only way to restore public confidence in them. Nevertheless, the next day he issued a new decree that increased the amount of import duties, paid in silver, from 5 to 10 percent. This undercut confidence further, and the workers demanded the complete withdrawal of the bills.[20]

Agitation also continued. Lima's postmen went on strike demanding that their wages be paid in silver, but after two days agreed to accept half in silver and half in notes. The workers on the Caudivilla estate near Lima refused to work when offered bills and returned only when they were offered silver. In the south, at Ica, shop owners accepted small bills while bakeries refused even these and sold bread only to customers with silver. In the north, at Trujillo, shop owners refused all bills and raised the price of bread and meat, triggering off demonstrations on January 1 and 2, 1888. In the neighboring town of Laredo, rioters looted Chinese shops and killed three owners who tried to defend their property. In the sierra, bills were not circulating for fear that the government might withdraw them. At Cerro de Pasco, local hacienda and mine workers rioted in December after the bills with which they were paid were refused by shop owners. Two thousand mine workers then went on strike, demanding to be paid in silver.[21]

As the bills were gradually withdrawn, the financial crisis eased and tension subsided. However, the workers' situation did not improve, and continuing economic problems quickly eroded any unity that the mutual aid societies might have established between the workers and their employers. In 1892 a decline in the price of silver led to new increases in prices and a new round of labor unrest as three groups of workers demanded better wages. Lima's typographical workers went on strike in June after their demands for a 50 percent increase were refused. Few workers participated, however, and those who did were replaced from the city's large pool of unemployed.[22]

A more serious and prolonged confrontation involved the bakery workers. Like bakery workers elsewhere, they exercised some influence because of their control over the production of an essential food item. But the Lima workers had the added experience of having agitated together with their employers against past increases in the price of imported flour and wheat and the benefit of an effective society in the "Estrella del Perú." In August 1892 the "Estrella" sought a 40 percent increase in the existing wage of 1.40 soles per day. The bakeries refused and received wide support with their argument that such an increase would raise the price of bread. *El Comercio* commented, "The present moment is most inauspicious for demands of this sort since every industry is threatened by the general decline and the entire country is living in poverty; furthermore, the situation is aggravated by an epidemic [of influenza] that has made it impossible for many people to make a living." The mayor described the workers' request as "unfounded and inopportune" and asked that they wait a month in view of the present unfavorable circumstances. The workers agreed to wait until September 1, but when the date passed with no agreement, they went on strike. Like the typographical workers, only a portion of the work force participated, but they began threatening the nonstrikers. The mayor warned the "Estrella's" president that he and the rest of the executive would be held responsible if any disorders resulted. The workers were not yet willing to risk this type of confrontation; the threats stopped, and the strike failed.[23]

The third group of Lima workers to strike for better wages had some influence because of their numbers. These were the cigarette workers, twenty-five hundred men and women employed in twelve factories of which the principal Lima companies were Cohen, Roldán, Juan Duany, and Oliva Hermanos. Paid on a piece-work, or *tarea* basis, the majority earned little—in 1890 an average day's work in this manual industry earned eight centavos for producing 3,000 cigarettes—and they had a history of unrest. In January 1888, because of the economic difficulties of that period, there had been a short strike resulting in a wage increase. Two years later, a demand by Roldán workers for a 50 percent increase produced a more serious strike that lasted a record eighteen days and marked the first time that the Confederación de Artesanos intervened in a strike to support financially one of its federated guilds. The strike failed, but Roldán later increased wages to one sol per tarea.[24]

The steady inflation produced demands for further increases, and in May 1892 Roldán's workers went on strike again, this time for 1.50 soles per tarea. At first the strike seemed to have little hope of success. Lima's other cigarette workers refused to get involved, and the owners threatened to close the factory rather than increase wages. They began replacing the strikers with apprentices, and the strike appeared to be over. Then, without warning, on May 25 the workers and apprentices laid down their tools and marched out of the factory, smashing work benches and windows as they left. They proceeded to the Oliva Hermanos factory where they won the support of their fellow workers, and the two groups then converged on the Duany factory where they won additional support. Workers who refused to participate were assaulted, and police had to be called in to end the disturbance.

The events revealed the potential strength of the workers but, at the same time, indicated some of the weaknesses that were common to all the workers' agitation at this time. Both leadership and unity were lacking; few of the Duany workers supported the strike for long. Nevertheless, it lasted until June 18 when the strikers accepted a 20 percent increase. Whether this was implemented is unclear, for in September 1894 the Oliva workers were only receiving eighty centavos per tarea while the Roldán workers were earning one sol. Rumors that the latter's wages were to be reduced to the Oliva level produced a new march on the Oliva factory to convince the workers to ask for more. This time, however, the police were prepared and quickly halted the demonstration.[25]

While the decline in wages was the principal reason behind the rise in workers' militancy in Lima, the cigarette workers were affected by an additional factor. Plans were afoot to mechanize the industry, which would eliminate many of the twenty-five hundred jobs. In January 1893 the government allowed Francisco García Calderón, a local businessman, to import cigarette-making machinery from Argentina. The cigarette-workers guild appealed to the government and to the municipality for a revocation of the concession, claiming it was illegal because it would deprive members of their livelihood. Four hundred workers meeting with the mayor argued:

> This concession . . . will result in the death of the manual cigarette manufacturing industry and thereby condemn thousands of workers to lose their means of subsistence and, perhaps, because of hunger

and want, to be transformed from honorable artisans to criminals and worse; it will force honorable women who now work themselves or depend on the work of their husbands to become prostitutes; it will condemn the elderly parents of those who cannot find work to become dependent on public charity; and, finally, it will pervert with innumerable vices children who have been abandoned, thereby preventing them from becoming honorable citizens charged with the defense of the homeland and its integrity. Instead, they will become corrupt vagrants who are an obscene leprosy on society and an affront to honorable men.

The workers also approached García Calderón to see if he would reconsider his plans. He was under some pressure from the government, which faced the task of having to relocate the workers and had presented their petition to the attorney general for comment. García Calderón argued that his plans were completely legal and proper, but he decided it might be politic to meet the workers' wishes; he postponed his plans.[26]

The manual industry was saved, but it was only a temporary reprieve, and everyone knew that mechanization was inevitable. When that happened, the number of cigarette workers would be reduced and so, it seemed, would their influence.

The economic difficulties affecting Peru during the decade after the War of the Pacific also produced labor unrest in Callao. The port had a sizeable work force employed in several industrial establishments including a brewery, a soap and candle factory, a cocaine factory, two foundries, a printing firm, and a gas company, as well as various artisan shops.[27] Between 1883 and 1895, many of these workers went on strike for better wages, although usually without success. More successful were Callao's railway and port workers. Their control over the flow of Peru's imports and exports gave them a great deal of bargaining power and caused the government to pay much closer attention to their demands than to those of other groups. The government also got involved because in both cases the employers were foreign companies: the Central Railway was operated after 1890 by the British Peruvian Corporation, while the docks were run by the French Muelle y Dársena Companía. Workers of the two companies had been involved in the postwar agitation and were at the center of Callao's most serious strikes in the early 1890s.

Trouble began among the Central Railway workers in May 1892 following a change in the pay system from fortnightly to monthly. The telegraph operators demanded that wages be increased by 15 percent, and when three of them were fired the rest went on strike. At first their chances of success seemed minimal for new workers were hired to replace the strikers and service was not greatly affected. However, other sectors of the work force began to lend support, demanding the reinstatement of the three operators. Three hundred workers from the Peruvian Corporation's Guadalupe foundry joined the strike. They, too, were upset by the change in the pay system which, they claimed, made it very difficult for those with families to budget effectively. In addition, they resented the treatment they had received in the past from the company's superintendent. The disruption of service and the refusal of the corporation to make any concessions drew a number of government officials including the president into the negotiations. The workers failed to win an increase, but eventually the company agreed to pay them every ten days and to rehire all those who had been fired during the strike.[28]

In the eyes of the government the most important workers in Callao were the harbor workers whose importance was indicated by the existence of a register designed to ensure an adequate supply of workers for loading and unloading ships. The register also benefited the workers by establishing a kind of closed shop for their unskilled labor; registered workers were guaranteed a certain amount of work since dock and shipping companies had to employ them before hiring any others. The register, however, did not guarantee adequate wages and, like port workers elsewhere, those in Callao became known for their militancy. In 1894 they twice managed to close the docks in attempts to get better pay.

The trouble began following the introduction of a new wage scale that reduced the rates for unloading coal, charcoal, and general merchandise. In February the workers went on strike for their old wages, but returned when the prefect explained that the higher rates had been set during better economic conditions and could not be expected now. The dissatisfaction remained, and in July the coal handlers struck after the company reneged on an agreement to pay a full day's wages whether the worker completed nine hours or not. Again the prefect intervened and suggested a return to the old rate of 2.40 soles for unloading coal, a forty-centavo increase on the new rate. The workers agreed, but the company refused and the strike continued. Attempts to use ships' crews to handle the coal then in port were forcefully resisted by the strikers whose ranks were growing as other elements of the harbor work force joined them. The disruption of all harbor activities drew the ministers of finance and foreign affairs into the negotiations, and with their participation the company agreed to reinstitute the old rates for the time being if the government issued a new official wage scale.

Although the strike had ended, tension remained high because there was still no agreement on the system of payment for a day's work. The workers insisted that they receive a day's pay whether they completed a full day or not, while the company wanted to divide the work day into three parts and pay only for each completed third. Also, there were rumors that the company planned to reduce the register from the present four hundred or more workers to two hundred because of lack of work. The tension erupted into violence in September when the government issued its wage scale that reduced wages even further, despite the recommendations of the workers. A strike followed, paralyzing the docks. Only a small amount of cargo was unloaded, and attempts to hire new workers failed when the strikers openly threatened the strikebreakers. After eleven days the workers were successful; the government reintroduced the old scale. The dock company now agreed because it was allowed to pass the increase on to the shipping companies in the form of higher handling fees.[29]

The strikes in Callao once more indicated the growing militancy of certain sectors of the Peruvian labor force. The intervention of government indicated its growing concern, especially when the economy was affected. In the case of the harbor workers' strike, there was an added political reason for government intervention. Peru was again split by civil war (1894–95), and the government could not afford a long strike that would deprive it of duties on which it was financially dependent. At the same time, it wanted to avoid alienating any sector of the population, particularly the dock company, a possible source of loans. Therefore, an agreement that satisfied both workers and management by passing the increases on to the foreign shipping companies was a politically astute move.[30]

The civil war marked the culmination of postwar dissatisfaction with military rule. The generals had proved unequal to the task of reestablishing Peru's economic stability, yet they seemed unwilling to permit a return to civilian rule. At the end of his term in 1890, President Cáceres chose Colonel Remigio Morales Bermúdez as his successor, expecting the favor to be returned in four years.[31] When Morales Bermúdez died unexpectedly in April 1894, shortly before the balloting, Cáceres staged a coup rather than trust the election to the civilian first vice-president and turned the government over to the second vice-president, another military man, who ensured Cáceres's reelection. This blatant manipulation of the electoral system sparked off antigovernment rebellions throughout the country. By October the rebels had united behind the Democratic party chief, Nicolás de Piérola, who had been the principal source of opposition to the military during the past decade. The Civilistas, who originally had backed Cáceres in the hope that he would solve Peru's economic problems, temporarily set aside their long-standing differences with Piérola and joined the rebellion. Fighting spread as support for the "coalitionist" forces grew. Cáceres alienated many of his remaining supporters by resorting to forced loans and impressing workers into the army. As a result, when Piérola invaded Lima in March 1895 he received assistance from the local inhabitants, many of whom were killed in the two days of fighting that brought an end to military rule.[32]

Piérola's success marked a turning point in Peruvian history and a new stage in the development of the labor movement. Civilian rule had been reestablished, and in the aftermath of victory there was widespread enthusiasm for "democracy" and electoral politics. There were plans to liberalize the nation's political system to allow wider popular participation. This reflected both Piérola's traditional ties with the lower classes as well as his recognition of the political debts he had incurred during the "revolution." He sought to repay these debts by offering "free" elections for president and for the legislative chambers.

It was an offer that appealed to Lima's workers. They had matured since the uncertain days following the war with Chile. Their growing unity was evident from their formation of societies and their participation in strikes. A labor elite had emerged with the reorganization of the Confederación de Artesanos that claimed leadership over the entire working class. The mutual aid societies were conservative entities, but they laid the bases for their more militant successors. They incorporated artisans and workers and claimed to represent the interests of both groups. They provided the early organizational experiences for many workers, and some of these societies eventually were transformed into more militant organizations.[33]

Despite this favorable beginning, the labor movement was still at an early stage. The workers lacked unity, identifiable leaders, and specific goals; their agitation was spontaneous and usually unsuccessful; and their influence was limited. The miserable state of their working and living conditions meant that they would continue to form societies and agitate. Moreover, Piérola's offer of free elections presented a new means of seeking improvements. Involvement in the nation's political life became a possibility, and beginning in 1895 the labor movement in Peru branched out in this new direction.

3 Political Involvement, 1895–1912

Like workers elsewhere in Latin America, Peru's labor force realized at an early date that involvement in the nation's political life could prove beneficial in obtaining needed improvements. Lima's artisans led the way in 1895 by participating in congressional and municipal elections. Success in their first attempt to elect representatives to public office increased enthusiasm and ensured continuing participation. Political contacts were promoted by growing demands for labor legislation, and successful passage of a law convinced even more workers that political involvement was essential to their future well-being.

But political involvement also had its negative side. The success of one candidate aroused the political ambitions of others, producing divisions within the working class that hindered the development of a united movement. Thus, while politics provided the workers with identifiable leaders to promote their interests at the centers of power and a new means of extending their influence, it also created serious problems that eventually caused many of them to look elsewhere for leadership and assistance.

Before 1895 Lima's workers had participated infrequently in the nation's political life. The control of the electoral apparatus by the elite and the military had not provided much of an incentive for involvement. During the presidency of Manuel Pardo (1872–1876), Lima's artisans had displayed some political interest, and at least two had been elected to the Chamber of Deputies. This had not been an organized political movement by the workers, and their political influence remained, according to one postwar observer, "insignificant" as they obeyed the orders and followed the views of "some personal favorite." Although some contacts occurred—Piérola and the Democrats enjoyed worker support while individual guilds or societies were known to participate in a campaign or political demonstration—for the most part the workers and the Confederación, their main society, remained apolitical.[1]

The situation changed dramatically in 1895 with Cáceres's overthrow and Piérola's promise of free elections. The workers would still look to the president for improvements, but their recent experiences—especially their participation in Cáceres's defeat—convinced them that they had to get more closely involved in the nation's political life. A letter signed by a group of artisans commented that failing to participate would be "criminal, for we have an obligation to defend our political rights that in the past have almost always been ignored, but now will earn the same respect that democratic countries show their producers and workers."[2] Their goal became the election of one of their number to political office.

They faced some problems: most notably, they lacked an organization to lead the political campaign. The obvious body, the Confederación de Artesanos, refused to get involved. In April, when the press reported that it was going to participate in a demonstration organized by the Democrats to honor Piérola, the executive replied that the federated guilds with party ties were free to fulfill their political obligations, but the Confederación intended to respect its statutes, which strictly prohibited involvement in political functions. The vacuum was filled in May when a group of artisans, many of them members of the Confederación and most of them supporters of Piérola, formed the Club de Artesanos y Obreros Unidos (United Artisans and Workers Club) to organize the city's workers for the congressional election. They agreed to nominate a candidate and a substitute for the Chamber of Deputies, plus candidates and substitutes for Lima's provincial council whose election was to follow in October.[3]

One thousand workers attended the nomination meeting on June 23. They were welcomed by the club's president, José Ramón Sánchez, who spoke of the hopes that the election had aroused. He concluded, "The disappointments suffered by Lima's working class, which consistently has had its hopes for improvements and prosperity crushed and been fed deceitful promises every time its valuable assistance was sought, plus the understanding that the workers have acquired of their political rights, have made us realize the need to unite the various groups to participate in the general election so that a worker will occupy a seat in Congress and represent our interests." From a list of fourteen nominees the workers chose a twenty-seven-year-old tailor, Rosendo Vidaurre, to be their congressional candidate. Sánchez was chosen as the substitute, and Leonidas Romero, a carpenter, Manuel Aduvire, a book binder, Félix Gutierrez, a glazier, and Manuel Bolívar were the council nominees, with Julio César, the president of the Confederación, and Horacio La Rosa, a typesetter, the substitutes. The meeting concluded with a march to the

Plaza de Armas where the participants applauded Piérola enthusiastically.[4]

Vidaurre's background is unknown. He had been a member of the tailors' guild executive when it joined the Confederación in 1888, and he was a secretary of the latter organization at the time of his nomination. The Democrats also chose him as a candidate, possibly to satisfy Piérola's promise to the masses, and since they dominated the ruling coalition, Vidaurre's success was assured. On August 10 the electoral college, after naming Piérola president, confirmed Vidaurre's election as one of the deputies from Lima.

There is little doubt that Vidaurre owed his success to his political affiliation. Yet it is also true that he owed his original nomination to the workers, and this created a special relationship. Although he was not the first artisan to sit in the Chamber of Deputies, his tie with the workers and their role in his election were unique. He became known as the "workers' deputy," and he expressed his determination to fulfill the obligations that the title entailed. In doing so he cemented the link between the workers and the political system and, thus, was a key factor in the workers' burgeoning interest in political action.

Following his election Vidaurre was still something of an unknown quantity, and one of his first tasks was to establish his credentials as a leading force in the labor movement. He did this by becoming involved in several worker-oriented activities, the first of which was the organization of a congress for workers from the province of Lima. The initiative for the congress came from a new organization, the Centro Nacional de Obreros (Workers National Center), and one of its leaders, Pedro Wolls, but Vidaurre and the Confederación soon assumed a leading role. Vidaurre was named to preside over the congress, and he set up a suggestion box in his shop for workers to submit proposals on its content and functions. The organizers eventually decided that the congress's general aim was to bring together representatives of the province's workers and artisans, owners of factories, presidents of workers societies, and the workers' elected representatives to discuss in a series of fifteen meetings a variety of topics ranging from protection of national industries, construction of workers' houses, and judicial reforms to workers' unity, maximum hours of work and minimum wage rates, and labor legislation.

When the congress opened on August 9, 1896, the topics discussed were more specific than the earlier suggestions. They covered the liberation of the provinces of Tacna and Arica, the cost of cemetery niches, the tobacco monopoly, direct and universal suffrage, a compulsory weekly day of rest, the isolation of Asian immigrants to prevent the spread of their "contagious vices," Sunday openings of the National Library for the benefit of the workers, night schools and gymnasia, rules of apprenticeship, working conditions for women, and the organization of a National Guard. There was even a proposal to reduce the workday to eight hours. At the second session, on August 16, José M. Guevara proposed that the workday last from seven to ten in the morning and noon to five in the afternoon. There is no indication what prompted the proposal, whether it was Guevara's response to a strictly local concern or whether he was influenced by workers from countries where the eight-hour day had become a primary goal. Whatever the reason, Guevara's proposal was not approved, and it was rarely mentioned in the subsequent struggle for the eight-hour day.

The rejection of the eight-hour day was typical of the congress. It was not a radical gathering, but rather followed the moderate and conciliatory line favored by the mutual aid societies. Indicative of this was a presentation relating to strikes that described them as a danger to public order and "pernicious and immoral," except when justified. Everyone had to act to prevent them: employers must set an adequate wage, and workers must not demand more than they deserved. When there was disagreement between the two, the best solution was arbitration, not agitation.[5]

This lack of militancy may account for the congress's limited impact on the development of the labor movement; it was rarely cited as a source of goals later set by the workers, although many of them were first discussed here. Yet, there were some positive results. The actions at the congress revealed the growing awareness of the workers as they gathered to discuss common concerns, and workers' unity was promoted. Most importantly, it established Rosendo Vidaurre's credentials as a leader of the working class.

Vidaurre strengthened his position by taking other initiatives on the workers' behalf. He pressed for the creation of a tribunal to settle disputes between workers and employers, and for a law to provide indemnities for workers who had been injured on the job and support for the families of workers who had been killed. This was part of a general labor code he introduced in 1903, designed to protect workers in factories and mines by limiting hours of work to ten for men, seven for women, and six for children. In addition, he wanted payment of wages in coupons and firing without justification or warning prohibited.[6] In neither case was he successful, but his demand for a law granting indemnities was part of a growing debate that eventually produced a law.

More frequently, Vidaurre's activities and recommendations were designed to assist the Confederación or one of its federated societies to whom he was more directly obligated. Shortly after his election he promised that he would "never do anything in the chamber except what the artisans directed him to do," and his subsequent initiatives bore out his pledge. He obtained a state-owned building for the Confederación as a new headquarters in 1896, and in 1902 he lobbied the Senate to grant the organization a subsidy of 1,000 soles that had already been approved by the Chamber of Deputies. To assist the federated societies, Vidaurre pushed for laws altering the duties on manufactured goods in order to stimulate the industries concerned.[7]

Another initiative focused on the cigarette workers and lasted several years. The industry was still facing the threat of mechanization, and in November 1895 Vidaurre introduced an amendment to a bill designed to reduce the export duty on cigarettes. He asked that this reduction be applied only to handmade cigarettes as mechanization had to be halted; in Europe it had produced the twin "evils" of socialism and anarchism, which were ruining the Old World. His intervention helped to delay mechanization once again, but the position of the workers remained uncertain. During 1899 many were laid off following an increase in the tax on tobacco that left the owners with insufficient funds to pay both the new tax on their existing stocks and wages. Vidaurre managed to obtain 260 soles from Piérola for some of the unemployed workers and later secured removal of the new tax. However, the end of the manual industry was in sight. In 1903, after the opening of cigarette factories in other parts of the country, the Lima owners decided that it was time to mechanize if they wished to remain competitive. Machinery was imported from Europe, and the factories began releasing their workers, who in turn appealed to the government for a tax on machine-made cigarettes and protection for their jobs, but without success. Facing the inevitable, they began looking for new jobs. Fortunately for them, this was a period of industrial expansion; alternative work was available, and the end of the manual industry occurred peacefully.[8]

Vidaurre also tried to establish closer ties between the Confederación de Artesanos and the government. The society already had a reputation for patriotism and government support that now became more pronounced. In the late 1890s it participated in projects promoted by both

Piérola and Vidaurre to colonize the still largely uninhabited selva. It formed a colonization society that, with the financial assistance of the government, sponsored a group of one hundred colonists who set out for the selva in May 1896. More directly supportive of the government were the frequent declarations of loyalty, prompted by the numerous antigovernment rebellions that marked Piérola's presidency. In 1899 following one in Iquitos, Piérola thanked the workers for their latest expression of support, concluding, "Many pusillanimous individuals have thought . . . that the attitude of the workers in forming societies could result in socialist movements; I am deeply gratified to note that, on the contrary, they try to ensure the continuation of peace."[9]

While strengthening its ties with the government, the Confederación continued to expand its influence among the workers by pursuing its normal activities of providing mutual aid benefits and acting as a social body, sponsoring picnics, dances, raffles, bull fights, and the like. To justify its claim that it represented the entire working class, it established relations with workers societies in all parts of Peru, opened a night school for workers, published a newspaper, *El Artesano*, which Vidaurre directed, and played a more active part in labor disputes. It also lent its weight to wider questions affecting the workers, like inflation and Asian immigration. In 1898 during a period of rising food prices the Confederación as the "representative of the working class" wrote to the mayor of Lima pointing to the lack of jobs and money and requesting that the municipality become involved in the sale of food in order to reduce prices. Because of the many markups between producers and sellers, prices in some instances had doubled. In 1906, following the importation of large numbers of Asian contract laborers for the coastal estates, the Confederación appealed to President Pardo to halt this migration which, it claimed, was ruining the nation. The society charged that the Asians were impregnated with "vices and physical defects too numerous to mention" and were competing for jobs, thereby threatening both "the improvement of the national race and its future prosperity."[10]

With Vidaurre and the Confederación leading the way, workers in Lima and elsewhere continued to be attracted to mutualism. The increasing size of the work force provided a further stimulus to their growth so that by 1911 there were sixty-two societies in Lima alone, each with an average of two hundred members.[11] Of these the Confederación remained the most important, but early in the twentieth century it began to face competition from another organization, the Asamblea de Sociedades Unidas (Assembly of United Societies). The Asamblea was not a new society: it was founded in 1891, but only rose to prominence in 1901. It was a product of the workers' interest in larger societies and initially formed as a loose directing body of twenty-five societies that included the Confederación. Like the Confederación, it remained a federation of societies whose main concerns were mutual aid and social activities; in 1907 it claimed forty-nine constituent societies with four thousand members.[12] It attracted large numbers of artisans together with individuals from middle sector groups like lawyers, teachers, and other professionals, but it claimed to represent the workers and like the Confederación tried to help them by obtaining lower food prices, establishing educational facilities, and providing assistance to strikers. Like the Confederación it was a moderate body that favored conciliation over confrontation. This became apparent early in its history, during the national workers congress it organized in 1901 to celebrate the new century and to establish its own credentials.

The 1901 congress imitated the earlier provincial congress, but at a national level. Delegates were invited from throughout the country to discuss many of the same topics as their predecessors. Sessions began on January 12 and were dominated by the large number of employers in attendance who initially refused to admit that Peru had any social problems. After three months of discussions the delegates were finally willing to accept that workers were engaged in a "desperate struggle for life," but their only solution—and the only concrete recommendation of the congress—was to control the price of foodstuffs and prosecute cheaters.[13]

Denying the existence of social problems at home, the Asamblea also rejected the more progressive ideas about labor mobilization then current in Europe. In 1911 one of its vice-presidents asserted, "Fortunately, our young American democracies are still uncontaminated by these truly diseased philosophies; and even when mad reformers have tried to introduce their confused theories, our culture has rejected them, for we know that there can be no social problems among us since there are no social classes, property is accessible to all, our laws consecrate every freedom, and our genuinely democratic institutions have erased the frontiers of race and genealogical distinctions by viewing everyone as elements of society and free and equal citizens."[14]

With this affinity in goals and ideas, there was little to differentiate between Lima's two major organizations. Even their membership lists were similar, for many workers belonged to both. With so much in common they could have been expected to work together, and on occasion they did. Together they expressed support for the government, urged an end to Asian immigration, assisted strikers, and appointed delegates to international conferences. Perhaps the most important of their united activities during this early period was to press the government for favorable labor legislation. They had some success in the field of indemnities for injured workers.

The Law of Professional Risk

Industry, agriculture, and mining were expanding at the turn of the century, as was the use of complex machinery and the number of accidents where workers, many of them children, were maimed or killed. Rarely did the victims or their families receive compensation. Under the civil code they could sue the employer for damages, but suits were costly, time consuming, and usually unsuccessful. Moreover, few workers were aware that this avenue lay open to them. What was needed was a clearly understood law that set out the obligations of the employer toward his injured workers.

Interest in a law granting indemnities to workers injured on the job grew with the size of the labor market. Legislative projects were discussed by the workers' congresses, and members of the Democratic party took up the question. In 1902 a senator, Joaquín Capelo, introduced a bill that included a clause granting medical assistance at the employer's expense to any worker who was injured or became ill on the job. The next year Vidaurre introduced his bill for indemnities in the Chamber of Deputies, and others followed. Some discussion was produced, but it did not lead to the passage of a law. Additional pressure came from the workers. In 1900, dock workers in Callao demanded indemnities for injured workers from their employers and won them by striking. Other workers made similar demands. Lawyers, too, expressed the need for a law, and in 1902 a Supreme Court judge added his voice to the growing list of proponents.[15]

In response to this mounting pressure, the government felt obliged to act. It sought information regarding employer liability in other countries, and in June 1903 President Eduardo López de Romaña (1899–1903) appointed a commission consisting of the minister of public works, the presidents of Lima's mining, agricultural, and industrial societies, three engineers, two academics, and two workers representatives to draw up a law on accidents for presentation to congress.[16] According to the decree, "the present state of the nation's various industries that use complicated machinery and employ numerous individuals in the tasks of extraction, preparation, and transportation of material and power, as well as in construction, manufacturing, and related jobs, makes it indispensable that precautions be adopted to reduce the professional risk, and that the responsibility of the contractors and employers, as well as the payment of indemnities to injured employees and workers, be determined by a specific law."[17]

The following year Serapio Calderón, the second vice-president and at that time acting president, appointed a new ad hoc committee headed by José Matías Manzanilla, a professor of political economy and economic legislation at the University of San Marcos, to draw up a complete code of labor legislation. Manzanilla and his committee produced ten separate projects that covered workers' hygiene and safety, female and child labor, compulsory days of rest, hours of work, work contracts, apprenticeship contracts, industrial and workers' associations, strikes, conciliation and arbitration, the formation of a national labor board, and indemnities for workers. At least some of these projects seemed likely to become laws, for the Civilistas' candidate in the 1904 presidential election, José Pardo, was a member of the party's more progressive wing, and he had indicated that he favored helping the workers through improved housing and wages, pensions for the old and sick, prohibiting employment of women and children in certain jobs, and employer responsibility for accidents suffered by workers.[18]

However, the passage of a bill through the Peruvian legislative network was a long and tortuous process, and even the support of the executive did not ensure a rapid or even successful passage. Manzanilla's projects were first introduced in the Chamber of Deputies, where they were referred to the legislation commission, which limited itself to discussing only the project on indemnities. After receiving the commission's approval, the project then went to the full chamber. Manzanilla could direct its passage through this body, having been elected to the Chamber of Deputies in 1905 as a member of the Civilista party. He received congressional support from Antonio and Luis Miró Quesada, but ran into stiff opposition from Lima's other deputy, Mariano Prado y Ugarteche, who argued that the civil law provided the workers with sufficient protection. The opposition proved too formidable when the bill first came up for debate in November 1905, and it was returned to committee for redrafting.[19]

It did not reappear until August 1907 and was again returned to committee without debate. This prompted an angry response from the workers societies. Until now they had played a minor role, commending the various officials for supporting a law and offering their assistance, but as late as November 1905 all they knew of the bill's contents was what they had read in the newspapers. Following the second delay they sent letters to congressmen asking that they do all in their power to satisfy the "cries of the proletariat," and in October 1907 the Confederación, the Asamblea, and the Confederación de Artesanos del Callao (Confederation of Callao Artisans) submitted a petition to Congress outlining the necessity for the bill's passage. They issued further protests in November when Congress closed without a decision on the bill.[20]

The following year, when it appeared that the bill was going to be shelved once again, the workers became more directly involved. President Pardo (1904–1908) had introduced a slightly modified bill, but four days of debate in early August failed to alter Prado's views. As a result, a large group of workers from Lima and Callao, led by the Confederación, congregated outside the Chamber on August 11 to support Manzanilla's attack on Prado's new motion to shelve. Those who could jammed into the spectators' gallery, which became so crowded that the surrounding wooden railing gave way and spectators spilled onto the floor. The show of force seemed to impress Prado: he withdrew his motion, debate proceeded, and that day the first article was approved. Three years had elapsed since the bill's introduction to the Chamber, but once the actual voting began passage proceeded rapidly, and on September 6 the final article was approved. It did so without the participation of the workers who after the incident on the eleventh were barred from the gallery.[21]

The bill now had to pass through the Senate. The new president, Augusto Leguía (1908–1912) was also a member of the progressive wing of the Civilista party, and he appeared determined to get Senate approval without delay. Indicative of his concern for the workers was a decree of March 1909 that required all companies involved in the construction and repair of railways to provide their workers with medical assistance and maintain their camps in a hygienic state in order to protect the workers' health. Despite the president's obvious interest, the Senate made no attempt to hurry, and by September 1909 debate had still not begun. The workers' congressional representative, Carlos Lora y Quiñones, warned that "a state of anxiety and justified alarm" was developing among the workers, while in a more melodramatic move the Asamblea declared itself to be in a state of mourning. It announced in November that until the law was passed the institutions comprising the Asamblea would fly their flags at half-mast and hang placards on their doors with the inscription, "Workers in mourning for the labor laws."[22]

The Senate finally turned to the bill on August 5, 1910, after further presidential pressure. The debate suddenly acquired an added sense of immediacy when reports arrived in Lima of a mining disaster in the Cerro de Pasco region. On August 10 an explosion in a coal mine at Goyllarisquizga resulted in the deaths of seventy miners, many of them children. It was the second disaster in seven months at this particular mine; in January, twenty-nine miners had been killed in a similar explosion. Leguía immediately appointed a special commission to investigate the cause of the explosion and, on the basis of its report, issued a decree requiring more stringent safety measures in the mine and listing the company's obligations to injured workers and the families of those who had been killed. In the Chamber of Deputies, Lora y Quiñones urged that the recommendations be extended to all of Peru's mines.[23]

With the mining disaster as a stimulus, the debate in the Senate went forward rapidly, and a slightly modified version of the Deputies' bill was passed. On October 18 the lower chamber approved the changes, and three months later, on January 20, 1911, President Leguía signed Law 1378, the Law of Professional Risk. From original inception to final signing it had taken almost eight years, but Peru was still the first country in Latin America to have such a law and, with Canada, only the second in all of the Western Hemisphere.

The law itself declared that employers were responsible for indemnifying their workers who were incapacitated while on the job, either absolutely or partially, permanently or temporarily. This applied to all workers who earned less than 1,200 soles per year and were employed in activities where machines were used; in agricultural work, but only where workmen were exposed to the danger of engines; loading and unloading on wharfs where mechanical apparatus operated by other than human power was employed; in mines where more than thirty-five workers were employed; in construction, repairing, and demolition companies, and factories, workshops, and industrial establishments. Indemnities took the form of a percentage of the worker's annual wage and were paid during convalescence or for life in the case of permanent incapacitation. In the case of fatal accidents, the family received a pension based on the dead worker's pay. Every worker, whatever his wage or his job, was to receive medical assistance provided by his employer and have his funeral expenses paid if he were killed on the job.[24]

The law had been passed, but would it be implemented? Manzanilla could point to a number of court cases that decided in the workers' favor. The first occurred in December 1912 and awarded the widow and children of a Southern Railway worker indemnities of 11 and 22 percent of his minimum wage respectively. Subsequent cases involved industrial, transport, plantation, and mining workers. Companies also paid voluntarily so that no legal action was necessary. Some avoided paying long-term indemnities by settling on a lump sum.

But there were negative indicators as well. *El Minero Ilustrado* of Cerro de Pasco reported in April 1911 that, although frequent accidents had occurred in the mines belonging to the Cerro de Pasco Mining Company, it had not indemnified the injured workers in accordance with the law. Cases were cited of widows receiving twenty-five and fifty soles. One man, after losing a hand in an accident, was offered one hundred soles instead of the one thousand and eighty he should have received.[25]

The main defects of the law seemed to lie in the initiation of legal proceedings and in its enforcement. Much was still left for the employers themselves to decide, and they invariably protected their own interests first. There seemed little likelihood that anything would be done about these defects, especially after the difficulties encountered in getting the law passed in the first place. But in July 1912 the Leguía government appointed a new commission to propose regulations to ensure that the workers were receiving the benefits that the law promised.[26] Leguía may have felt that after the time and effort spent on the law it should at least be effective. His actions also indicated the government's continuing concern about the labor scene and its belief that advantages could be gained by providing the workers with some benefits, minimal though they may have been.

The passage of the law of professional risk was a long, arduous, and only partially successful process. In some ways it resembled the election of Vidaurre: a token gesture by the government in recognition of an emerging group with potential influence. Both owed more to the government than to the workers societies. Both also drew the workers and their societies more firmly into politics. Despite their still limited impact on the political system, the workers were becoming more and more committed to the idea of political action to obtain improvements. With the election of representatives to public office and the passage of favorable legislation, politics seemed a logical route to follow. It might have had the additional effect of uniting them, by bringing them together in a labor party for example. However, rather than uniting them, political involvement created serious divisions both between and within the mutual aid societies and, in the process, hindered the development of the labor movement.

Widespread interest in electoral participation followed Vidaurre's election in 1895. His success, apparently with the workers' support, and his subsequent rise to prominence aroused the ambitions of other politically motivated workers, especially members of the Confederación who believed that they, too, could become successful politicians with its support. The organization was seen as a steppingstone to political office as it changed its attitude to political participation. It reversed its original opposition immediately after Vidaurre's election, absorbing the Artisans Club as a federated society, and then assisted in the election of three artisans to the provincial council in October. By 1904 its constitution called for active electoral involvement.[27]

However, the organization could not prevent the divisions that were becoming apparent by the 1899 congressional elections. One cause of disunity was Vidaurre's indecision about seeking reelection, which produced groups supporting other possible candidates. Another was the continuing political coalition between the Democrats and the Civilistas, which meant that candidates of the two parties and the Unión Cívica (Civic Union, a branch of the Civilistas) had some chance of electoral success. Thus, by the time of the nomination meeting in March, three prominent members of the Confederación representing the three parties had significant backing: Vidaurre for the Democrats, who had decided to seek reelection, Adrian Zubiaga for the Civilistas, and Manuel S. Valcarcel for the Unión Cívica. All agreed that the one receiving the most votes at the nomination meeting would be the candidate for the deputy's seat, and the runner-up would be the substitute.

The nomination had aroused intense interest, and two thousand workers attended the meeting. However, supporters of Vidaurre and Zubiaga, who were about equal in number, began fighting for first cast of their ballots, prompting the club's executive to suspend the proceedings. They then nominated Vidaurre, probably because his political affiliation made him seem the better bet. They also named Zubiaga as substitute, but he and his followers were outraged. A group of one hundred who claimed to represent thirteen hundred others charged that the executive had ignored the wishes of the majority and had fixed the results of the nomination. Zubiaga accused the executive of having done everything in its power to ensure Vidaurre's success and resigned from the club, although he continued to run as substitute.[28]

It was an unfortunate beginning to the campaign, and Vidaurre encountered further opposition before the voting took place. A group of five hundred artisans threw their support behind an alternative candidate, while in the closing weeks of the campaign several members of the Confederación who were shareholders in the company that published *El Artesano* attacked Vidaurre over his management of the paper. They introduced a motion to terminate its authorization as the Confederación's official organ, charging that it had become a political rag designed to support certain parties and to secure Vidaurre's reelection. They claimed its loss of editorial independence had followed receipt of 250 soles from the government without the shareholders' consent; that Vidaurre had taken to running it himself and appointing his own people to vacant positions, although the paper was supposed to be run by an elected board of artisans. He had taken charge of the accounts despite the appointment of a treasurer; debts of 1,250 soles had been contracted in the name of the company; and, because of bad service, subscriptions had fallen to half the original thirteen hundred.

Vidaurre denied the accusations. He explained that the government grant had come after a meeting of the shareholders and amounted to 200 soles per month; all positions had been filled by men elected by a committee of the shareholders; all debts had been authorized by the company; and the books were presently being examined by a commission.[29]

The dispute had little bearing on the election results. The Democrats still dominated the coalition, and their candidates, including Vidaurre, were elected in May. Zubiaga, on the other hand, was defeated.

Vidaurre remained the "workers' deputy," but the election once again underlined his dependence on Democratic control of the electoral apparatus, and this was beginning to slip. The Civilistas were making a determined effort to return to power, and by 1901 they had attracted Piérola's hand-picked successor, Eduardo López de Romaña, to their views. The president's deviation from Piérola's policies caused Vidaurre and other Democrats in the Chamber of Deputies to censure his cabinet in August, but Romaña refused to accept his ministers' resignations, and workers demonstrated against those who had introduced the motion. A group from the Confederación condemned Vidaurre for supporting the motion and accused him of compromising the good name and honor of the working class whom he represented and of breaking "the harmonious ties that happily exist between the government and the people." They called for his resignation as the "workers' deputy," and invited all the members of the Confederación to support the government with a vote of confidence.[30]

Vidaurre's political stock continued to plummet as the coalition between the Democrats and the Civilistas disintegrated and a new political alliance between the Civilistas and ex-President Cáceres's Constitutional party was formed. In the congressional elections of 1903 it was the new coalition's candidates who were elected. At the same time, the workers' opposition to Vidaurre was hardening. In 1904 Adrian Zubiaga and other opponents formed the Partido Obrero Independiente (Independent Labor Party) to assist Zubiaga's political ambitions. In May he resigned from the Confederación, charging that its electoral participation had produced animosity and rancor that he found offensive. The growing divisions seemed to convince Vidaurre that he would be wise to step aside. In October he informed the Artisans Club that he did not intend to run again in the following year although he still felt it essential for the workers to nominate a candidate, regardless of party affiliation, and retain control of the seat.[31]

The internal problems facing the Confederación came at a critical time, for it was now facing an external challenge as well with the emergence of the Asamblea de Sociedades Unidas, which also supported the idea of having representatives in elected office, but ones whom it would not share with the Confederación. The Asamblea's attitude became apparent during the provincial council election of 1904 when it refused to cooperate with the Confederación in naming candidates, supporting instead councilors who had backed its projects.[32]

Independent political action was to be the pattern, but in 1905 particular circumstances brought the two organizations together to defend the workers' seat in the Chamber. Regardless of whom the workers chose as their candidate, success depended upon support from the Civilista party, and in March it named José Matías Manzanilla and Mariano Ignacio Prado y Ugarteche to be its candidates for the two vacant Lima seats. This decision killed any chance of a worker being elected to the Chamber. However, the workers were now committed to the idea of having a congressional representative and the setback drew all the societies together to support whatever candidate was nominated. They still could hope for an upset, since Democratic voters outnumbered Civilistas by ten to one.

At the nomination meeting the workers avoided any possible divisions by nominating both of the leading contenders, Vidaurre and Fidel P. Cáceres.[33] For the first time the workers presented a program that they expected their candidates to introduce if elected. It called for legislation limiting the hours of work, providing indemnities for injured workers, and protecting female and child workers. If elected, the two candidates would differ in their approach to the program. Vidaurre was the more conservative of the two. He opposed both socialism and anarchism and had described redistributing income from the rich to the poor as "patently unjust." In accepting the workers' nomination he mentioned the need for further labor laws, but dwelt on the peaceful nature of the workers and their opposition to violence. Cáceres was more militant. He also spoke of the need for more laws but, in addition, urged worker unity and complained of the inequities in the present system where the majority worked for the benefit of the few. He promised to abolish some of the more unjust taxes, increase wages, defend the workers, and propose the implementation of the eight-hour work day as had been declared by the Socialist Congress in Paris in 1888.

Neither candidate really had a chance. The Civilistas' control of the electoral machinery was all-important, and the workers were further frustrated by the enumeration boards that operated only during working hours, disenfranchising many of them. The results were hardly surprising: Manzanilla received 9,734 votes, Prado 9,693, Vidaurre 119, and Cáceres 71. For the first time since 1895, the workers did not have a representative in the Chamber of Deputies.[34]

The electoral defeat split what at best had been a flimsy alliance between the workers societies. No longer was there a seat to defend, and it was now apparent to all that any future success depended upon the support of the Civilista party rather than a particular workers society. It was essential to find a candidate who appealed to the Civilistas, and this did not require cooperation. With the political situation as it was, the societies had no reservations about establishing ties with the party of the elite. There was little remaining loyalty to the Democrats since Piérola had done little to assist the workers while he had been in power, whereas the Civilistas with their support of the law of professional risk appeared to have some interest. But the competition for Civilista backing soured relations between the societies and, at the same time, created havoc within them.

The friction became apparent during the 1907 congressional election campaign as the societies began nominating candidates. The Confederación named its wayward son, Adrian Zubiaga, with Luis B. Castañeda, a master weaver at the El Inca textile mill, as substitute. Zubiaga had severed his ties with his Labor party some years earlier and returned to the Confederación to be elected president in 1905 and 1906. The Asamblea nominated Federico Elguera, the mayor of Lima, for the deputy's seat and Carlos Lora y Quiñones and Arturo Fernández Martínez as substitutes. Elguera was not a worker and the Asamblea's choice produced widespread opposition, which the Confederación fomented and from which Zubiaga sought to benefit. At the nomination meeting they secured a ruling that only recognized workers could be candidates or voters, thereby blocking Elguera's candidacy. The announcement touched off fighting between his supporters and Zubiaga's; the meeting was suspended; and the Asamblea refused to cooperate further with the Confederación. This ensured Zubiaga's nomination, although his supporters made certain by stuffing the ballot boxes.

At this time the Civilista party was willing to allow a new representative of the workers in the Chamber of Deputies, but the violence and fraud of the nomination meetings raised questions about the suitability of their candidates. Instead, it invited Lora y Quiñones, who as a past president of the Confederación had ties with both societies, to run for the deputy's seat and Castañeda as the substitute. The decision outraged the Asamblea, which had originally nominated Elguera, a member of the party, on the Civilistas' recommendation. The objection that Elguera was not a worker now seemed rather hollow, and after apologizing to him the Asamblea announced that it would not participate further in the election. This was of little concern to Lora y Quiñones and Castañeda who with Civilista support were easily elected in May.[35]

The electoral setback suffered by the Asamblea was followed by even more harmful internal divisions that almost led to a suspension of operations in 1908. Yet, despite these embarrassments and divisions, it continued to involve itself in politics. In the provincial elections of 1908 it nominated ten of its members, two of whom were elected as substitutes. In 1909 it considered nominating candidates for two vacant substitute deputy seats, but again refused to cooperate with the Confederación, which had been organizing a workers' nomination meeting. The Asamblea accused its rival of slighting the workers institutions and of organizing the meeting only to secure the nomination of its own members. The Confederación retorted that the Asamblea was "an institution composed mainly of brotherhoods and humanitarian societies and fifty-one imaginary societies whose directors are doctors and pedagogues who have no other object than to cause divisions among the workers in order to satisfy their own political ends."[36]

The effect of the squabbling was to damage the societies and, in the process, hinder the establishment of a united labor movement. Political involvement drew the workers into an area where benefits could be won—and the passage of the law of professional risk was proof of this—but it left the movement, and particularly the mutual aid societies, badly weakened. They were much discredited because of their great attention to electoral participation and their pandering to the political parties, especially the upper-class Civilista party. It was a necessity within the context of Peruvian politics at this time, but it alienated many. Most affected was the Confederación, which had shown itself willing to associate with any party to further its ends. It had first tied itself to the Democrats through Vidaurre, and when the political winds shifted it showed that it was quite prepared to float with the current. In 1905 it accepted a monthly subsidy of 80 soles from the Civilista government for its night school, and in 1911 it received a further 600 soles "to cancel a credit."[37] This financial support indicated that the Civilistas had decided there was nothing to fear from the mutual aid societies and there might be some benefit by supporting their continued existence. The passage of the law of professional risk and the Civilistas' eventual willingness to support workers' candidates also indicated an awareness of the workers and a desire to maintain some contact with and control over them.

Why was this so? There may have been some sympathy for the workers and their societies, especially since they were now allies of the government. There was also the potential electoral support of the organizations, for although their effectiveness declined as their squabbling grew, they were still popular organizations with large memberships. Probably of more concern to the government, however, was the fact that as the effectiveness of the mutual aid societies declined, the workers turned to other means to achieve the improvements that they wanted, and these other means presented a far greater threat to the government than the mutual aid societies. Many workers had begun taking matters into their own hands, and strikes became increasingly common after 1895. Of equal concern was the emergence of more militant organizations stimulated by the anarchist and syndicalist ideas then current in Latin America. As the mutual aid societies declined, resistance societies and syndicates influenced by anarchists began to appear, offering the workers an ideology and goals with a more radical flavor. In these circumstances some kind of connection between the Civilistas and the mutual aid societies was to be expected. The societies had shown that their concern was to participate within the existing system, not challenge it. Therefore, the government was keen to support them, to ensure their survival for combating the more extreme proposals of the militants. As a result, in spite of internal factionalism and external attacks, the mutual aid societies continued to survive and remained an important force within the labor movement.

4 The Influence of Anarchism, 1895–1912

Under the direction of the mutual aid societies the labor movement in Lima and Callao was following a slow and uncertain path toward change. It was a path increasing numbers of workers found both frustrating and unsatisfactory. They wanted something more dynamic, something that would offer leadership as well as the real possiblity of rapid and fundamental reforms. Some of them found what they were seeking in anarchism.

In the late nineteenth and early twentieth centuries, anarchism had a profound impact on labor movements throughout Latin America, and Peru was no exception. As in other Latin American countries, it was the anarcho-syndicalists with their emphasis on the formation of militant workers organizations who had the greatest influence. Under their direction, resistance societies, study groups, and newpapers appeared, and with them came an ideologically based militancy. During this early period of mobilizatin the Peruvian anarchists could not challenge the mutual aid societies in terms of popularity, but their influence was undeniable and they provided the heretofore missing component of radicalism to the Peruvian movement.

The early success of anarchism among the Peruvian workers owed much to the ineffectiveness of the mutual aid societies and their growing addiction to political involvement. Public dissatisfaction because of these shortcomings first appeared in August 1898 when a number of Lima newspapers reported a speech that charged, "The Lima artisans who sit between the simple workers (whom they despise) and the upper class (whom they adulate) constitute a pseudo-aristocracy with all the ignorance of the poor and all the depravities of the rich. When they meet, they establish fraternities or electoral clubs and since they express no convictions, for they do not have the slightest idea of their social mission or their rights, . . . the Lima artisans can be viewed as courtiers or lackeys to any authority, legal or otherwise."[1]

The author of the attack was the controversial Lima writer and intellectual, Manuel González Prada, recently returned from seven years in Europe where he had become a confirmed anarchist. Although of upper-class background, González Prada was one of Peru's foremost freethinkers and a recognized defender of the country's underprivileged and oppressed. Before the War of the Pacific, he had established a literary reputation and afterwards formed the Circulo Literario (Literary Circle) with a group of socially aware writers who were disillusioned by the debacle and "welcomed the more advanced ideas of the time." The society was more than a literary society and soon acquired notoriety for its attacks on the church and the military governments of the period. In 1891 it had been transformed into a political party, the Unión Nacional (National Union), with González Prada as leader, with a program of opposition to the government of Morales Bermúdez and his Civilista supporters and defense of the country's underprivileged, especially the sierra Indians and the working class. However, it did not win much support, partly because of the intellectual focus of the party and its consequent organizational deficiencies, partly because of the greater popularity of Piérola and the Democrats at this time.

González Prada had left for Europe shortly after the founding of the Unión Nacional. Europe in the 1890s was reverberating with new ideas and new movements that challenged "the political, moral, and artistic conventions of the previous generation." Anarchism, with its goal of a just society and individual freedom and its call for a "total revolt against the established order," was particularly popular and had a great impact on the Peruvian rebel and freethinker. In France and Spain he established personal contacts with local anarchists and found that their ideas about the state and social development coincided with his own.[2]

González Prada's attack on the artisans in 1898 came as a great shock to the artisans; even though his ideas did not have much support among the mutual aid societies' leaders who were solidly committed to operating within the existing system, he had earned their respect for his past defense of the workers. Rosendo Vidaurre sprang to the artisans' defense, calling González Prada "a lunatic," refuting the charges of adulation, and demanding an apology. With the support of the Confederación de Artesanos, he decided to treat the affair as a case of honor, appointing seconds to demand "ample satisfaction" from the writer. The latter replied that his words had been misinterpreted, that he had been making an appeal for the victims of society, but now because of the speech he had been threatened and calumnied. Vidaurre continued to press for an apology, but González Prada, despite the support of many artisans, refused to get involved further.[3]

Although the Peruvian intellectual remained the most visible personality and foremost interpreter of anarchism in Peru, it was local conditions and not his reputation that caused his views to win support among the workers. Anarchism, it is claimed, appealed to all sections of the Latin American working class: to artisans who "valued self-teaching and individual enterprise, and therefore saw in the rise of industry a threat to [their] way of life," and to the proletariat who were the product of this industrialization and found their working and living conditions unbearable.[4] Both groups were present in Peru at the turn of the century as the industrial sector expanded. Also pushing workers towards anarchism were the economic conditions. The cost of living was being driven up by the growth of primary production, industry, commerce, and finance and the adoption of the gold standard. Price rises were sufficiently dramatic for the Lima Chamber of Commerce to appoint commissions of enquiry in 1899, 1904, and 1906. A survey of their findings (see table 7) indicates that although the increases between 1897 and 1906 were not particularly steep, sharp, short-term fluctuations must have created hardships for the country's low-paid workers.

The economic expansion ended in 1908 with a severe commercial depression linked to a financial crisis in the United States. Trade stagnated and unemployment worsened as the country's commercial houses, which had become overstocked as a result of the prosperity of the preceding years, suspended operations. This forced factories and other establishments to close or to reduce working hours and wages. Transport workers were particularly affected. One observer noted, "Credit has been rudely shaken, the result of the over-trading in the previous year. Whereas over 500 laborers were employed daily in Callao in the discharging of cargo in 1908, in October 1909, on some days scarcely 20 men passed the gates."[5]

In the urban centers there was already an excess of workers. In the late 1890s, officials in Lima and Callao frequently complained of the "plague" of vagrants and unemployed, numbering some two thousand, who wandered the streets. The industrial expansion of the following years created many new jobs, but the unemployment problem remained and was worsening by 1908 as industrialization slowed. In that year the Lima census listed 2,181 men and 24,594 women over the age of fourteen who were without jobs. The situation was worsened by the arrival of large numbers of immigrants. Many of these were Asians imported to work on

Table 7: Increases in the Cost of Food in Lima, 1897–1906 (in soles)

	Apr. 1897	Apr. 1898	1902	1903	1904	1905	1906
Beef (kilo)	.26–.32	.31–.39	.30[a]	.30[a]	.36[a]	.23–.50[b]	.30–.54[c]
Lamb (kilo)	—	—	.28[a]	.26[a]	.32[a]	.26–.48[b]	.34–.60[c]
Potatoes (100 kilos)	8–8.50	9	—	9.25[a]	10.5[a]	—	—
Wheat (135 lbs.)	5	6.80–7	—	—	—	—	—
Rice (190 lbs.)	8–13	13–17	12.50–13.50	17	16	—	12.50–13
Butter (lb.)	.20	.26	—	—	—	—	—
Milk (liter)	.15	.20	—	—	—	—	—
Chickpeas (quintal)	4.50	8	—	—	—	—	—
Lentils (quintal)	7	11–11.50	—	—	—	—	—
Beans (quintal)	4.50	6	—	6.50	6–6.50	—	14–15
Sugar (quintal)	—	—	4.56	4.75	5.20	—	7.20
Flour (quintal)	—	—	—	5.80	6.40	6.70	6.25

Sources: Lima, Cámara de Comercio, *Memoria presentada por el Consejo de Administración de la Cámara de Comercio de Lima a la Junta General del 11 de Febrero de 1899 siendo presidente el señor D. Manuel Candamo* (Lima, 1899), pp. 36–38, *Memoria presentada . . . el 5 de Abril de 1905 siendo presidente el señor Ernesto F. Ayulo* (Lima, 1905), pp. 50–57, *Memoria presentada . . . el 6 de Abril de 1907 siendo presidente el señor Ernesto F. Ayulo* (Lima, 1907), pp. 27–44; *El Comercio,* Apr. 20a, 1898.

a. Average for April and May.
b. Average for the year.
c. For January.

the coastal plantations, but who often ended up in the urban centers. There were also Peruvian refugees from Ecuador and Chile. A large group arrived in 1908 from the former Peruvian province of Iquique following a strike in the nitrate fields in which fifteen hundred miners were massacred. There was another wave of Peruvian refugees in 1911 following attacks by Chilean nationalists on the Peruvian communities in the former southern provinces. The newcomers were offered jobs in the rural areas, but few accepted, and the majority remained in Lima and Callao where they competed with the locals for any available work.[6]

The excess of labor meant that wages remained low during this period. Over the years some improvements occurred, largely as a result of labor agitation, but wages were still not high enough to meet more than basic needs. One 1904 study calculated that a family with two children required 1.13 soles per day for food. Another reckoned a higher amount: that a couple with one child required 1.32 soles for food, and when clothing, accommodation, entertainment, and extras were added, 3.30 soles per day or 85.85 soles per month.[7] Few workers were earning as much as this (see tables 8 and 9), and there were probably few who had only three or four mouths to feed.

Competition for jobs was high, wages were low, and working conditions were harsh. The hours of work, especially in the new textile mills, were long and hard. At Vitarte, for example, the work day lasted thirteen and a half hours, while at San Jacinto the workers labored from seven in the morning until ten at night. At Santa Catalina those who worked the day shift had a relatively easy work day of nine hours split by a one hour lunch break. The night shift worked for twelve hours straight, although they received 25 percent more in pay.[8]

Living conditions, which had undergone few improvements since the war, were equally harsh. Some textile mills like Vitarte and La Victoria and the La Luciernaga match factory built houses for their workers, but these were of the poorest type and no improvement on those already found in Lima. They continued to be small, dark, damp, airless, without running water and toilets, and now increasingly expensive. They were situated in the most unsanitary parts of the city where diseases like typhoid, intestinal disorders, tuberculosis, plague, and malaria were endemic: on the edge of the Rimac River, near the hospital and the camp for incurables, and close to the lazaretto where those suffering from plague were isolated. Dung heaps were a common sight in these areas, adding to the health risk.[9]

It was because of these factors that some of Lima's workers turned to

Table 8: Wages of Lima and Callao Workers, 1895–1911 (in soles per day, except where specified otherwise)

	1895	1896	1899	1900	1901	1903	1904	1905	1906	1907	1908	1911
Lima												
Bakery workers	—	—	—	1.60	—	2.00	2.25	—	3.00	3.50	—	—
Vitarte	—	—	—	—	—	—	—	—	—	—	—	11–12w
La Victoria	—	—	—	—	—	—	1.20	—	—	5–12w	—	—
La Providencia/El Inca	—	—	—	—	—	—	1.20	—	—	1.50	7–9w	—
Santa Catalina	—	—	—	—	—	1.70	2.00	—	—	—	—	—
Coach drivers	—	—	—	—	1.50 or 45m	—	—	—	2 or 60m	75m	2.30	—
Tram drivers	—	—	—	—	—	—	—	1.50–2	1.60–2.50	—	—	—
Tanners	—	—	—	—	—	1.50	1.80	—	—	—	—	—
Callao												
Central Railway workers												
Brakemen	1.30–1.50 or 39m	45–50m	—	1.20	—	—	—	1.20+.01k or 70m	90–100m	105–110m	—	—
Laborers	—	—	1.20	—	—	—	1.80	—	1.80	1.80	—	—
Firemen	—	—	—	—	—	—	—	60m	70–90m	—	—	—
Conductors	170m	—	—	—	—	—	—	—	—	180m	—	—
Customs workers	35m	—	—	—	35m	40m	45m	—	—	60m	66m	—
Gas workers	—	—	—	—	—	—	—	—	—	—	—	2.00
Santa Rosa	—	—	—	—	1.50	1.70	1.70	—	—	—	—	—
Bellavista	—	—	1.60	—	—	2.00	—	—	2.00	2.00	—	—
Dock handlers												
Wood	—	—	—	2.20	—	—	2.60	—	—	—	—	—
Coal	—	—	—	3.00	—	2.60	3.20	—	—	—	—	—
Cement	—	—	—	—	—	—	—	—	2.60	3.00	—	—
Metals	—	—	—	4.00	—	—	4.00	—	—	—	—	—

k = per kilometer, w = per week, m = per month.

anarchism. They were attracted by its commitment to change and its goals to "ennoble" work and redistribute wealth for the benefit of the oppressed. González Prada explained, "The anarchic ideal can be summed up in two lines: unlimited liberty, and the greatest possible comfort for the individual with the abolition of the State and private property." This would not occur spontaneously, but had to be secured by the workers themselves, which required prior education and organization. The final victory would come after continuous propaganda and agitation, the formation of organizations of true workers—not ambitious politicians—and an ultimate, revolutionary general strike involving the vast majority of the workers who would take over the means of production. Strikes were the principal weapon of the workers in their struggle. Glicerio Tassara, a follower of González Prada, explained, "Strikes do not resolve the economic conflict, nor do they eliminate the workers' discontent, but they

Table 9: Wages in Lima, 1911 (in soles)

Bakery workers	2–4	Jewelers	1.50–2.50
Barbers	1.50–3	Laborers	1.20–1.50
Biscuit makers	2–4	Masons	1.80–4
Bookbinders	1.50–3	Modelers	1.50–3
Brakemen	1.50–3	Painters	1.20–3
Cabinetmakers	3–5	Paperhangers	2–4
Carpenters	1.80–5	Pavers	1.50–2
Carters	1.50–3	Postmen	2
Children	.60–1	Printers	2–5
Coachmen	2–6	Saddlers	1.50–3
Decorators	2.50–4	Shoemakers	1.50–4
Dustmen	1	Smiths	2–3.50
Engineers	3–5	Stevedores	2–4
Engravers	2–4	Tailors	1.50–5
Founders	2–4	Tanners	1.20–4
Fruiterers	1.50–9	Textile workers	1.80–3
Gas fitters	2–4	Upholsterers	2–4
Female Workers		*Monthly Wage Earners (includes room and board)*	
Cigarette workers	1.20–1.50		
Knitters	1.20–2.50	Carriage drivers	25–80
Laundresses	1–3	Cooks	10–50
Pressers	1–3	Maids	8–15
Salesgirls	1.20–2	Servants	10–40
Seamstresses	.60–1.80	Wet nurses	30–45

Source: Cisneros, *Provincia de Lima,* p. 197.

are responsible for a profound evolution in our societies: they awaken the conscience of the worker, make him understand his value as a human being, as a social factor, as an element of production; they link the destiny of the workers of every country, and by teaching them that they are the largest and strongest element in this absurd and egotistical society, they prepare them for the social revolution when the workers will no longer be the slaves of capital, but capital will be subordinated to the needs of all men."[10]

These ideas spread to various parts of Peru, attracting supporters on route. The established press carried reports of the more lurid activities of anarchists in Europe and America, and anarchist newspapers from Spain and books by Proudhon, Bakunin, Kropotkin, Réclus, Malatesta, and other anarchists were available. A British traveler in Arequipa noted with some amazement, "I was surprised to find, in such a stronghold of Roman Catholicism as Arequipa, plentifully displayed in the windows of book-shops, numerous works of modern scientists, philosophers, freethinkers, evolutionists, materialists, etc., including those of Darwin, Spender, Draper, Réclus, Renan, Haeckel, Schopenhauer, Kropotkin, and many others. These are all in cheap paper-covered editions with good type, and all issued by a publisher in Madrid." On the other hand, works by Marxist writers seem to have been rare and largely restricted to Lima.[11]

The spread of anarchism in Peru may also have been influenced by immigrants from Spain and Italy, as was the case in other Latin American countries. Between 1891 and 1901 there was a particular influx of Italians, and their total number may have risen as high as thirteen thousand. Many of the names associated with the Peruvian anarchist movement were of Italian origin, suggesting that immigrants had some influence. However, many of these were born in Peru and may have been influenced more by local conditions than by the ideas of their parents. Some, like Manuel Caracciolo Lévano, were former supporters of Piérola who became dissatisfied because of the Democratic chief's failure to achieve any real change and turned to anarchism as the only route to social justice. Others, like Ismael Gacitúa, had been members of the Confederación de Artesanos and became anarchists because of its ineffectiveness.[12]

In 1904 the anarchists made their first real impact on the labor scene in Lima. By that time, although their numbers were still small, they were holding meetings in several Peruvian cities. The Lima anarchists felt they had sufficient support to publish a newspaper, and in March the first issue of *Los Parias* appeared under the direction of González Prada. In May the anarchists participated in a strike in Callao which provided them with an opportunity to present their ideas. More importantly, the strike produced the local labor movement's first martyr whom the anarchists also used to great advantage.

The strike involved several sectors of the Callao labor force that wanted higher wages to offset the rising prices. The leaders of the strike were the harbor workers who demanded three soles for unloading general merchandise, wood, and charcoal and four soles for coal, as well as other improvements including indemnities for injured workers and the eight-hour work day. When their demands were rejected, three hundred workers went on strike on May 6. Other strikes followed in the Central Railway, the Aguila and Cox foundries, the Santa Rosa flour mill, and the tram company, all for higher wages. Despite the common demands of the workers, there was no united action, and each group tried to settle its claims separately.

The momentum of the strike was also disrupted by the death of the Peruvian president on May 7. Manuel Candamo had been in office only seven months, and the news of his death, followed by the state funeral, directed attention away from the demands of the strikers. Some began returning to work and then, still dissatisfied, rejoined the strike; others joined for a time and then returned to work. None of the strikers appeared particularly militant, for they were all prepared to negotiate with their employers and had met with a number of outside arbiters including local officials, the chamber of commerce, members of the cabinet, even ex-President Cáceres. There was also a lack of commitment among the leaders of the strike. The head of the Guadalupe factory workers deserted his followers to return to work when the factory reopened and offered jobs to the first 300 applicants. The leader of the harbor workers began urging his members to return to work after being accused of instigating the strike. As a result, some factories were reopening, and on May 19 work was set to resume on the docks after a number of workers accepted an offer of 2.50 soles per day. In anticipation of this the dock company requested police protection for the returning workers.

To this point there had been little violence except for a few rocks thrown at trains. However, the reopening of the docks led to a clash between strikers and police. *El Comercio* described it as "a real battle" as strikers hurled rocks at the police who responded by firing first over the heads of the strikers and then into their ranks. About forty shots were fired, and then a cavalry charge dispersed the workers. Seven workers were badly injured and two had to be hospitalized. Fifteen police and soldiers were also hurt, and eight workers were arrested.

It was ironic and tragic that as the strikers battled in the streets their negotiators were accepting an offer of 2.60 soles for merchandise, wood, and charcoal, 3.20 soles for coal, and better overtime pay. The company agreed to provide medical assistance for injured workers and in return got the reintroduction of the register, which had been dropped eight years earlier.

The strike, although it had secured some improvements for the workers, revealed the basic lack of unity that still affected the labor movement. The fragmented action had allowed the companies to deal separately with the groups, to the workers' disadvantage. There had also been little support from nonstriking groups, especially those in Lima; only the employees of a lumber yard had joined the strike, while the bakery workers had furnished some financial support. *Los Parias*, in criticizing the Lima workers for their lack of solidarity and "criminal indifference" to the strikers, felt their immersion in the "infected pond of cretinism and political servility" was to blame.[13]

Despite this negative aspect, the strike also produced an important rallying point for the movement. One of those shot in the clash on May 19, a thirty-six-year-old harbor worker from Cañete named Florencio Aliaga, died from his wounds. The movement had its first martyr, or, as the anarchists claimed, it had undergone its "baptism of blood".[14] While the mutual aid societies were willing only to issue a "protest at the sad events that occurred in Callao," the anarchists took advantage of the situation to present their ideas to a now-receptive audience. Five hundred workers attended Aliaga's funeral and heard eulogies delivered by a number of local anarchists, including Manuel Caracciolo Lévano, Leopoldo Urmachea, and Pantaleón Salcedo. Urmachea declaimed:

> We are not sad as we gather today to render homage to the first martyr of our Social Redemption, to this heroic worker who, like the rest of us, struggled tirelessly, until he shed his blood and lost his life, sacrificing it for his ideals in defense of our right to life.
>
> We do not cry; there is no reason to be sad: instead, we renew our determination and point out to our children the future that awaits them if they do not imitate Florencio Aliaga who at the height of the struggle succumbed but was not humbled. *Compañeros,* this blood must be fecund; we are here at the first stage of the great universal

social redemption that grows daily. . . . The sides are drawn. Let us organize resistance funds so that our future struggles will be better, more merciless, and more enduring. . . . Centavo by centavo we shall accumulate capital and then set ours against that other capital and against that brute force called the armed forces who assassinate us in the streets. Be strong, compañeros, and best wishes! Guard your sacred hatreds for the great day of social revindication.[15]

This first public appearance by the anarchists was followed by an even more impressive demonstration the following year on May 1. Lévano invited all the societies and guilds of Lima and Callao to attend celebrations in honor of the martyrs of the Chicago General Strike of 1886 and their own martyr of the previous year. This was not the first celebration of May Day in Peru, but it was the first time that the entire working population was invited to participate, and it was a great success.[16] Four hundred workers, including representatives from the Confederación de Artesanos, the Asamblea de Sociedades Unidas, and other societies in Lima, Callao, and even Trujillo, congregated at Aliaga's grave where wreaths were laid and eulogies delivered. That evening in the Confederación's hall, bedecked with red flags, the workers heard a number of speeches by prominent anarchists.

González Prada delivered the keynote address. His thesis was the necessity of an alliance between the workers and intellectuals to bring about a revolution. He stressed that the workers had to secure their own emancipation, but rejected the idea of class conflict, calling instead for the liberation of all classes from their present state. "The emancipation of the working class must be simultaneous with the emancipation of the other classes," he argued. This was not to be an apocalyptic transformation, but would require time and education in order to eradicate what he described as "two equally abominable plagues: the custom to obey and the desire to command." Without this the workers' revolution would produce the same result as an election or a military coup: the triumphant workers would be converted into agents of the bourgeoisie. The only route to total emancipation was not egoistic individualism nor socialism—which González Prada viewed as a kind of slavery—it was anarchy.

The working class speakers stressed the need for working class solidarity and effective societies to bring an end to the existing inequalities in society. Caracciolo Lévano condemned the mutual aid societies as disunited and "atrophied organisms" that had done nothing for the workers.

"Our guilds are amorphous corpses, indolent and incapable of the least activity to fulfill their obligations, and they stir only in response to the humiliating voice of the manager, the candidate, or the employer." He urged the creation of "resistance societies" that would defend the workers in their disputes with management. Some societies already had begun to organize along more militant lines, and he listed groups in Trujillo, Tarma, and Mollendo, the Unión Jornaleros (Laborers Union), an organization formed by the dock workers during the 1904 strike, in Callao, and the Gremio de Fideleros y Molineros (Guild of Pastamakers and Millers), the Empleados de Comercio (Commerce Employees), the Unión Obreros de Tejidos "33 Amigos" (Textile Workers Union "33 Friends"), and the "Estrella del Perú" in Lima. He urged the workers to observe and imitate the examples of their fellow workers in the United States, Argentina, and Chile, to establish strike funds, and to employ other forms of industrial action like protests, boycotts, and sabotage to back their demands.

The evening concluded with the election of a new executive for the "Estrella del Perú." The anarchists were in the ascendancy in this particular organization, and they were elected to a number of the executive positions: Lévano as president, Urmachea as director of the resistance fund, and Lévano's son, Delfín, as one of the secretaries. The society issued a manifesto that indicated its new direction. It called for the development of cameraderie and solidarity among the members, improvements in their economic, intellectual, and social conditions, the establishment of relations with workers around the world to combat "the exploitation of monopoly capitalism" and to vindicate the rights of the working class, the adoption of the motto of the International that the emancipation of the workers was the task of the workers themselves, and the exclusion of everything that did not embody advanced socialism since "all the workers of the planet are brothers."[17]

From these beginnings the influence of the anarchists spread. A number of newspapers with a libertarian flavor appeared in Trujillo, Arequipa, and Chiclayo, as well as Lima. New resistance societies or anarchist-influenced organizations were formed. In Lima there were anarchist study groups like Humanidad (Humanity) with its newspaper of the same name and the Centro Socialista Primero de Mayo (Socialist Center First of May). In 1908 the two groups fused to form the Centro de Estudios Sociales Primero de Mayo (Center of Social Studies First of May) with a new paper, *El Oprimido*.[18]

The most active of the anarchist organizations was the "Estrella del

Perú." Complying with the objectives enunciated in 1905, it established relations with anarchist groups in Europe and the Western Hemisphere. It also sought to separate from the Confederación de Artesanos. This was not unexpected following the anarchists' takeover of the "Estrella," for their dissatisfaction with the parent body had become apparent to all. In November 1905 members of the "Estrella" called for secession from the Confederación which, they claimed, had "done absolutely nothing for the advancement of the bakery workers guild." They encountered some opposition, for although anarchism promised to improve the workers' conditions it had not been widely accepted in Peru. The vast majority of the workers remained satisfied with the old mutual aid organizations and their attempts to secure improvements through the existing system. Even some bakery workers opposed the idea of independent action, preferring the concept of larger confederations. However, they were in a minority, and on December 28 their more militant colleagues, now calling themselves the Federación de Obreros Panaderos "Estrella del Perú" (Federation of Bakery Workers "Star of Peru"), unanimously approved separation. The Confederación refused to accept it, claiming that it was the work of only a few members, and formed a new executive from the dissidents despite anarchist opposition. As a result, two organizations now represented the bakery workers.[19]

The separation of the "Estrella" from the Confederación was indicative of the type of divisions that the anarchists were to produce in the labor movement as radicals confronted moderates. An equally divisive element was the anarchists' refusal to participate in politics. This set them apart not only from the mutual aid societies, but from more radical groups that also favored political participation by the workers. Opposition to the state and political parties lay at the core of anarchist philosophy and was rigidly adopted by the Peruvian anarchists. Caracciolo Lévano and the bakery workers called for a completely nonpolitical role even before they separated from the Confederación, and González Prada constantly urged the workers to follow their example. He argued that to vote in elections was to sanction the established order. Instead, the workers should declare war on politics since "nothing has degraded and continues to debase the nation's workers as much as politics: it divides them, debilitates them, and reduces them to impotence by making them squander their energies on useless and counterproductive struggles." Past political activities by the workers were described as a complete waste of time; Vidaurre had been "impotent," a deputy whose presence in the Chamber had signified "absolutely nothing."[20]

Initiatives taken by the government on the workers' behalf were viewed by the anarchists with equal cynicism. Lévano greeted Manzanilla's project on indemnities as "nothing more than an illusion, an obvious lure that entices us in order to lull us to sleep and mislead us into expecting better times that will never arrive." The bill eventually approved by the Chamber of Deputies was criticized for sanctioning inequalities among the workers by leaving some with no protection and providing the industrialists, owners, and managers with easy means of avoiding compliance. The final law was no better: "Article by article it was indefatigably opposed, postponed, written and rewritten, and finally reduced to its lowest common denominator, and thus we have the law of professional risk: a list of mutilated, incoherent, and useless articles, each having more than one loophole for the exploiter to avoid responsibility."[21]

The frequent criticism and divisive attacks by the anarchists give the impression that their contribution to the labor movement at this time was largely negative. In fact, there was also a positive side as they made recommendations that even the mutual aid societies accepted, and introduced goals that brought the workers together. The anarchists were constantly supporting strikers since strikes provided them with a fertile ground for agitation and propaganda. Their moral and material assistance may not have won many converts, but it produced an awareness of the anarchists' commitment to the workers and an idea of their aims. Involvement in strikes remained an important activity, and their fortunes seemed to rise and fall according to the frequency of strikes.

The anarchists' organization of May Day celebrations also had important repercussions. The format of the celebrations in subsequent years followed that established in 1905 with a march to Aliaga's tomb and then speeches together with entertainment in the evening. The number of participants grew as employers began giving their workers half-day holidays. Outside Lima celebrations were also being held. In 1906 Arequipa was completely shut down on May 1 as every firm gave its workers the afternoon off, and artisans closed their shops.[22]

The real effect of these celebrations is difficult to evaluate. A large part of the labor force probably viewed them simply as an excuse for a fiesta. But, at the same time, they must have produced a certain sense of unity and class consciousness as the workers came together to honor the internationally recognized labor day and to recall their colleagues who had died in labor struggles.

Another campaign headed by the anarchists that the mutual aid societies adopted was the winning of the eight-hour work day. This goal had been one of the principal objectives of the Chicago strikers in 1886 and, subsequently, workers everywhere had adopted it. Already some Peruvian workers had demanded it, most recently the Callao dock workers in May 1904 and Fidel Cáceres in his political campaign in 1905. The public campaign under anarchist direction began in May 1906.[23] As part of his May Day editorial in *Los Parias,* González Prada wrote:

> In accordance with the initiative that seems to have emanated from the French socialists, all the demonstrations made by the workers today should focus on creating an irresistible movement for winning the eight-hour day. Certainly, within the complete emancipation proposed by anarchy this does not amount to much; but in relation to the economic state of the nations and the mental development of the workers it has a profound significance: it is a great leap forward in almost impenetrable terrain. If the social revolution has to be achieved gradually, inch by inch, the conquest of the eight hours must be seen as a giant step; if it has to be won violently and spontaneously, the diminution of the time dedicated to material tasks is a preparatory stage: some of the hours that the proletariat presently dedicate to manual labor could be used to cultivate their intelligence, making them conscious, aware of their rights, and, consequently, revolutionaries.[24]

The eight-hour day became a rallying cry for the anarchists in Lima and elsewhere in the following years, and it was soon accepted by the mutual aid societies. In November 1908 the Asamblea de Sociedades Unidas approved a project introduced by delegates of the bakery workers calling for a maximum work day of eight hours.[25] With the backing of "respectable" groups, the demands for the eight-hour day grew in volume and increased its chance of some future success.

As the anarchists' influence spread, there was another, not altogether unexpected, result: the authorities began to show increasing interest in their activities. The anarchists' philosophical rejection of the state, their fundamental opposition to all forms of government, and their participation in labor disputes also served to attract official attention. Yet, initially the government displayed a notable lack of concern, suggesting that either it misunderstood their aims, or the number of anarchists was still very small and their influence limited. Government policy seemed designed to let them know that their existence had not gone unnoticed, but to avoid any action that might produce new martyrs for the anarchists to exploit. Persecution was minimal and usually directed at foreigners. In March 1907 the authorities arrested Carlos Zevallos Agüero after he delivered a speech at a libertarian gathering praising socialism and urging the immediate declaration of a general strike and an armed attack on the police to avenge the death of Florencio Aliaga. When Cirilo Martín, a Spaniard and an avowed socialist, tried to obtain Zevallos's release, he, too, was arrested, but they were both released within a short time and allowed to continue with their activities. In September 1908 José Briggs, an Englishman who had been one of the leaders of the 1907 Iquique strike, was arrested in Lima and accused of being an anarchist and writing anarchist poetry. He denied both charges and, according to one report, claimed that he was presently engaged in prospecting for gold relics in the ruins of Pachacamac. He, too, was released shortly, to reappear as one of the editors of the anarchist newspaper, *El Hambriento*. In February 1909 a Mexican was arrested for being an anarchist and held for a week.[26]

By its actions the government seemed to view anarchism as strictly a foreign import that could be eradicated by intimidating the existing sources of supply and preventing further imports. In 1910 President Leguía proposed a law that would allow the authorities to expel "pernicious foreigners." Referring to a recent explosion in a Buenos Aires theatre that had injured a large number of people and had been the work of "foreign criminals," he warned that "these evil elements" on being expelled from Buenos Aires and other cities of America might turn their attention to Peru, and this had to be prevented. However, his urgings aroused little enthusiasm among the legislators, and no law was passed.[27]

The lack of support for the law may have been because the anarchists no longer seemed much of a threat. From 1907 their influence suffered a notable decline, and by 1910 they appeared to be in danger of disappearing as an influential group. The reasons for this are less clear than those for the anarchists' rise. One writer has argued that anarchism followed a cyclical pattern of rise and decline, which suggests that the anarchist movement had inherent strengths and weaknesses directing it along an inevitable course. As has been shown in the case of Mexico where the movement followed such a cyclical pattern, there were also concrete local factors that determined its direction.[28]

This was true as well of Peru where one important factor was the lack of effective leadership. The recognized ideological figurehead of the anarchists, González Prada, was a writer and an intellectual, not an activist who could command the masses. He did not even address them; because of a poor speaking voice he allowed someone else to deliver his fiery words. And was he really committed to a revolution? The paternalism he frequently displayed in his dealings with the workers indicates that his aristocratic background had a much greater impact than his social conscience.[29] Moreover, by 1910 he was sixty-two years old and past the age for mounting the barricades. At that time the working class leaders, the Lévanos and Urmachea, were also ineffective because they no longer had any organized group behind them, having resigned from the "Estrella del Perú" early in 1909.

The reasons for their departure point to another problem affecting the Peruvian anarchists: limited worker commitment to militant organizations. This may have reflected a lack of confidence in the anarchist societies that so far had failed to accomplish their goals. A more important reason was the economic downturn in 1908 that produced high unemployment and made the workers very protective of their jobs. They were not willing to risk them by supporting militant action. They returned to the mutual aid societies or transformed their resistance societies into more moderate organizations. This was the fate of the "Estrella del Perú" and the reason for the anarchists' resignations. Further problems followed in 1911 when its president absconded with the society's funds, leaving it powerless to assist the workers. Delfín Lévano described the society at this time as "shameful and forlorn," the result of the "bad administration of some and the gossip, calumny, and intrigues of others who have removed the healthy and altruistic elements and given protection to the reactionaries in order to return to the mutual aid routine which provides little or nothing for the economic interests of the group."[30]

There were other factors limiting the anarchists' influence. Competition came from the left in 1907 when Cirilo Martín formed a Socialist party. It expressed many of the same aims regarding the working class as the anarchists. However, its commitment to political participation meant that it became a rival rather than an ally and, although it attracted only a few supporters, its appearance at a difficult time created confusion that hurt the anarchists.[31] Of more importance was the fact that the decade of industrial growth that stimulated interest in anarchism came to an end; industrial agitation declined because of the high unemployment, reducing the anarchists' primary means of assisting the workers and winning converts. And, finally, the government gave the impression that the existing system was responsive to the workers' interests by pushing for the law of professional risk.

Resurgence followed decline, and during the early months of 1911 the anarchists recovered their initiative. Strikes were now occurring again as the country's economic conditions deteriorated to a point where the workers were willing to risk their jobs and follow more militant leadership. The mutual aid societies had failed to provide adequate leadership, leaving a gap the anarchists would try to fill. New study groups, such as the Grupo de Luchadores por la Verdad (Group of Fighters for the Truth) of Lima and "Luz y Amor" ("Light and Love") of Callao were formed, and in 1911 a new newspaper, *La Protesta,* began publication under the direction of Delfín Lévano. The focus of the revitalized anarchist movement had not changed: the formation of effective, militant workers organizations continued to be one of its primary goals. *La Protesta* published a number of articles on the necessity and advantages of syndicalism and even explained how to set up an industrial union. The "Estrella del Perú" was organized along these lines once again, and it was joined by the Gremio Liberal de Empleados (Liberal Guild of Employees), which incorporated the hotel and restaurant workers, the Unificación Proletaria Textil de Santa Catalina (Textile Proletariat Union of Santa Catalina), and the Unificación Obrera Textil de Vitarte (Textile Workers Union of Vitarte). In January 1912 a local anarchist, Eulogio Otazú, urged the formation of a Federación Obrera Regional del Perú (Workers Regional Federation of Peru) to incorporate these groups and centralize their efforts.[32]

The resurgence of the anarchists in 1911 meant that once more there was a radical group exerting its influence on the workers. They still constituted only a small minority of the working class, and they could not claim leadership of the local movement, but a militant and active alternative to the mutual aid societies was operating again and offering advice and leadership. Already the anarchists had produced an identifiable impact on the Peruvian labor movement. They had introduced new goals for the workers, sponsored activities that attracted them, and provided an explanation of their plight that even the mutual aid societies were beginning to accept. Increasingly, condemnation of capitalism and its exploitative aspects was finding its way into the memorials and speeches of all working class leaders.

The rise of the anarchists was one of the reasons why the government began to view the more conservative mutual aid societies with greater favor and why it considered making some gestures in the workers' direction. There was a second factor behind this decision that also was linked to the spread of anarchism: strikes had become an increasingly common feature of Peruvian labor relations. They caused the government to pay closer attention not only to the anarchists, but the working class as a whole.

5 The Intensification of Industrial Action, 1895–1912

An indication of the growing militancy of the labor movement after 1895 was the increasing frequency and intensity of strikes. The agitation was a logical reaction to the workers' poor wages and harsh working and living conditions that continued to deteriorate with further increases in the cost of living. It was also stimulated by the mutual aid societies' apparent inability to obtain more than minimal improvements for the workers. The societies remained ambivalent about the efficacy of labor agitation, but they did not divorce themselves from strikers: frequently they provided moral and material assistance and interceded with the government on their behalf, thereby maintaining some contact and influence.[1] Much more supportive were the anarchists. Strikes were an integral part of their revolutionary strategy and, therefore, the anarchists assisted striking workers whenever possible. It was not coincidence that the spread of anarchism and the intensification of industrial action occurred simultaneously.

The primary goal of strikers during this period was to achieve better wages to offset the rising cost of living. They also began to demand improvements in their working conditions in the form of a shorter work day, compensation for injured workers, and the removal of unpopular foremen. The outstanding feature of this period of agitation was the workers' growing awareness of the need for united action. They usually faced great obstacles—that ranged from their own lack of experience to the opposition of hostile officials and unsympathetic employers—and they came to realize that success could be achieved only through the support of all the workers of a factory, an industry, or even a city. This continued growth in the militancy and consciousness of the workers culminated in April 1911 when Lima's workers staged Peru's first general strike and clearly showed the advances that had been made by the local labor movement.

Strikes in Callao

In the port of Callao the most militant workers continued to be those employed by the Central Railway and by the dock company (see table 10). Both were vital to Peru's export-oriented economy, so they enjoyed a certain amount of power. However, the results of their agitation differed, largely because of differences in the degree of worker unity. The railway workers comprised a number of groups who went on strike individually, allowing the company to replace the strikers with workers from other sectors of the operations and thereby maintain services. The dock workers, on the other hand, displayed relative cohesion and as a result enjoyed greater success. Nevertheless, both groups were dependent on the flow of imports and exports for their jobs, and when the commercial crisis of 1908 hit they suffered similarly.

During the period poor wages brought about the first strikes on the Central Railway. In 1895 brakemen's pay was so low they were personally carrying produce from Lima to sell in the sierra.[2] The strikes had little success: strikers were either replaced or threatened with replacement, their leaders were arrested, and their conditions remained unchanged. It was not until 1906 that they managed to win some improvements but, as the anarchists later pointed out, even these were limited because of the workers' inability to act together.

A series of strikes involving the separate sectors of the railway labor force began in July when the brakemen demanded a wage increase on the grounds that they had to maintain houses in Callao and up the line in Chosica because of the nature of their work. They also wanted some form of workmen's compensation since accidents were frequent and four workers had been killed already that year. By disrupting rail traffic they managed to win one of their demands, a wage increase to 90 and 100 soles per month for the two ranks of brakemen. Two months later the firemen demanded the same amount plus indemnities, but settled for 70 to 90 soles per month depending upon rank, the opportunity to rise to the top rank in five years, and better overtime pay. The general laborers, who were earning from 1.70 to 1.80 soles for an eleven-hour day, followed with demands for an increase to between 2.20 and 2.50 soles, better overtime pay, free medical assistance, and indemnities for injured workers. This time the manager balked and offered only a minimal increase, claiming he had the backing of his "friend," President Pardo. Although the strikers stopped replacements from being hired and disrupted rail traffic, they were unable to win more. In October the firemen struck for a second time. They claimed they were not receiving the overtime that had been promised, that it was being calculated only on the time the engines were in motion, not when the firemen arrived at work. When the strike threatened to spread to the brakemen and laborers, the company gave in once again.³

The experience stood the railway workers in good stead when the company began introducing changes in its operations, designed to increase profits and usually at the expense of the workers. In 1907 it introduced a system to pay according to mileage, but was prevented by a strike of the conductors and brakemen whose combined action also secured new salary increases. In October 1908 it introduced a new overtime rule: the workers had to complete a total of 312 hours per month based on a twelve-hour day and a twenty-six-day month before earning any overtime. Again, the brakemen and conductors went on strike, but this time they were unsuccessful.⁴

The company was now displaying much greater rigidity in its labor relations. William Morkill, the local representative of the Peruvian Corporation that operated the railroad, was determined to show the workers who was boss. Assisted by the depression in world trade that reduced the amount of goods being carried and the number of workers the company needed, he was unsympathetic when the workers began making new demands in June 1909, seemed to relish the prospect of a confrontation, and could afford even the disruption of traffic.

As in the past, the sectors of the labor force went on strike individually. On June 17 the Guadalupe foundry workers struck after a reduction in their work week by fourteen hours because of a collapsed bridge. They wanted the lost hours restored as well as weekly instead of fortnightly pay. Morkill was prepared to restore only one hour per day, and he warned the strikers that they would lose their rating in the service if they did not return to work immediately and unconditionally. Two days later, when most had complied, the brakemen went on strike. They were protesting the hours of work, the treatment they received from one of the foremen, and company regulations that made them responsible for any damage done to the trains yet denied them the right to compensation for work-related injuries. They demanded wages of 115 and 110 soles per month, a reduction in the number of monthly work days to twenty-six and daily hours to ten. Morkill considered their demands "exorbitant" and opposed any concession, claiming that he would lose all control over the workers if he acceded. He threatened that if they did not return to work they would never be hired again and began hiring replacements to back up

Table 10: Strikes in Callao, August 1895–April 1912

	1895	1896	1897	1898	1899	1900	1901	1902	1903	1904	1905	1906	1907	1908	1909	1910	1911
Central Railway workers																	
Brakemen	Oct.	Aug.	—	—	—	Dec.	—	—	—	—	—	July	July	Oct., Nov.	June–Aug.	—	—
Laborers	—	—	—	—	Oct.	—	—	—	—	—	—	Sept.	May, July	—	July	—	—
Linemen	—	—	—	—	—	—	—	—	—	Sept.	—	—	—	—	—	—	—
Firemen	—	—	—	—	—	—	—	—	—	—	—	Sept., Oct.	—	—	July	—	—
Conductors	—	—	—	—	—	—	—	—	—	—	—	—	July	Oct., Nov.	July	—	—
Engineers	—	—	—	—	—	—	—	—	—	—	—	—	—	—	July	—	—
Guadalupe foundry	—	—	—	—	—	—	—	—	—	May	—	—	—	—	June	—	—
Dock handlers	—	—	—	—	—	Dec.	—	—	—	May	—	Nov.	Apr.–May	Feb.	—	—	Apr.
English Railway Co.	—	—	—	—	Oct. Dec.	—	—	—	—	May	—	—	—	—	—	—	—
Customs workers	—	—	—	—	—	Dec.	—	—	Nov.	—	—	—	—	Dec.	—	—	—
Santa Rosa	—	—	—	—	—	—	Sept.–Oct.	—	Nov.	May	—	—	May	—	—	—	—
Bellavista	—	—	—	—	Oct.	—	—	—	Nov.	—	—	May	May, Sept.	—	—	—	—
Coach drivers	—	—	—	—	—	Dec.	—	—	—	—	—	—	—	—	—	—	—
Aguila foundry	—	—	—	—	—	—	—	—	—	May	—	—	—	—	—	—	—
Cox foundry	—	—	—	—	—	—	—	—	—	May	—	—	—	—	—	—	—
Municipal workers	Aug.	—	—	Oct.	May	—	—	—	—	May	—	—	—	—	—	—	—
Cocaine factory	—	May	—	—	—	—	—	—	—	—	—	—	—	—	·	—	—
Cerro de Pasco	—	—	—	—	—	—	—	—	—	—	—	—	—	—	Mar., Apr.	—	—
Gas workers	—	—	—	—	—	—	—	—	—	—	—	—	—	—	—	—	Apr.

his threat. He remained unmoved by the fact that the strikers were receiving assistance from several societies, including the dock workers' Unión de Jornaleros, the Confederación de Artesanos, the Asamblea de Sociedades Unidas, and the "Estrella del Perú," and eventually forced them back to work.

In mid-July a new strike by 170 drivers, firemen, conductors, and brakemen, objecting to the company's renewed attempt to introduce a pay by mileage scheme, disrupted traffic once again. Violence accompanied this walkout: a group of strikers attacked a train carrying a number of company representatives. Police responded by shooting into the crowd and injured five of them. The following day rail service was restored when crews were brought in from other regions and the strike leader, Samuel Ballesteros, was arrested.

The anarchists blamed Ballesteros for the defeat; they accused him of accepting fifty pounds sterling and a first class ticket to Buenos Aires from the company. A more obvious reason for the defeat was the strikers' inability to keep out scab labor, a difficult task when jobs were scarce and unemployment high. The actions of Morkill should also have been considered. During the strike he resisted not only the strikers but also the government, which felt the company was responsible for the trouble and had threatened to fine it if service was not restored immediately. He noted afterward, when operations were again proceeding smoothly, "To produce this state of harmony in the working of the line severe measures had to be resorted to, and many men, with large families, who had long served the Railway, but who had served it as it suited them and not us, and who went on strike after being warned not to do so, are still suffering the consequences."[5] Management was now firmly in the driver's seat, and agitation among the railway workers ceased until the trade depression ended.

Callao's dock workers also suffered from the trade depression, although they had previously displayed more of the unity that was essential to strike success. When the register was abolished in 1895, leaving them without the small protection it had afforded, they remained a united group determined to protect their rights. In December 1900, when the wood handlers went on strike for a wage increase, the other stevedores joined them almost immediately, paralyzing the docks and resisting attempts by the dock and shipping companies and the government to break the strike. The companies found few applicants when they tried to hire replacements. In the one instance when they managed to hire some, the strikers boarded the ship to prevent any unloading. The dock company's offer of a monthly salary of sixty soles to the first 130 strikers who returned to work was equally unsuccessful, for the strikers refused to split ranks. And when the government brought in troops to unload the ships, only a police cordon prevented the strikers from marching into Lima.

After a week there was no solution in sight. President Romaña met with representatives of the two sides and told the workers he could not grant a wage increase at this time, but would recommend one as soon as the economic conditions improved. The dock company was now willing to offer free medical assistance for injured workers and financial support during convalescence which, although not the strikers' primary demand, was offered for the first time, and they accepted. Moreover, Romaña promised that no worker would lose his job for participating in the strike.[6]

Romaña also urged the reintroduction of the register, but it was not until after the May 1904 strike and the death of Florencio Aliaga that this took place. The aim seemed to be to establish greater control over the workers, for the decrees of June and November 1904 reestablishing the register placed them under the direction of the military. Dock workers would be subject to the military code, and any offence would be tried by a military tribunal. Many workers refused to sign and, as a result, were not allowed access to the docks after registration closed on December 31. The workers, with the assistance of the Confederación de Artesanos, managed to get clarification of some aspects of the decrees—in the case of "peaceful strikes" they would not come under military jurisdication—but uncertainty and hostility remained.[7]

Another source of trouble was the handling of winches and gangways when loading and unloading ships. In November 1906 the dock workers went on strike to secure control of both. The shipping companies claimed that company crews should be responsible because it was unclear who would indemnify dock workers injured while working on board a ship. Nationalistic feelings were also involved in the dispute since most of the ships' crews were Chileans, whom the Peruvian stevedores did not trust. After a week President Pardo offered a compromise solution: the workers would handle the gangways and the crews the winches. This ended the strike, but the stevedores still refused to unload ships that would not allow them to handle the winches, and eventually the shipping companies agreed to this as well.[8]

Increases in the cost of living produced demands of a different sort. In April 1907 the dock workers went on strike for sixty centavos, raising the rate to 3.20 soles for unloading cement. All harbor activities were halted as the dock and shipping companies refused to allow any cargo to move while the cement remained idle. The government backed the companies, charging that the strikers had failed to present their demands in writing, had no justification for striking, and had prevented others from working. It issued a decree ordering them back to work and then hired sailors at three soles per day to unload the cement. Six hundred strikers retaliated by marching on Lima, but were stopped at the outskirts of the city by troops and cavalry who charged into their ranks, injuring three and arresting thirty. A delegation of strikers finally managed to meet President Pardo a few days later. However, he showed little sympathy, urging them to return to work, and offered only to send money to the families of those who had been injured in the confrontation.

Pardo's refusal to intervene seemed to strengthen the strikers' resolve. They set up a camp near the docks, which had its own administration and police force and an office to collect donations. Other sectors of the Callao labor force began striking, partly in sympathy, partly to obtain their own wage increases. On May 17, after the strike had lasted almost a month, the government tried once more to end it, this time by abolishing the register. It reasoned that with the work open to everyone the strikers would have to return to protect their jobs. However, the workers remained firm and continued on strike for another week, when they accepted an offer of three soles.[9]

United, the dock workers had shown that they could confront their employers successfully, but new challenges began to undermine that unity. The abolition of the register meant that the companies were free to hire whom they wished, and many of the former workers found themselves without jobs. One thousand workers were competing for six hundred jobs, a situation that worsened with the arrival of hundreds of refugees from Iquique after the December 1907 nitrate workers strike. The Pacific Steam Navigation Company tried to take advantage of the situation by hiring some of the refugees at lower wages. This triggered off a strike in February 1908 that once more paralyzed the docks. Soldiers and sailors, together with refugees, tried to replace the strikers, but they managed to move only a portion of the goods. The refugees claimed that they had not intended to cause trouble and offered to leave if they were given one month's pay and passage back to Iquique. The locals were unimpressed. They remained on strike until the company agreed to terminate the refugees' contracts after a month, at which time they would have to compete for the jobs like any other worker. The agreement was almost undone on the day of its signing by the minister of government, Germán Arenas, who ordered the arrest of the strike leaders and suspended the strikers' rights. Fortunately, the Asamblea, the Unión de Jornaleros, and the Civilistas' presidential candidate, Augusto Leguía, managed to get Arenas's order repealed almost immediately, and the strike was settled.[10]

The former privileges enjoyed by the dock workers continued to be eroded. The Pacific Steam Navigation Company was still hiring outside workers and paying them fixed wages instead of the tariff rate. On ships owned by the Kosmos and Grace companies, cargo was being unloaded by the ships' crews. Without the protection offered by the register, the workers had little defense, and their efforts to get it reintroduced were unsuccessful. Their strength and unity were also being undermined by the 1908 trade depression. Unemployment on the docks was so high that agitation became too great a risk to take. The situation was exacerbated by changes in local business practices, especially the movement of mercantile houses from Callao to Lima following the construction of an inter-urban electric tramway, which produced a further loss of jobs in the port. As a result, it was not uncommon at the height of the financial crisis to find dock workers, who in the past had been noted for their militancy, acting as scab labor and replacing workers who were still prepared to go on strike.[11] Until the trade depression ended, Callao's labor movement made no further advances.

Strikes in Lima

The concerns and demands of the labor force were the same in Lima as in the port, strikes increased in both frequency and severity, and workers' success depended upon united action (see table 11). One important difference was that Lima's workers were not as closely tied to commerce, so that the trade depression had less of an impact on them. As a result, by 1911 they were the more militant group and the ones responsible for Peru's first general strike.

The bakery workers continued to be one of the most effective labor groups in Lima. Their success was largely a result of their society, the "Estrella del Perú," which represented most of them, presented their demands, and assisted them when they went on strike. Its importance was clearly demonstrated during the successful bakery workers' strike in April 1901. The society issued the workers' demands for an increase of forty centavos on the basic wage of 1.60 soles, bringing it up to 2 soles for each quintal of flour processed or an equivalent increase in the daily wage, a reduction in the work day that presently averaged twelve hours and in some instances stretched from 3 P.M. to 6:30 A.M., and compensation for injured workers. The society expected little from the owners for it had been collecting fifty centavos daily from the workers in a strike fund since the previous July. Its expectations were well founded: the employers insisted that most workers earned between 70 and 90 soles per month and offered only a 10 percent increase. On April 14 the workers went on strike, closing all the bakeries except those already paying 2 soles per quintal to their workers.

With their substantial strike fund, the workers were prepared for a long dispute. They received fifty centavos daily from the fund, which was replenished by workers who returned to their jobs when their employers accepted the strike demands. They also received moral and material assistance from Lima's other societies, from Callao's bakers who refused to ship bread to Lima, and from the national workers congress, which was meeting at this time. Several bakeries agreed to striker-suggested arbitration and met with Santiago Giraldo, a deputy with proworker views, who represented the workers.[12] Negotiations proceeded, and after twelve days only a small number of owners continued to resist the workers' demands.

On April 26 the "Estrella" invited all the workers of the city to a meeting to announce the official end to what was labeled a successful strike. *La Idea Libre* noted that it "had demonstrated the solidarity of the working class as all the guilds had acted promptly in assisting their brothers not only morally but financially." It had been the first strike in which arbitration had been used with some success and, according to the newspaper, it had been a defeat for capitalism. There were still the few owners who had not accepted the two soles, but they came under renewed pressure from the workers to conform to the agreement.[13]

The authorities viewed the developments with some misgivings. In a year-end report on the labor scene, Lima's prefect commented:

> The so-called social question, a subject that presently is of the greatest interest in the old societies of Europe, has been imported into our midst by wild-eyed revolutionaries who are more or less ignorant of the grief they are causing the very classes in whom they express interest.
>
> The "cooperative societies of workers," the "confederated guilds of artisans," the so-called "National Workers Congress," all institutions of recent date, are less interested in the moral and material development of the working class than in socialist prop-

Table 11: Strikes in Lima, August 1895–April 1912

	1895	1896	1897	1898	1899	1900	1901	1902	1903	1904	1905	1906	1907	1908	1909	1910	1911[a]	1912
Slaughterhouse workers	Sept.	—	—	—	—	—	—	—	Mar.	—	—	—	—	—	—	Mar.	—	—
Bakery workers	—	Oct.	Apr.	—	—	—	Apr.	—	—	Jan.	—	—	—	—	—	—	—	—
Dustmen	—	—	—	Jan.	—	—	—	—	Apr.	Apr.	—	—	July	—	—	—	Apr.	—
Colliers	—	—	—	—	—	—	—	—	Nov.	—	—	—	Jan.	—	—	—	—	—
Lumber workers	—	—	—	—	—	—	—	—	—	May	—	—	—	—	—	—	—	—
Tanners	—	—	—	—	—	—	—	—	—	June	—	—	Aug.	—	—	—	—	—
Backus & Johnston	Nov.	—	—	—	—	—	—	—	—	—	—	—	—	—	—	—	—	—
Typographical workers	—	Sept.	—	—	—	—	—	—	—	—	—	—	—	—	—	—	—	—
Cigarette workers	—	—	Jan.	—	—	—	—	—	—	—	—	—	—	—	—	—	—	—
Telegraph operators	—	—	—	—	Aug.	—	—	—	—	—	—	—	—	—	—	—	—	—
Tailors	—	—	—	—	—	—	—	—	—	—	—	—	—	—	—	—	Dec.–Jan.	—
Suppliers	—	—	—	—	—	—	—	—	—	—	—	—	—	—	—	—	Oct.	—
Marble workers	—	—	—	—	—	—	—	—	—	—	—	—	—	—	—	Mar.	—	—
Confectioners	—	—	—	—	—	—	—	—	—	—	—	—	—	—	—	—	Oct.	—
Hotel employees	—	—	—	—	—	—	—	—	—	—	—	—	—	—	—	—	Feb.	—

Coach drivers	—	—	—	—	—	—	—	—	—	Dec.–Jan., Oct.	Mar.	—	—	—	Apr.	—	Oct.	Nov.	—
Coach conductors	—	—	—	—	—	—	—	—	—	—	Mar.	—	—	—	—	—	—	—	—
Tram Company workers																			
Linemen	—	—	—	—	—	—	—	—	—	—	—	—	Aug., Oct.	—	—	—	—	—	—
Drivers	—	—	—	—	—	—	—	—	—	—	—	—	—	—	Dec.	Jan.	—	—	—
Conductors	—	—	—	—	—	—	—	—	—	—	—	—	—	—	Dec.	Jan.	—	—	—
La Victoria	—	—	—	—	—	—	—	—	—	—	—	Feb.–Mar.	—	—	—	Mar.–Apr.	—	—	—
El Progreso	—	—	—	—	—	—	—	—	—	—	—	—	—	Dec.–Jan.	—	—	Dec.	Nov.	—
La Providencia/El Inca	—	—	—	—	—	—	—	—	—	—	—	Feb.–Mar.	—	—	—	Oct.	Mar., Nov.–Dec.	—	Mar.	—
Vitarte	Aug.–Sept.	—	—	—	—	—	—	Dec.	—	—	—	—	—	—	Dec.–Jan., May	Dec.	—	Mar.–Apr., May	—
San Jacinto	—	—	—	—	—	—	—	—	—	—	—	—	—	—	Jan.	Dec.	—	—	—

a. General strike in April 1911.

aganda and principles that are largely misrepresented and badly misunderstood by the masses and that, since they do not meet any of our social or economic needs, only serve to anarchize further the various classes and races that comprise our *ethnic* and social order.

The men of state and the intelligent classes of the nation have watched with contempt this exotic movement that has no significance, historic antecedent or economic basis in our country; nevertheless. . . . I believe it my duty to draw the attention of the government to the *strikes* of the employees of the Tram company and the bakeries that occurred this year and to their real importance—the lack of special legislation to regulate and define the rights and the duties of these societies or assemblies of workers, to limit the orbit of the semiofficial influence they exercise today over the authorities and the public powers in all questions that interest them, to compel them to present their statutes for government approval and not to recognize them as legal entities until they do so, thereby placing these societies, their meetings, and public demonstrations under the care and scrutiny of the authorities.[14]

The successful strike almost terminated agitation by the bakery workers. The effectiveness of their organization had been shown and, as it fell under the even more militant leadership of the anarchists, the bakery owners may have decided that negotiation and concession were a wiser approach than confrontation. In January 1904 there was a short strike as a result of increases in the cost of living and the work load. Representatives of the "Estrella" met with the owners and won an increase of twenty-five centavos on the basic wage of 2 soles in return for a promise not to demand further increases and to settle any subsequent problems through negotiation. They broke the agreement only once. In July 1907, following further increases in the cost of living, they went on strike and won an increase to 3.50 soles.[15] Thereafter the bakery workers avoided strikes, possibly because of the more conservative approach adopted by the society and the consequent divisions within it, possibly because the system of negotiations was continuing to work.

While limiting its own industrial action, the "Estrella" continued to provide assistance to other workers who went on strike. Between 1895 and 1912 this was most frequently the textile workers, who comprised the largest single sector of industrial workers in the country. Although divided among a number of factories, the various groups of textile workers

The Intensification of Industrial Action, 1895–1912

wanted similar improvements, and their frequent disputes gradually brought them together. In June 1911 it was this group that provided the focus and the leadership for Peru's first general strike.

Serious labor trouble involving the textile workers began in 1896 in Lima's first mill, Vitarte. The dispute brought to light the miserable conditions of the workers, as well as the lack of sympathy of the reputedly proworker president, Piérola. The mill was located in the town of Vitarte, a short distance from Lima along the Central Railway. It was owned by the London-based Peruvian Cotton Manufacturing Company whose local agents were W. R. Grace and Company. It employed around three hundred workers, providing them with food and lodging in addition to their wages. The wages were very low; according to one report, they amounted to only thirty centavos for a workday of sixteen hours, and it was for higher pay as well as fewer hours of work and better food that the workers went on strike on August 24. The manager insisted that they were already earning between six and ten soles per week plus food and lodging, so that there was no justification for an increase. The strikers hoped that President Piérola would support them since the workers had supported his revolution and election the previous year. However, a fire in the factory on the night of August 27 showed him to be firmly on the side of the company and foreign investment. The blaze destroyed only eighty sacks of cotton and the strikers assisted in extinguishing it, but arson was suspected and four strikers were arrested. When a delegation of workers met with Piérola the following day, his primary concern was the fire which, he claimed, not only hurt the factory owners but discredited the entire country. As for the strike, he was not prepared to intervene; the two parties would have to find their own solution.

While Piérola was unwilling, some deputies tried to get congressional intervention to end the dispute. Rosendo Vidaurre, who had been personally involved in all the negotiations, attempted to convince his fellow deputies by claiming that even the strikers had opposed the arson attempt. Most of the deputies, however, showed the same lack of sympathy as the president. They charged that the strike indicated a new militancy among Peru's workers, a spread of socialism and "Proudhonian communism," and feared that there might be greater violence, with dynamite and gasoline bomb attacks.

Without external support and faced by employers who resisted any concessions except for some improvements in their food, the strikers had to give in. By September 5 work at Vitarte was all but back to normal. For the four workers who had been arrested, however, the effects of the strike had not run their full course. They were found guilty of arson and sentenced to six years in prison.[16]

It was almost a decade before another strike was called in the textile industry. The later outbursts were a result of the growth of the industry and, more importantly, the abysmal working conditions in the mills. In addition to long hours of work and low wages, the workers had to pay their section heads up to 30 soles for their machines. They could be fined for a variety of reasons that included missing a day's work, for which they also lost the day's pay, or spotting the cloth, which was virtually assured by the nature of the machinery. The worst mill for fining its workers seems to have been Santa Catalina. In 1908 the Asamblea de Sociedades Unidas tried to get the fines removed after the amount was raised from 1 sol to 1.50 soles, but managed only to get the maximum reduced to fifty centavos. Further pressure by the workers to get the fines removed resulted in threats to fire any worker who protested.

Intimidation of this sort kept Santa Catalina relatively free of labor agitation. There were no strikes, and the workers refused even to cooperate with their striking colleagues in the other mills, possibly also because they earned slightly more than the other textile workers (see table 8). Furthermore, the work force was a varied lot that made united action difficult. The factory employed men, women, Japanese, Italians, and sierra Indians. The latter had recently completed their military service at the nearby Santa Catalina barracks and, accustomed to the discipline and hardships of army life, they must have found the work regime in the mill an improvement.[17]

The rest of the textile workers became increasingly militant and developed a sense of solidarity. Like other workers, they began responding to the rising cost of living by going on strike for better wages. In February 1904 the workers at La Providencia and La Victoria went on strike for a 25 percent wage increase. They received financial support from the Vitarte and El Progreso workers and the Asamblea, but their employers refused any increase, arguing that the depressed state of the industry at this time made it impossible. The strikers were also opposed by the government, which arrested their leaders, and as a result, they had to return to work. The owners now promised to increase wages when conditions improved, abolish fines, and contribute 200 soles to help cover some of the strike costs.[18]

The strikes were followed by further signs of the growing unity among the textile workers. They formed a society, the Unión Obreros de Tejidos

"33 Amigos," which the anarchists considered to be one of the city's more militant organizations. In December 1905 when Santiago Carthy Caballero, a member of the society's executive and a leader of the 1904 strike, was fired together with two other El Progreso workers, the rest of the mill went on strike. They called for the implementation of the promised wage increase and abolition of fines, extra pay for night work, and more time for meals. One hundred and twenty workers participated and, with the support of other sections of Lima's labor force, they won a wage increase and the establishment of a canteen where workers could obtain cheap meals.[19]

Beginning in December 1906, the industry was hit by a series of strikes. The Vitarte workers were first, demanding the same wages as Lima's other textile workers and better food. They presently had to pay sixty centavos daily for a breakfast of two cups of tea and a piece of bread; a lunch of soup, scraps of meat, and potatoes; and a dinner of noodle soup, a little rice, and beans that were "harder than a usurer's conscience." The strikers were successful with the assistance of the Confederación de Artesanos, with which they were affiliated, other societies and factories, the anarchist groups, and individuals like the president of the Confederación, Adrian Zubiaga, and the presidents of the textile workers' two societies, Luis B. Castañeda and Pedro Malpartida. In January 1907 fifty San Jacinto workers went on strike and won a wage increase with the support of the other mills. In March it was the turn of La Victoria. The workers demanded twenty-five centavos more for all those earning over 1.20 soles per day and a 50 percent increase for the rest. They felt such an increase was justified because the cost of food and accommodation had risen by some 50 percent in recent years while their wages, which in some cases ranged as low as sixty centavos per day, had remained unchanged. They had been planning the strike for some time and, following the pattern for success developed by the bakery workers, they had formed a strike fund and sought assistance from the rest of the work force. They also discussed the possibility of sympathy strikes throughout the industry and even considered a general strike. At a meeting on March 31 of representatives from various sectors of the labor force in Lima and Callao, Luis Rios Castell, a carpenter at the Maurer sawmill, proposed this as a means to end the strike. However, his proposal received little support, and instead the La Victoria workers agreed to continue as before with the assistance of the other workers. Luis Pardo, the owner of the factory and brother of the president, tried to break the strike by hiring apprentices as replacements. They were frightened off by the strikers who, after a month, finally succeeded when Pardo capitulated and granted most of their demands.[20]

Not every section of the textile labor force enjoyed success during this round of agitation. The workers at El Inca (formerly La Providencia) went on strike three times and each time failed. They had to deal with an unsympathetic foreman in Luis B. Castañeda who, despite his election to the Chamber of Deputies as a representative of the workers and leadership of one of the textile unions, was prepared to fire any worker who agitated. They also failed to win unanimous support within the mill and by 1908 were facing the effects of the commercial depression. In November they had the support of the Vitarte, El Progreso, and San Jacinto workers, but their strike still failed.[21]

As in Callao, the commercial depression with its attendant unemployment reduced strike activity throughout the industrial sector in Lima. Some agitation continued, but the target shifted from employers to those whom the workers viewed as threats to their jobs. Their primary target was the local Asian community that had expanded noticeably since the importation of Japanese and Chinese contract laborers for work on the coastal plantations. On completing their contracts, most of the Asians left the estates and migrated to the urban centers, especially to Lima and Callao where large Asian *barrios* (ghettos) developed. The immigrants aroused enormous hostility because of local racial and economic fears. The Asians were thought to carry numerous communicable vices and diseases; they were accused of monopolizing small businesses and some occupations, and since many of them owned small grocery shops, they were held responsible for increases in the price of foodstuffs.

Opposition to the Asians became acute as the full effects of the commercial depression were felt. Despite the lack of jobs there were plans to import several thousand more Asians. In May 1909 riots in Lima followed rumors that a ship carrying one thousand new immigrants was about to dock in Callao, and twenty shops suffered 10,258 soles damage during attacks on the Asian community. Despite assurances from the government that immigration would be halted, further attacks occurred during the following year.[22]

The anti-Asian demonstrations once again indicated that the Lima workers still had much to learn: the government or the planters who were responsible for the immigration should have been the target, not the Asians. Nevertheless, the movement had made significant advances since Piérola's revolution. Strikes were now better organized and more successful, and they had produced increased unity and attracted widespread support as a means of obtaining improvements. In 1911 all of these factors came together in the general strike that marked the culmination of this period of growing industrial unrest.

By the early months of 1911 labor agitation had resumed in Lima. In the textile industry there were strikes in two mills that succeeded because of worker unity.[23] Then on March 18 the Vitarte workers went on strike to back demands for better wages, a reduction in the work day from thirteen hours to ten, and the elimination of night work. They put the lessons learned from previous successful strikes to work by naming a strike committee headed by Gustavo Castillo to lead the strike and obtain assistance from Lima's societies, organizing a strike fund to which every worker contributed five soles, setting up a camp near the factory to collect donations, and asking the Asamblea to intercede on their behalf with the authorities. The company retaliated on March 23 by terminating the leases on the workers' accommodations and giving them ten days to vacate. The prefect ordered them out of the town immediately and arrested the strike committee.

The workers made their way to Lima where the news of the expulsion solidified support behind them and created the groundswell for the general strike. On March 26 representatives of the textile mills, the bakery workers, the coach drivers, and the anarchist groups agreed to join the Vitarte workers in a general strike if the owners delayed much longer in making a suitable offer. The latter did little to deflect the workers from their chosen path. They refused to make any wage increase; then, on the recommendation of the acting British consul, they refused any concession until the strikers returned to work and directed their arbitrator to follow this line after the two sides agreed to arbitration. As a result, the workers voted to declare a general strike for Monday, April 10.

The decision produced some frenzied action by President Leguía who had shown sympathy in the past for the workers' cause. On the ninth he met with Castillo and representatives of the Asamblea and told them he supported their demands for a shorter work day and the abolition of night work, but he asked them to accept a work day one-half hour longer than demanded. If they did, he personally would give each worker five soles. The proposal aroused little enthusiasm among the workers who pressed ahead with their plans for the strike. It was to be a purely social demonstration—all political manifestations were prohibited—and the strike committee issued handbills urging the workers and the public at large to join the strike as an act of protest and solidarity against the "brutal egoism of evil capital."[24]

At 8 A.M. on April 10 the first general strike in Peruvian history began. Almost the entire work force in Lima's textile mills, lumber yards, bottling plants, slaughterhouses, printing firms, factories, and other establishments stopped work. Hotel and restaurant staffs and coach drivers joined them. Shops closed. Only a few including one owned by Manuel Mazzi, a past president of the Asamblea, remained open. The trams, too, continued to operate under the protection of armed guards, but they, like Mazzi's shop, became a target for demonstrators and soon closed. Six thousand workers congregated in the Paseo Colón to cheer the general strike, the Vitarte strike, and the solidarity of the workers. They then marched to the Plaza de Armas waving red flags, having rejected the plea of the minister of government that they carry the national bicolor instead, and once more presented their demands to Leguía.

On the eleventh the strike continued. Lima resembled "a city in mourning" as no one ventured forth for fear of the unknown. Shops remained closed, and the only people in the streets were patrols of police and soldiers. Behind the scenes, however, negotiations had been proceeding, and in the face of the workers' resolve the authorities gave in. They granted everything: the abolition of night work, the opening of a canteen, the reinstatement of all the workers, and better wages. The company still had to agree, but since the government had accepted, this was only a formality.

Castillo was convinced that the general strike had achieved all that it could, and on the afternoon of the eleventh he declared it over, despite the desire of some Vitarte workers to continue until the owners accepted the agreement. By that evening Lima was back to normal. The Vitarte workers remained on strike a few days longer while their employers argued over some terms of the agreement, but by the seventeenth they had returned to work, with only the size of the wage increase still to be resolved.

The general strike had been a tremendous success. The anarchists complained that more could have been achieved if it had continued, but they recognized that the Vitarte workers had won all they had demanded. The strike was followed by the formation of two new societies for the textile workers, the Unificación Obrera Textil de Vitarte and the Unificación Proletaria Textil de Santa Catalina, both of which were dedicated to the socioeconomic struggle of the workers and to the formation of other syndicalist organizations.[25] The general strike had once again demonstrated the value of united action and, perhaps more importantly, had revealed to the government, the employers, and the rest of the country that the workers could unite to get their interests recognized. In the words of *La Prensa*, "The workers have given a demonstration of their strength which although still modest is now visible; a bit confused perhaps, lacking in orientation, possibly without energetic direction, but they have succeeded in showing to everyone the spirit and effect of a fine and commendable test of solidarity."[26]

The success of the strike was not a signal for new agitation since, as *La Prensa* had noted, the strength of the workers was still limited. During the following months two workers at Vitarte were fired for assaulting another who had not participated in the strike, and Luis F. Grillo, a worker at El Progreso who had been one of the organizers of the general strike, was also fired. In both cases attempts were made to organize strikes to force their reinstatement, but without success.[27] Nevertheless, employers on the whole now appeared more willing to respond to their workers' demands, and other strikes during the year were quickly settled to the workers' satisfaction.

The year 1911 had been an important one for the Peruvian labor movement. The general strike had revealed the potential strength of Lima's workers and at the same time had shown that they could unite to defend their interests and improvements could be won by direct action. That same year the law of professional risk was passed, indicating improvements could be won by the political route. Also in 1911 the anarchists began to recover some of their earlier enthusiasm so that the most militant leaders regained their voice. The different foci of these developments pointed to the likelihood of further divisions among the workers, but they also meant the movement was more vibrant and active than ever before. In the following year it was to be drawn in a new direction with the election of Guillermo Billinghurst as president of Peru. Populism now became a factor in the Peruvian labor movement and although its roots lay in past developments, its impact was to be as significant as mutualism, anarchism, or industrial action.

6 The Impact of Guillermo Billinghurst, 1912–1914[1]

The year 1912 marked a new milestone in the development of the Peruvian labor movement with the election of Guillermo E. Billinghurst to the nation's top office. Billinghurst's electoral success was largely a result of the intervention of Lima's workers, and his presidency can be seen as an early example of populism. It exhibited many of the characteristics associated with the populist movements that emerged in Latin America beginning in the 1930s.[2] There was a multiclass alliance involving the workers and their leader, the wealthy Billinghurst. The workers won some notable improvements as they pressed their demands on a sympathetic and indebted president. Their achievements reflected Billinghurst's desire to assist them, their own growing strength, and the elite's recognition of both. This period also demonstrated the workers' continuing lack of confidence in their own leaders and their readiness to turn from labor agitation to political pressure when it seemed more likely to satisfy their needs. Moreover, the Peruvian workers, like Latin American workers operating under later populist regimes, did not destroy the power of the elite; in fact, they hardly dented it. As a result, they could not prevent the elite, who saw the new developments as a threat to their traditional political and economic power, from organizing a coup that removed Billinghurst from office in February 1914 and ended this early experiment in social reform.

Guillermo Billinghurst was not a typical member of the Peruvian upper class. Born in 1851 in the southern province of Arica, he was the grandson of a British hero of the independence wars and the son of a wealthy businessman. His money came largely from the nitrate trade of Tarapacá, in sharp contrast to the estate-based wealth of Peru's traditional elite. The loss of the southern province to Chile following the War of the Pacific set Billinghurst further apart for his wealth was now centered in the country that was Peru's archenemy. Billinghurst certainly had no affection for Peru's leading families or their political party, and he remained a staunch opponent of *civilismo* throughout his life. Politically, he was a member of the Democratic party and, initially, a loyal follower of Piérola. He financed and participated in several of Piérola's rebellions and following the successful revolution of 1895 was rewarded for his loyalty and generosity by being named first vice-president. His efforts to solve the thorny question of the captive provinces of Tacna and Arica during this period enhanced his reputation, and it was generally assumed he would succeed Piérola in 1899. However, the Democratic chief, in order to guarantee his future political ambitions, wanted to maintain the alliance between his party and the Civilistas that had been established in 1895, and in this scheme of things there was no place for a sworn enemy of the Civilistas. As a result, Piérola chose the less controversial Romaña as his successor.

His decision destroyed the long-standing friendship. Billinghurst withdrew from politics and for a time devoted himself to his business concerns. During this period he seems to have developed his interest in the working class. He already had some contacts through his membership in the Democratic party, his ties with Piérola, and his hostility towards the Civilistas. He was also a member of at least one mutual aid society and had been elected president of the Sociedad Peruana de Socorros Mutuos (Peruvian Society of Mutual Aid) of Iquique in 1891. During his years in the political wilderness he established further contacts. The 1907 Iquique strike aroused his concern, and he was associated with the Chilean Democratic party that had ties with local artisans.

Billinghurst's interest in the workers was fully apparent when he reappeared on the Peruvian political scene as mayor of Lima in 1909. During his two years in office he introduced a number of reforms designed to help them. He established outlets in the poorer districts to sell meat at cost price; he prosecuted vendors who defrauded the public; he ordered the demolition of the city's slums, particularly parts of the Chinese barrio, and began replacing them with cheap, sanitary housing for workers; he improved the city's potable water supply; and he intervened in strikes on the workers' behalf. As a result, he won the affection of the urban workers. In 1912 he was to ride this support to the presidency.[3]

In the context of Peruvian politics it seemed unlikely that an outsider, and especially a person like Billinghurst, could ever become president. But 1912 was not a typical election year, and the particular circumstances surrounding the election created the possibility of an upset. During the presidency of Augusto Leguía, the Civilista party split over Leguía's policies, with the result that Leguía's chosen successor, a wealthy estate owner named Antero Aspíllaga, had the support only of the Leguiísta wing. Yet, even this reduced support appeared more than adequate until the end of April for the Independent Civilistas and the other parties were unable to find an alternative candidate.[4] It was at this point, with only a month remaining until the election, that Billinghurst's name began to be mentioned as a possible candidate, and a campaign led by the workers developed.

Lima's workers were already in an excited state from the previous year's general strike and were further aroused by a deputy's blatant attempt to take over the two main workers societies in April. The Confederación de Artesanos and the Asamblea de Sociedades Unidas, in a rare display of unity, had agreed to cooperate in naming candidates for the 1912 municipal election, but in the process they attracted the attention of Luis B. Castañeda, the unpopular deputy originally elected with worker backing. Seeing the alliance as potentially valuable to his own political ambitions, he tried with government support to seize control of the two organizations by intervening in their nomination meetings and having the Confederación's president arrested. He was stopped when the workers threatened a new general strike and subsequently expelled from the Confederación, but the government that had backed him remained a target of worker animosity.[5]

Another indication of the workers' spirit was the May Day celebrations. Thousands of workers participated, moving Caracciolo Lévano to comment, "The brilliant manifestation of *compañerismo* [comradeship] and solidarity effected to celebrate the glorious date of May 1 is tangible proof that the seed of socialism sown in the proletarian furrow on May 1, 1905 has germinated prodigiously and with insuperable vigor."[6]

It was in this atmosphere that Billinghurst emerged as a possible presidential candidate. The movement supporting him was at first a provincial phenomenon, but by May 6 it was in the hands of Lima's workers. That day five hundred of them marched to his house to express their support and during the following weeks progressively larger demonstrations occurred daily. To assist his candidacy the workers also formed political clubs such as the Centro Obrero Guillermo Billinghurst (Workers Center Guillermo Billinghurst) and the Artesanos Billinghurst No. 1 (Billinghurst Artisans No. 1); by mid-May there were over thirty of these clubs in Lima and Callao alone. Demonstrations held for the candidates on May 19, the last Sunday before the election, indicated the extent of Billinghurst's growing popularity: Aspíllaga attracted at most two thousand supporters; Billinghurst attracted over twenty thousand.

Aspíllaga had not been ignoring the workers. In his election manifesto he recognized them as an important sector of the population and expressed his support for programs such as the construction of houses, reduced prices for staples, increased employment opportunities, and improved educational facilities. He promised to work with the municipalities to improve sanitary conditions in work areas and in the workers' homes, to stimulate savings habits, and to ensure the implementation of the law of professional risk. However, his appeal for support aroused little enthusiasm among the workers whose feelings were graphically illustrated by members of the Club "Motoristas y Conductores" ("Motormen and Conductors" Club) during the demonstration on the nineteenth. They carried two poles. On one was a diminutive loaf of bread with the inscription, "This will cost 20 centavos if Aspíllaga wins." On the other was a loaf a meter in length with the caption, "This will cost 5 centavos if Billinghurst wins."[7]

"*Pan grande,*" as he came to be called, had the support of the masses, but he recognized that this did not necessarily mean political success in Peru. On May 4 he stated that if the people wished it, then his duty was to accept the electoral challenge. However, he refused to commit himself because he needed time to organize his campaign, win the backing of the parties, and sound out Leguía, whose support for Aspíllaga had been minimal so far. Charging that blatant irregularities had occurred in the electoral process, Billinghurst urged that the election be postponed so the authorities could make corrections and thereby ensure the election of a truly representative candidate. His campaign to delay the election won popular support, but failed where it counted most. According to the constitution, only the president could order a postponement, and Leguía refused to intervene. Aspíllaga's victory seemed assured.

It was at this point that the workers decided to take matters into their own hands. They had been roused by the recent demonstrations and the prospect of Billinghurst as president, and they now refused to accept the imposition of a preselected candidate. Aware that more than one-third of the registered voters had to cast their ballots for an election to be constitutionally valid, they voted to hold a general strike on the two days of the election, ostensibly to protest against the illegalities surrounding it, but in fact to prevent its occurrence.

Their plan succeeded admirably. On May 25 and 26 they paralyzed Lima and Callao and overturned the few voting tables officials managed to set up so that no votes were cast in the two cities. In the other urban centers the story was the same as workers disrupted the voting. The necessary one-third votes were not cast; Aspíllaga's election was prevented; and, in the words of *La Prensa,* the "popular will" had triumphed.

In default of an election, Congress now had to choose the president. Aspíllaga made a last ditch effort to get his claim recognized, but Congress was hesitant to challenge the workers who were continuing to demonstrate and threatening new general strikes if their wishes were ignored. The upper class may have been suspicious of Billinghurst because of his links with the masses and his dependence on their support, but unlike the workers they were not united at that time. Moreover, they may have believed that once in power he could be controlled by Congress and would not prejudice the interests of his own class. A deal between Billinghurst and the Leguiístas who composed the majority in Congress cleared the way for his election. The first vice-presidency was given to the retiring president's brother in return for Leguiísta support in the congressional election, and on August 9 Congress confirmed the popular choice for president by a vote of 130 to 4 with 26 abstentions.[8]

The intervention of the workers had succeeded: their candidate was now president of the country. Billinghurst recognized his debt to the workers and was willing to repay it. At a banquet in his honor in July he told an audience composed of the "better social, commercial, banking, and industrial circles" of Lima that he intended to change the election laws to ensure that all sectors of the population were guaranteed political representation; he was going to introduce laws to protect the workers, build them cheap, sanitary housing, amplify and clarify the law of professional risk, find jobs for the unemployed, and provide assistance to those who were sick or permanently disabled. In his inauguration speech on September 24 he repeated his intention to assist this particular group.[9]

The workers, however, had already decided to take matters into their own hands. They had seen once again that direct action could produce advantageous results, and now with a sympathetic and obligated president in power the way seemed open for more profitable labor agitation. Even before Billinghurst's inauguration, strikes began. In early September the tram workers and electricians of the Empresas Eléctricas Asociadas went on strike for higher wages and better working conditions and managed to win some improvements. When Billinghurst took the oath of office the Santa Catalina workers were on strike protesting against the mill's working conditions and system of fines. Three weeks of fruitless negotiations were followed by a new general strike on October 8, this time involving workers from both Lima and Callao. It lasted only a day, as Billinghurst stepped in and agreed to arbitrate the Santa Catalina strike, which he ended by obtaining a small wage increase for the workers and promising governmental assistance to the industry. Before the end of the year he was drawn into further disputes involving Lima's bakery workers and employees of a biscuit factory.[10]

The agitation culminated in January 1913 when the Callao harbor workers went on strike. Trouble had been brewing on the docks for some time. The large number of workers meant that jobs were being apportioned on a rota system that placed the workers at the mercy of unscrupulous bosses. In early December 1912 agitation began for better working conditions, higher wages, and the reintroduction of the register. The workers at first saw the government as their potential savior and petitioned it for assistance. But then, in response to anarchist pressure, their attitude changed and they decided to rely on their own resources. At a meeting on December 15 they altered their demands from improvements in their working conditions to the introduction of the eight-hour day. This change was a result of the influence of two Italian anarchists, José Spagnoli and Antonio Gustinelli, representatives of the Federación Obrera Regional Argentina (Workers Regional Federation of Argentina) who were in Callao at this time as guests of the local anarchist groups.[11] Spagnoli described the eight-hour day as "the basis of all conquests that can be won by the proletariat in their struggles," and as neither the government nor management had agreed to the workers' initial demands, the idea won wide acceptance. When the harbor workers finally went on strike on January 7 after further futile negotiations, they demanded the eight-hour day plus a 10 percent wage increase and better overtime pay, and they had the support of all of Callao's workers together with the more militant of the Lima groups.

The direction of the strike seemed to suggest that the anarchists were firmly in control. However, the potential influence of Billinghurst was too great to be ignored, and on January 9 the strikers arranged to meet him. There was little pressure to do anything more than try to arrange some sort of compromise: the strike was but two days old; it involved only the harbor workers, although they did have some outside support; management had expressed its willingness to negotiate; and the strikers obviously were not confident that they could succeed on their own. Yet Billinghurst granted them everything that they had demanded. He told them that he would issue a supreme decree establishing the eight-hour day and would meet with their employers to obtain an equitable wage increase.

With this high-level backing, management had little choice but to agree. On the tenth they notified the workers they would accept Billinghurst's decision if it was confirmed by a supreme decree. The president complied immediately, ordering that "the unloading on the wharf and dock and in the bay of Callao will take place . . . from 7 to 11 A.M. and from 1 to 5 P.M."[12]

By granting the eight-hour day Billinghurst indicated once more his commitment to the workers and his intention to repay his political debt. At the same time he laid a claim to leading the workers in their socioeconomic struggles. This was a claim he needed to establish more firmly, for many were wondering who was really in charge. The granting of the eight-hour day to the harbor workers triggered off a rash of strikes, first in Callao and then in Lima, as other sectors of the labor force now tried to win it. In Callao the flour mills, foundries, Central Railway, gas company, bottling plants, brewery, shipping companies, lumber yards, tobacco deposits, customs, a bakery, and the municipality were all hit by strikes. In Lima the strikes involved employees of the textile mills, foundries, lumber yards, breweries, bakeries, coal yards, and the telephone company, as well as confectioners, carpenters, and carters. Some plantation workers also joined. All of them wanted a shorter work day— some were willing to accept more than eight hours—and they also demanded better wages. How was Billinghurst going to respond?

On January 17 he assured a delegation of industrialists, mine owners, and landholders, who argued that the extension of the eight-hour day to other sectors of the labor force would have ruinous effects on the country, that he had no intention of becoming involved in these new disputes and that the strikers would not be receiving his assistance.[13] However, more resolute action was essential to convince the business community and to confirm his control over the workers. On January 24 he issued a second decree. It recognized the right of the workers to strike while establishing specific guidelines that had to be followed both before the strike and during it, for the strikers to receive official recognition. The workers first had to go to arbitration. If this was rejected by their employers, they could then consider strike action, but could declare a strike only if three-quarters of the workers agreed. Written notice of the strike had to be posted with the authorities, and strike votes had to be taken every four days during the strike. If employers wanted to declare a lockout in the face of worker hostility, they first had to inform the authorities in writing. A supplementary edict on January 30 established special Labor Sections in the police departments of Lima and Callao to collect data on the labor scene for further government action.

According to Billinghurst, the strike decree was designed to end the conflict between capital and labor, which was compromising the interests of the country's economic and financial sectors. It became operative on January 27 and had an immediate impact as most of the strikes ended within days. Some of the Callao workers, including the customs workers and employees of the gas company, the flour mills, lumber yards, bottling plants, and a printing firm, managed to win the eight-hour day from their employers. In Lima, however, although some workers won wage improvements, none won the eight-hour day. According to the anarchists, this was because "capitalism had time to prepare a defense and . . . the government actively cooperated with the draconian decree of the twenty-fourth."[14]

The strikes and Billinghurst's response to them had set the guidelines the workers had to follow in the future if they wanted his assistance. In effect, he had shown them that they were not free to operate as they wished. At the same time, he had indicated to the business community that he was prepared to act resolutely in controlling the workers and that he was not under their control.

His decrees had some success. Workers complied with the strike decree, and employers seemed more willing to meet workers' demands so that the frequency of disputes declined. The Labor Sections were also operating. The head of the Lima section intervened in a strike involving the El Inca workers who wanted higher wages and an end to the company's system of fines. The strike dragged on for several weeks, but with the continuous involvement of the official a satisfactory compromise was finally reached and the strike did not expand into a wider conflict. With the assistance of this new office a clearer picture of the work force also began to emerge. In June the Callao section reported that there were seventy-six centers of work in the port employing 2,667 men, 36 women, and 442 children in nonagricultural work. The average work day was nine hours. The lowest paid workers were child apprentices of the Aguila foundry, the El Sol match factory, and the La Estrella soap factory. The foundry paid twenty-five centavos per day, while the two factories paid sixty centavos. The highest wages were paid by the Peruvian Steamship Company, the White foundry, and the Guadalupe foundry: 6.60, 6.30, and 5.13 soles per day respectively. The section also found that there were nineteen workers societies in the port with a total membership of 3,973.[15]

In addition to maintaining closer control over the workers, Billinghurst undertook a number of initiatives to ensure that he retained their support.

First, he tried to fulfill the promises he had made during his election campaign. After his inauguration he introduced a bill to improve the congressional representation of the workers by establishing a system of occupational representation. However, the bill which Congress finally passed merely altered the bureaucracy in charge of elections to reduce electoral corruption. In July 1913 Billinghurst issued a series of decrees that clarified the law of professional risk, and he asked Congress for laws to supplant his decree of January 24 and to fill the enormous gap in labor legislation. He repeated his intention to find a job with a fair wage for every worker, and he pursued his plans to build them cheap houses. Although his efforts resulted in the construction of only a few units, one harbor worker felt that what Billinghurst had accomplished made him "Peru's first worker" and the "incarnation of an ideal for the proletariat."[16]

Billinghurst's efforts on behalf of the workers also extended to promoting relations between the workers of Peru and Chile. With his links to both countries he was in an ideal position to pursue this goal. In 1913 Víctor A. Pujazón, a printer and member of the Confederación de Artesanos, was sent to Chile to invite a delegation of Chilean workers to Peru's independence day celebrations on July 28. A delegation of Peruvian workers returned the visit in September. The visits were a great success and momentarily helped to reduce the tension between the two countries. The delegates signed a solidarity pact whose purpose was to end the differences between their nations and to foment closer relations among all the workers of Latin America. Another result was the formation of a new workers society, the Centro Internacional Obrero de Solidaridad Latino-Americana del Perú (International Workers Center for Latin American Solidarity of Peru), in November 1913 under the direction of Pujazón. Its objectives included uniting the workers of all the American republics, organizing congresses of Latin American workers, and educating local workers in their rights and obligations.[17]

With Billinghurst playing such an effective role on behalf of the workers, there was a decline in the importance of the old working-class leaders, the mutual aid societies, and the anarchist resistance societies. Most seriously affected were the mutual aid societies, which had been experiencing problems for some years and were now almost completely eclipsed. Their enthusiasm for political activity and their determination to have a representative of the working class in Congress had waned. In the congressional and municipal elections of 1913 they supported doctors, lawyers, engineers, newspapermen, and politicians, but very few workers. The Confederación de Artesanos did not even participate in the municipal election.[18]

This lack of interest may have been a result of the ineffectiveness of their past choices. The most recent workers deputies, Carlos Lora y Quiñones and Luis B. Castañeda, had achieved little for the workers, and a pro-Billinghurst newspaper, *La Acción Popular,* charged that "the workers' representatives have so far never responded to the workers' needs nor have they been the genuine and spontaneous fruit of the working masses; they were always the result of political opportunism since their election depended upon the party entities or party groupings, not the working class." The few representatives of the masses who had been elected to the Chamber of Deputies were nothing more than "a symbol or a decoration."[19] The presence of Billinghurst in the nation's highest office may also have reduced the societies' interest in expending energy on electing representatives to lesser bodies.

Reduced political involvement, however, removed the mutual aid societies from what had been one of their few areas of influence. Only their mutual aid activities survived and these provided little opportunity for action. The Confederación de Artesanos suffered a particular decline, undergoing an internal power struggle that almost destroyed it and led to its reorganization in 1913.[20]

The situation called for more aggressive leadership, and in 1913 a group of mutual aid society members sought to meet this challenge by forming a new society, the Confederación General de Trabajadores del Perú (General Confederation of Peruvian Workers). It was led by the long-time labor leader, Juan Goachet. In structure it resembled the old mutual aid federations, but it supported more militant goals such as the transformation of member guilds into resistance societies, the passage of more labor legislation, the creation of cooperatives to sell food to the poor at reduced prices, and the construction of houses for workers. It also fully supported the anarchist goal of the eight-hour work day.[21]

More successful in facing the challenge presented by Billinghurst's leadership were the anarchist organizations. In March 1913 they installed their own federation, the Federación Obrera Regional del Perú (FORP), which comprised the city's biscuit workers, textile workers, the Gremio Liberal de Empleados, and some other sectors of the urban work force; the two study groups, "Luz y Amor" and "La Protesta"; and the workers of the nearby "La Estrella" plantation. The goals of the federation were to unite the workers of each industry or profession in resistance societies, combine these societies in order to fight capitalism, assist the federated societies, and elevate the intellectual and moral level of the workers through education and emancipatory propaganda. The FORP spearheaded anarchist activities. It directed attacks on the mutual aid societies and chose a representative, Eulogio Otazú, to accompany the Peruvian delegation to Chile in September 1913. Otazú's participation did not go unnoticed. In Santiago local anarchists disrupted a meeting to insist that he be allowed to speak. In Valparaíso he got involved in a strike, was arrested, and sent back to Peru. In Callao he was met by hostile demonstrators, whom the anarchists later claimed had been paid by the government.[22]

The FORP also provided assistance to striking workers, an activity that remained one of the anarchists' primary means of influencing the labor force. The anarchists' involvement in the January 1913 strike in Callao was crucial, and although opportunities of this sort declined for a time, they offered assistance when they could. In July 1913 they led a boycott directed at the ships of Duncan Fox and Company, the Lima agent of the London and Pacific Petroleum Company. There had been strikes recently in the oil fields, and the latter company had reneged on an agreement not to fire any of the strikers. The FORP, together with the Federación Obrera Maritima y Terrestre del Callao (Maritime and Shore Workers' Federation of Callao), a new organization formed after the January 1913 strikes, declared a boycott that succeeded in forcing the company to reinstate the workers.[23]

Despite successes of this sort, the influence of the anarchists was still limited, especially when compared with that of Billinghurst, and they were aware of the fact. Their aims were still limited: "to set forth the ideas and aspirations of the proletariat, to awaken and fortify feelings of solidarity . . , and to introduce real and practical means of struggle."[24] If this resulted in the emergence of working-class leaders for the labor movement, they would be satisfied, but at the moment they recognized the dominant position enjoyed by the president.

Billinghurst's leadership of the workers was thus undisputed and, as a result, he could satisfy his desire to assist them and in the process repay his electoral debt. There was, moreover, an additional factor that ensured a continuing relationship between the workers and the president: just as his election had depended upon their intervention, so too did his continuing political effectiveness. While in office Billinghurst failed to establish either some kind of working relationship with one of the existing parties or a party of his own, so he had no control over Congress and little likelihood of ever establishing any. Thus, he could not guarantee approval of any of his legislative proposals. But through the workers he had an unofficial means of creating pressure and influencing congressional decisions in a manner reminiscent of his 1912 political campaign.

The institution responsible for this pressure was the Comité de Salud Pública (Committee of Public Welfare), a semi-official body that the British minister to Peru described as "a mysterious numerous body of men for whom work is said to be found by the Government on some sanitation works but who are also generally held to be kept in readiness to give expression to the wishes of the President—or what are supposed to be his wishes—as conveyed to them by one or two go-betweens of their own class reported to be in His Excellency's political confidence." Members included some participants in the presidential campaign, as well as a number of recent refugees from Tarapacá.

The main targets of the Comité were ex-President Leguía and his followers who comprised the majority in Congress and who were held responsible for blocking Billinghurst's planned reforms. In December 1912 the Comité attacked the offices of the pro-Leguía weekly, *Mosquito*, while members of the police force watched. In June 1913 it attempted to influence the results of the congressional elections in Ica and Arequipa by demonstrating outside the Palacio de Justicia while the Supreme Court was deciding on the successful candidates. On July 24, after the Senate approved the credentials of a recently elected anti-Billinghurst senator, the Comité first occupied the chamber and then attacked the houses of Leguía and the president of the Senate. The ex-president defended himself against the mob and shot and killed one of them. Arrested and deported, he arrived in Panama charging that Peru was in a "state of anarchy where the desires of the populace reign supreme and where the *descamisados* [masses] have usurped all the prerogatives of government."[25]

The direct participation of the masses in the political process did, in fact, seem to be altering the old system of government. The traditional control exercised by the small ruling elite appeared threatened, so that many of this group shared Leguía's views. Dissatisfaction with Billinghurst was becoming increasingly evident, and as early as July 1913 there were rumors of his imminent deposition.[26] Opposition grew in response to other factors that equally threatened the elite. During the second half of 1913 labor agitation resumed, raising again the question of who really was in control. At the same time a constitutional crisis provided Billinghurst's enemies with ammunition to attack him publicly and a rallying point to draw the alienated into a conspiracy that ultimately succeeded in removing him from office.

The renewed labor agitation, resulting mainly from price increases, began with the Duncan Fox boycott in August. It was followed by a series of strikes involving the Santa Rosa mill workers, the harbor workers, the Callao brewery workers, and the Guadalupe foundry workers. The strikes received wide support and threatened to broaden into general strikes. The representative of the Peruvian Corporation reported, "Our men [are] in a dangerously unsatisfied state, as is the entire working class here at the present time." He blamed the unrest on the government for its "pampering of the working class during the last year."[27]

The agitation placed Billinghurst in an extremely difficult position. On no account did he want to antagonize his working-class support, yet at the same time he was under pressure from both the business community and factors related to his 1914 budget to establish firm control. The budget was supposed to be passed by Congress, but Billinghurst was hesitant to present it because of almost certain resistance from the Leguiísta majority in retaliation for deporting their leader. To avoid a confrontation, he turned to other sources and began negotiating a loan of 500,000 pounds sterling from English and French financiers through the firm of W. R. Grace and Company. In this situation, as the British minister observed, "any raising of the labour question would certainly be detrimental to the prospects of that advance."[28]

This was the dilemma confronting Billinghurst when a new strike broke out among the Callao workers in November. Fortunately for him, the circumstances surrounding the dispute permitted him to crush it without affecting his working-class support. The strike began among the brewery workers who demanded the removal of a foreman who had refused to join their society. Other sectors of the labor force joined, and the Federación Maritima y Terrestre began organizing a general strike for November 27 to try to force a favorable solution. The Federación, however, was not a united body at this time because recent decisions by the executive had alienated some of the membership. They had objected to the choice of representatives for the Peruvian delegation to Chile, the imposition of weekly dues (reportedly for a strike fund but controlled only by the executive), and the executive's insistence upon the removal of a popular foreman. Consequently, the general strike attracted only limited support that permitted Billinghurst to use uncharacteristically tough measures to bring it under control. With the president's approval, the

Callao prefect declared the strike illegal, gave assistance to those who wanted to work, issued a number of decrees restricting the movements of the strikers, and arrested ten of their leaders including the Federación's president, Fernando Vera, and secretary, José Robles.

This may have been something of a gamble for Billinghurst, but it succeeded: the strike was broken without the loss of worker support. He lectured a delegation of strikers that if they had complied with his strike decree, they would have received an immediate and equitable offer from their employers; by interfering with shipping as they had done, they were only "killing the goose that lays the golden eggs." They admitted that the strike had been a mistake and contrary to the "high intentions" of his regime and accepted the subsequent deportation of Vera and Robles with little comment.[29]

Billinghurst's response to the strike met with the approval of the business community, but it failed to save his presidency.[30] Already a small group of conspirators headed by the leader of the Liberal party, Augusto Durand, had begun plotting his overthrow. The focus of the conspiracy was a constitutional question that had developed from Billinghurst's budget problems. Despite receiving his stopgap loan, he still had to get his budget passed.[31] Two alternatives lay open to him: he could either avoid Congress altogether by declaring his budget operative by decree, as certain of his predecessors had done, or he could dissolve Congress and call an election in order to obtain more compliant representatives. He decided on the former, but many congressmen believed the charges then appearing in *La Prensa*, that he was also going to proceed with the latter, and accused him of unconstitutionality.[32]

Billinghurst was not oblivious to the growing threat. His response was to mobilize the only group whom he could trust, the workers. From late December demonstrations organized by the Comité de Salud Pública began to occur in a manner reminiscent of May 1912, with the participants calling for the dissolution of Congress and new elections. Workers societies like the Asamblea and even the Federación Marítima expressed complete confidence in the president, while representatives of the Confederación de Artesanos offered him their unconditional assistance "to safeguard the most cherished interests of the country" that, they claimed, were being "threatened by the ambitions of unscrupulous politicians." Outside Lima the response was the same as workers in Arequipa, Trujillo, and other centers held demonstrations in support of the president and new elections. In Cuzco a pro-Billinghurst rally attracted ten thousand participants.[33]

The demonstrations aroused fears of a new mass movement, and Billinghurst did little to dispell the impression. In an interview in the English-language weekly, *The West Coast Leader,* on January 29, he denied that he had engineered the demonstrations or that he was arousing "the masses against the classes." However, he had a "deep and abiding interest in seeing the people rule" and would do all in his power to achieve this since he believed that "the equality . . . of all Peruvians must be realized sooner or later." The editors of the paper commented that what was happening was in fact a "social revolution" and that the tradition of "the concentration of power in the hands of the few, the elimination of the great mass of the people as anything but a passive factor in the government" was being "undermined and overthrown." They seemed willing to accept this, but they disliked the way the political uncertainty was detrimentally affecting business.[34]

Peru's ruling groups, on the other hand, were not at all happy with the idea of a social revolution. The plotting intensified, and the ranks of the conspirators grew to include officers of the Lima garrison. In early February Billinghurst resorted to firmer action to counter the threat. He ordered the arrest of some of the conspirators and forced others into hiding. On February 3 he closed *La Prensa*. Popular demonstrations had been continuing, and on the afternoon of the third arms and blank ammunition were distributed to his supporters. For the rest of the day and into the early hours of the morning they drove through the streets firing volleys into the air and cheering Billinghurst. It was the last gasp of a doomed regime.

No sooner had the demonstration ended than the conspirators acted. The Lima garrison led by Colonel Oscar Benavides attacked the presidential palace and, after overcoming some loyalist resistance, arrested Billinghurst and forced him to resign. Firing continued for a short time, but by 6 A.M. the city was quiet. The Billinghurst presidency had ended.[35]

The speed of the coup indicated the strength and organization of the conspirators and the weakness and disorganization of the Billinghurst forces. The conspiracy involved members of all the political parties, except the Democrats, together with representatives of the business community and elements of the army. The stated reason for the coup was "the decision of the Executive to cancel dictatorially the powers of Congress and to convoke a general election of senators and deputies in order to substitute one legal parliament with another. This would constitute the gravest crime against the National Sovereignty whose most substantive manifestation is the Legislative Power exercised by Congress." A decree for the dissolution of Congress was presented by the conspirators following the coup, although Billinghurst subsequently denied that he had planned such an action.[36]

There is little question that some of the participants in the coup genuinely believed that the constitution was in danger, but this argument was used to cover a variety of other, more self-centered reasons. Basically, opposition resulted from Billinghurst's challenge to the old order. Under his tutelage the workers were becoming too bold, too disrespectful. In the process they were altering the rules of the traditional political game and affecting the economic position of the business community. This trend towards greater popular participation had to be halted.[37]

Billinghurst later claimed that some of the leaders of the coup had acted solely out of personal ambition for the presidency. This was certainly true of Durand, who had been involved in plots and rebellions throughout his life. In 1912 he had supported Billinghurst, expecting perquisites in return for his party and support for Liberal candidates in congressional elections. Billinghurst, however, had refused and thereby transformed Durand into an implacable enemy. As leader of the coup, he expected to succeed Billinghurst as president, but the Civilistas had no desire to see the Liberal leader in the nation's top office and managed to have Benavides named provisional president.[38]

The army officers had become involved because of a growing disenchantment with Billinghurst. Although he increased military spending during his first year in office, there was always the suspicion that one day he would make cuts in order to meet his commitments to the lower classes.[39] Statements such as one he made in October 1913 while distributing houses to workers in Callao did little to create confidence among the professionalized officer corps. "Of what use," he asked, "is the acquisition of large naval units . . . or of all the costly material of war if we do not conserve the health, the physical energy, and the spiritual vigor of the citizens who are called on to defend the Homeland?" Their suspicions seemed confirmed in December 1913 when Billinghurst issued his 1914 budget proposals containing cuts in military spending. This attack on the military came at a crucial moment and almost certainly won support for the conspirators.

There was also some question about Billinghurst's loyalty because of his contacts with the archenemy, Chile. Rumors spread that he intended to sell the captive provinces of Tacna and Arica to Chile, and his postponement of a plebiscite designed to decide the ultimate future of the provinces antagonized all the nationalistic elements in the country.

Finally, the discipline-minded officers were disturbed by the growing militancy and agitation of the masses. One thing they would not permit was the creation of a popular militia and, therefore, the arming of the workers on February 3 was the last straw. It confirmed the decision of the Lima garrison to support the conspiracy and ensured that other elements of the armed forces throughout the country remained neutral during the coup.[40]

While politicians, military officers, and the business community all united to overthrow Billinghurst, the workers did little to prevent it. During the fighting their involvement was minimal and civilian casualties few.[41] It seemed that even though the workers were mobilized in the expectation of some type of confrontation, they had not expected the military to intervene. When it did, they were not prepared to challenge it. Moreover, the speed of the coup gave them little time to organize any resistance. In fact, there was really no one to organize them. The events since May 1912 had established Billinghurst as their leader, but by 6 A.M. on Feburary 4 he had resigned and was under lock and key. The workers had no one to replace him.

The end of the Billinghurst presidency had a number of immediate effects upon the local labor movement. Workers societies issued statements denying that they had had any ties with Billinghurst, while some workers tried to ingratiate themselves with the new rulers. The executive of the Confederación de Artesanos resigned, and Billinghurst supporters in the Asamblea came under pressure to follow suit. Exiles like Fernando Vera were allowed to return. His first act was to form a workers club affiliated with the Liberal party.[42]

The coup had other important implications. It had indicated to the workers that although they were now a more influential group within society, they were still not sufficiently strong to challenge the combined might of the oligarchy and military, even with the backing of the president. The social structure remained largely intact, and it seemed that further organization and mobilization were essential if fundamental changes were to occur. The Billinghurst period had been a profitable one for the workers. Sections of the labor force now enjoyed the eight-hour day, international contacts had been established, a new vitality was evident within the movement, and the events of these eighteen months had aroused greater class consciousness. Yet, the ultimate failure raised questions about the efficacy of establishing political alliances that could produce short-term benefits but tied the workers into what was still an elitist and unrepresentative political system. There had been a growing emphasis upon political involvement since 1895, but the events of February 1914 clearly demonstrated the shortcomings of this path where the ties were with upper-class individuals. As a result, although workers were still attracted to politics and presidential contacts, many felt that working-class leaders and parties were more appropriate.

These feelings were reinforced by developments following the Billinghurst presidency. Within six months of the coup, war had broken out in Europe. Although Peru remained neutral, the effects of the war on the workers and the country as a whole were extensive. Billinghurst and his goals were not forgotten, but very quickly new factors came into play. In some cases they had an equal and even greater impact than this early populist figure.

Billinghurst had no further personal contact with the Peruvian workers. Exiled to Chile following the coup, he died there on June 28, 1915. On receiving the news, the workers societies in Lima declared a period of mourning. The following year, when his remains were returned to Peru, his supporters once more filled the streets of the capital. Thousands accompanied the coffin to the cemetery in a final demonstration of respect for the man who had claimed that his constant wish had been to ameliorate the lot of Peru's working class.[43]

7 The First World War

The years of the First World War were not auspicious ones for the labor movement in Lima and Callao. The outbreak of war negatively affected all sectors of Peruvian society; the country's economic dependence meant that the cutbacks and restrictions imposed by the Great Powers in August 1914 brought nationwide economic chaos and hardships. Some months later, when the belligerents realized the war was going to last much longer than originally anticipated, the economy began to recover, and the demand for raw materials produced a boom in Peru's primary sector. Some elements of the population prospered enormously from this, but there was no relief for the urban workers. Rising prices accompanied the export boom, while wages remained more or less stagnant. The conditions seemed ripe for a new round of labor agitation, yet few strikes occurred, partly because of high unemployment, partly because of government action, and partly because of pressures within the labor movement that kept the workers quiet. It was not until the final months of the war that the urban movement once more showed signs of militancy.

Before the outbreak of war the workers were in a disorganized state. They were still leaderless, and with the country under the control of army officers who valued order and discipline and Civilistas who wanted their political and economic prerogatives restored, the situation was hardly propitious for any kind of labor agitation. The deportation of a prominent anarchist in March for an article criticizing the government was a warning to any potential agitator. The workers seemed to recognize the difficulties of the situation, for they focused their attention on noncontroversial subjects; they issued protests at the American invasion of Mexico in April 1914 and the assassination of the French socialist, Juan Jaurés, in August; May Day was celebrated as usual but, according to *La Protesta,* with less enthusiasm than in the past. The tranquility of the labor scene prompted William Morkill to report in June that "there is considerably more willingness on the part of the men to do their duty than has been evident for some years past; in fact, the agitating element would appear to have been practically eliminated."[1]

The war had an immediate impact on Peru. Sources of loans and manufactured goods were cut off while shipping all but disappeared, pushing up freight rates and prices of all imports. Exports suffered as buyers canceled their orders in the belief that it would be a quick war and they had sufficient supplies on hand. President Benavides's response to the crisis was to declare a bank holiday and a moratorium on bank withdrawals to prevent the exporting and hoarding of gold. Factories and shops followed suit and closed the first days following the declaration of war. On reopening, they found their operations restricted by the lack of money in circulation and the uncertain financial situation. To conserve cash, firms began distributing work on a rota basis, reducing hours of work, cutting wages, and releasing workers. Unemployment soared, and by August 10 there were four thousand unemployed workers in Lima alone. In an attempt to halt this, the government issued a decree, based on Billinghurst's strike decree, that prohibited firms from releasing workers without giving them a day's notice and required them to inform the authorities of the reasons for the cuts and the names of those affected. The government also announced it would find jobs for the unemployed on public works projects.

The cost of essential goods rose as money, jobs, and shipping disappeared, freight rates increased, and merchants hoarded goods in the hope of future price increases. Under public pressure the government tried to combat the inflation by prohibiting the export of coal, rice, flour, beans, fat, corn, potatoes, wheat, and meat and instructing the municipalities to set prices for commodities at prewar levels, which were to remain in effect for the duration of the crisis.

There was still a cash shortage, which some observers felt was the principal cause of the difficulties. As the government declared new moratoria, pressure grew for the issuance of a paper currency despite popular distrust of banknotes. On August 22 the government authorized banks to issue circular checks, and subsequently paper currency became the main circulating medium. The new currency permitted the reestablishment of commercial transactions and the reopening of factories, but it also helped to inflate prices. As soon as the bills were issued, silver and gold coins disappeared from circulation and, equally quickly, the bills began depreciating in value. Moreover, they did not solve the country's financial difficulties; there was still not enough money to meet the foreign debt, payments had to be suspended, and Peru's international credit was affected.[2]

The economic uncertainty lasted almost a year. It was an important factor in the resignation of President Benavides, who found himself the target of increasing public hostility because of his inability to solve the crisis. He resigned in August 1915 following a convention of the various parties that named José Pardo to succeed him.

Under Pardo, the economy began to recover, especially the export sector. The prolongation of the war produced renewed demands for raw materials, and their value rose enormously with sugar, cotton, copper, and petroleum leading the way (see tables 1 and 2). However, the benefits produced by this expansion were not spread evenly throughout Peruvian society. While landholders, mine owners, and trading companies were making handsome profits, workers received little. Wages remained virtually unchanged, and the buying power of the sol declined with the rise in the cost of living (see tables 12 and 13). Increases in food prices caused

Table 12: Daily Wages in Lima and Callao, 1912–1918 (in soles)

	1912	1913	1915	1917	1918
Lima					
Bakery workers	3.20–3.50	3.40	3.20	—	3.75–5
Tram drivers	2–2.50	—	—	—	—
Telegraph operators	—	69–80m	—	—	—
Postal workers	—	1.20–1.50	—	—	—
El Inca	—	2–3	—	12.50w	—
Vitarte	—	—	1.75	—	—
Santa Catalina	—	—	—	15w	—
Shoemakers	—	—	2	—	—
Candle makers					
Men	—	—	2	—	—
Women	—	—	1.50	—	—
Callao					
Santa Rosa mill	1.80	—	—	—	—
Otero mill	—	—	—	—	1.60
Railway linemen	—	—	—	1.60	2
Dock workers					
Merchandise	—	—	—	2.80	—
Wood	—	—	—	2.86	3.56
Coal	—	—	—	3.52	—
Metal	—	—	—	4.40	—

m = per month, w = per week.

particular distress, while the further depreciation of the paper sol added to the workers' woes.³

In this situation direct action by the workers seemed almost inevitable, and there was some agitation following the initial measures taken by employers and government. The bank holiday prompted those still working to demand overtime pay. The workers societies protested the rise in prices and loss of jobs, demanded price controls, and threatened strikes if nothing was done. Two new organizations, the Comité de Defensa Obrera (Workers' Defense Committee), headed by Luis B. Castañeda, and the Asamblea de Solidaridad Obrera (Assembly of Workers' Solidarity), which incorporated the anarchist groups, were formed and pressed the municipality to reduce its rents on accommodation, shops, and market stalls. At the end of August the lack of money in circulation led to a rent strike. Requests by the mayor to the archbishop and beneficent society that they reduce their rents by 30 percent failed to satisfy the Asamblea, which wanted the rents for August and September wiped out altogether and subsequent rents reduced by 50 percent. Accusing the government of being interested only in safeguarding "the interests of the capitalists" at the expense of the workers who had lost their jobs and charging that landlords had failed to reduce their rents, it called for a general rent strike. Only the city's meat vendors participated, but some rents began to fall in response to the workers' continued pressure.⁴

This early agitation was not typical of the urban labor movement during the war years. A number of strikes occurred and there were threats of others but, in general, the situation remained calm because of increased government participation and a decrease in labor militancy. The workers accepted governmental intervention because of the leadership gap left by the fall of Billinghurst. Both Benavides and Pardo tried to win working-class support and impressed many workers who turned to the government for help rather than depend on their own resources. The

Table 13: Increases in the Cost of Living, 1913–1920

Category of Costs	%	1913	1914	1915	1916	1917	1918	1919	1920
Food	55	100	107	115	123	145	162	188	208
Housing	18	100	100	100	115	130	150	180	200
Clothing	12	100	100	117	129	146	192	223	268
Various	15	100	98	109	125	144	169	172	182
Cost of living	100	100	104	112	123	142	164	188	210

Source: Arrús, *El Costo de la Vida en Lima y Causas de su Carestía*, pp. 15–20.

general economic conditions and particularly the high unemployment rate also helped keep the situation calm. With the presence of a large pool of unemployed willing to accept work under almost any circumstances, those with jobs resisted any show of militancy. This benefited both the government and the mutual aid societies, which experienced something of a recovery during the war, and hurt the more radical organizations whose popularity declined even more because of wartime conditions and increased government persecution. As a result, the urban workers remained relatively quiet throughout most of the war and accomplished little.

The intervention of the government on the workers' behalf began almost immediately war was declared. The measures taken to assist the workers during the first weeks were followed by further directives designed to prevent the export of foodstuffs and regulate the supply and price of commodities. In 1917 the government set up depots in the poorer sections of the city to sell rice, sugar, and salt. The following year it commissioned a number of popular markets to sell goods at cost price, which meant savings of up to 75 percent. When the dock company, the Backus and Johnston brewery, the Ciurlizza y Maurer lumber yard, and the La Victoria textile mill established workers' cooperatives on their premises to sell produce at reduced prices, the government named a commission to look into the possibility of establishing similar cooperatives in every factory.[5]

The government also implemented existing projects and laws affecting workers. The construction of workers' houses remained popular. In 1915 a company was formed with government approval to issue shares to the workers and to use the accumulated capital to build 500 houses that would be sold to shareholders. However, the scheme failed, probably because few workers had money to invest. In March 1917 President Pardo ordered the completion of the 27 houses begun by Billinghurst and the construction of others, and the following year Congress approved a project to sell state land to construction companies at one sol per square meter for the construction of 100 model homes for workers and public employees.[6]

The government also tried amending the law of professional risk, whose numerous shortcomings had become apparent since its passage in 1911. The most common shortcoming was the refusal of companies to pay compensation if they believed the worker responsible for the accident. This could be rectified by judicial intervention, but in some areas no judge was available and there was confusion where the worker could go for legal redress. Companies also ignored judicial decisions. In one notorious case, the Morococha Mining Company refused to pay any compensation to an employee who had lost an arm and a hand in an accident. Assisted by the local workers societies, he went to Lima to commence legal action. At every level of the judicial system, including the Supreme Court, he was judged entitled to compensation, but the company still refused to pay. The law was later clarified by Billinghurst to some extent, and a decree in July 1914 ordered that details of industrial accidents be submitted to the authorities within thirty days. A more comprehensive amendment in October 1916 identified which judicial authorities should be used in instances that had produced confusion in the past, ordered the commencement of indemnities from the day of the accident, and denied any relationship between worker responsibility and payment of compensation. A firm trying to avoid its legal obligations by using this excuse would be fined the cost of any subsequent legal action.

This may have reduced the number of violations of the law and guaranteed more indemnities for injured workers, but many were still being denied their legal rights. Frequently they were reduced to begging in order to survive. In November 1918 *La Prensa* commented, "In the doors of our churches, in the barrios of our capital, and in various parts of the city we encounter the blind and mutilated who beg public charity, having left parts of their bodies in the mines, factories, or fields that have enriched and continue to enrich those wealthy owners who very easily could have maintained these unfortunates . . . in a more equitable state."[7]

President Pardo's attempts to assist the workers also extended to reintroducing some of the labor projects of José Matías Manzanilla, in particular those relating to female and child workers, a weekly day of rest, labor contracts, and strikes. Debate began on the first two, but by the end of the war no laws had been passed.[8]

In fact, few of the initiatives taken by the government had much success. Despite "new decrees, numerous circulars, repeated reports, copious expositions, [and] long conferences," food prices continued to rise, houses remained unbuilt, injured workers lacked compensation, and labor laws were a hope for the future. Nevertheless, the workers seemed to feel that Pardo and his government were honestly trying, and they issued frequent testimonials of their support. In 1918 the Confederación General de Trabajadores del Perú named Pardo honorary president of the organization and thanked him and the minister of finance for their efforts to reduce prices. When the military garrison at Ancón revolted in August

1918 to try to force Pardo to declare war on Germany, the workers societies condemned the mutineers and expressed their complete satisfactin with the government.[9]

The workers' wartime conservatism, as indicated by their dependence on the government, was also evident in the recovery of the mutual aid societies. Perhaps this would have occurred without the war since the Billinghurst presidency had shown that more aggressive involvement in the labor movement was needed if they wanted to reassume their leadership position, but it was confirmed by the developments of the war that produced widespread opposition to militancy. The societies began playing a more active role and in the process regained much of their old support. In August 1914 they were prominent in demanding price controls and rent reductions, and after they succeeded in obtaining the former they remained in close contact with the municipality to see that there was strict compliance. In their campaign for lower prices they pressed for lower freight rates, especially on foodstuffs, a prohibition on food exports, abolition of import duties on essential goods, the establishment of state shops to sell goods at cost price, and prosecution of those who speculated on the price of drugs. In 1916 a presidential commission, which included the three main societies' presidents, was formed to examine ways to reduce prices and, subsequently, the societies submitted several memorials and requests on the subject.[10]

The societies also tried to find jobs for the city's large number of unemployed. The Confederación de Artesanos suggested the formation of a labor exchange that would compile lists of available jobs and names of unemployed workers and might also serve as a mediator in labor disputes. The proposal appealed to the government, but Congress was slow in providing the necessary financing, so by 1917 interest had all but disappeared and only the Confederación General was pursuing the idea. The Confederación de Artesanos also suggested that in order to create jobs the municipality undertake a public works program and the beneficent and religious organizations repair and reconstruct their buildings. When Callao's El Sol match factory and its 120 jobs were threatened as a result of a new law imposing import duties on materials used in the manufacture of matches and eliminating duties on imported matches, all the societies in Lima and Callao urged President Pardo to amend the law. He agreed to reduce the duties over a period of three years, which temporarily saved some jobs. Another plan of the Confederación was to stimulate industrialization and in the process create new jobs. The society asked the government to prohibit the export of petroleum and use it instead to expand the nation's industrial base. However, this, like the other proposals of the societies, created little in the way of new jobs, and in 1918 it was reported that, although workers were willing to accept any wage, they could find no jobs.[11]

The crisis in employment again drew the attention of the societies to the continuing influx of Asian immigrants. It prompted renewed racialistic charges and attempts to limit the number of Asians in the country and the labor force. The societies issued memorials demanding that the government end further immigration by "this repugnant race." In December 1916 the Confederación called a meeting that appointed a propaganda committee headed by the president of the tailors guild and composed of representatives of various societies, including Nicolás Gutarra and Carlos Barba for the anarchist groups, to lead the campaign against the Asians. Two years later an anti-Asiatic league was formed, with the express purpose of stopping any further Asian immigration.[12]

In spite of the workers' pressure, the flow of immigrants continued. They were being imported by the coastal plantation owners who wanted more workers during this boom period and had failed to attract unemployed urban workers because of the hard work and low wages on the estates. The planters had no desire to see the Asian immigration halted, and they enjoyed the support of the president who was an estate owner himself.

Other projects that occupied the energies of the mutual aid societies met with an equal lack of success. Following the amendment of the law of professional risk, the Confederación de Artesanos directed one of its members, Víctor Herrera y Vera, to assist injured workers and help them to obtain the compensation they deserved. Herrera y Vera made several trips around the country assisting injured workers and insisting that employers fulfill their legal obligations and, although he was successful on occasion, many companies still refused to comply with the law.[13]

Most of the problems involving the mutual aid societies during the war were far too complex for them to solve alone; even the government proved unsuccessful in dealing with many of them. Perhaps if the societies had been willing to follow a more aggressive path, they would have accomplished more, but they never considered this. As the war progressed their limited ability to influence events declined further still as their popularity and effectiveness began to wane. Weakened by internal difficulties, by 1918 they were no longer capable of offering themselves as leaders of the working class.

Divisiveness caused by political involvement hurt them during the war as it had in the past and was the major reason for their decline. At first it appeared that the societies were making an effort to overcome this problem; in 1914 they urged united action in electing representatives to the 1915 municipal council and established a company to publish a new workers newspaper. However, the movement towards unity disappeared as the municipal election neared. The Confederación and Asamblea nominated their own candidates, and in the subsequent congressional election they also acted independently, supporting a variety of candidates, few of whom were workers.

Following the elections there was renewed cooperation. The three main societies discussed the possibility of physical unification; a National Labor party comprising workers and foremen was established to elect workers or those who were sympathetic to the workers' cause and would follow the example set by Billinghurst; and the workers newspaper, *La Verdad,* began publishing in January 1916. Together they appealed to President Pardo for scholarships for the children of working-class families; the Asamblea began organizing a second national workers congress with the active participation of the other societies; and their various representatives on the municipal council operated as a group.

Then elections disrupted the process once again. As the 1917 congressional elections approached, the president of the Asamblea and one of the principal forces behind unification, was forced to resign by a number of politically motivated members. Several of the federated societies reacted by withdrawing their delegations from the parent body, which in 1916 was reported to be in a state of complete anarchy. The societies attempted to nominate common candidates, but by the time of the election only the Asamblea and the Confederación General, which had been suffering internal problems of its own, were cooperating. Even they made little effort to name workers as their representatives, choosing two lawyers, Luis Miró Quesada and Gerardo Balbuena, as their candidates for the deputies' seats and turning to members of their societies only for substitutes.[14] The Confederación de Artesanos restricted itself to nominating its president as a candidate for substitute deputy.

The societies' official involvement in the election may have been limited, but working-class political support was now seen as important, even by elite candidates. Jorge Prado, running as an independent, and Miró Quesada claimed to have backing among the workers and their societies, which they listed in newspaper advertisements. Their claims may have been exaggerated, for the president of the Confederación General subsequently denied that he had authorized use of his name, while the president of the Asamblea who, according to rumors, had been receiving bribes from congressional candidates, admitted that he had not obtained the society's permission to use its name and was forced to resign. Although the advertisements were of questionable verisimilitude, they indicated the importance of working-class political support, and in this election it may have been vital because Prado was elected only after a recount. Miró Quesada, too, was elected, but only one worker was successful.[15]

Political involvement was not the only factor hurting the mutual aid societies. As the war continued many of them faced financial difficulties that threatened their survival. Increases in the cost of their services, particularly drugs, were severely reducing their working capital. In 1917 the mutual aid societies in Lima paid out over 150,000 soles in sick benefits and funerals. Meanwhile, their income remained frozen because of limited increases in their members' wages. They had to dip into their cash reserves, but several were caught short, and by August 1918 many were on the verge of bankruptcy and had suspended their services.[16] As a result, at the end of the war these proponents of working class moderation were in a much weakened state.

With the mutual aid societies in difficulties, leadership might have fallen to the Centro Internacional Obrero de Solidaridad Latino-Americana del Perú. It had managed to avoid the dislocations of political involvement and had established itself as an important institution by drawing Lima's mutual aid societies into its operations, appointing Víctor A. Pujazón as its resident delegate in Santiago to maintain its Chilean ties, and assuming responsibility for the organization of Lima's May Day celebrations—although it transformed them from a day of remembrance into a day of festivities with picnics, dances, and games for children. Under the Centro's auspices, May Day acquired respectability, and in 1916 Enrique de la Riva-Agüero, the foreign minister and president of the cabinet, became the first cabinet minister to participate in the celebrations.

However, the Centro soon began to follow the path of its constituent organizations. In 1918 critics complained that its president, Alberto J. Montes, had done little to establish links with workers throughout all of Latin America. A power struggle between Montes and José Cahuas of the Confederación de Artesanos ended with Cahuas also under attack and the Centro suspending operations as two groups claimed to be the legitimate executive. May Day celebrations that year were organized by the individual societies and it was not until August that the Centro was reactivated by Pujazón.

The source of the conflict is unclear. It may have been over the right to appoint delegates to a number of international workers congresses to be held in 1918. On the other hand, the problem may have been more fundamental. The Centro shared with Lima's mutual aid societies a characteristic that one commentator felt was central to their constant difficulties: the executive positions of several societies were monopolized by a small group of individuals who were unable to operate efficiently because of the weight of their various duties. The executive of the Centro had been and continued to be drawn from the executives of its constituent organizations so that if this were the reason for its difficulties, its influence was likely to remain limited in the future.[17]

At the end of the war a further problem affected the Centro's operations. Peruvian hopes for the recovery of Tacna and Arica were aroused as a result of President Woodrow Wilson's appeal for the return of all captive territories. Chile's response to Peru's renewed demands for a plebiscite on the future status of the area was an intensification of its efforts to "Chileanize" the captive provinces. Peruvians were assaulted and expelled from the area, and a new wave of refugees streamed into Lima, worsening the already critical employment situation. The conflict destroyed the relationship between the workers of the two countries and particularly affected the organization that had fostered the relationship. The now nationalistic Centro accused the Chilean workers of lacking sincerity in their past offers of friendship, backed Callao's stevedores who had begun boycotting Chilean ships, and sought international condemnation of Chile.[18]

The Centro survived, but it needed to reorganize its international connections and rethink its local role. All of the mutual aid societies, in fact, were going to have to change if they were to regain the leadership position and influence they had enjoyed in the early years of the war. Greater militancy now seemed a possibility since the mutual aid societies had begun adopting more and more of the goals as well as the rhetoric of the radical groups: during the war most of them joined the struggle for the eight-hour day. Some began discussing the formation of a workers' socialist party.[19] There were undoubtedly many members of the mutual aid societies with their long involvement in politics who would support such an entity, especially since the societies themselves had proven ineffective as political vehicles and the party would be operating within the existing political system.

While the fortunes of the mutual aid societies rose and fell during the war, those of the anarchists followed almost the opposite pattern. Faced by the workers' conservatism, the renewed attraction of the mutual aid societies, internal problems, and increased government harassment, the anarchists exerted little influence. At times they were virtually forced underground, and it was only towards the end of the war that they managed to reassert themselves as a significant component of the labor movement.

The economic hardships that accompanied the outbreak of war seemed to offer the anarchists an excellent opportunity for expanding their influence. Initially they had some success, introducing an apparently new type of labor organization, the "syndicate," which, in fact, was the old resistance society under a new name. The first syndicate was established by Lima's shoemakers who had been a rather disorganized section of the labor force. Twenty of them were employed by Lima's one shoe factory while the rest worked in small artisan shops or at home. They were considering forming a federated guild of the Confederación de Artesanos when Carlos Barba, Delfín Lévano, and other anarchists pointed to the Confederación's past history of political involvement and internal friction and suggested instead they form a "syndicate." The rank and file were uncertain what this meant, but in September 1914 they founded the Sindicato de Obreros Zapateros y Anexos (Syndicate of Shoemakers and Associates) with Barba as secretary general. Its general objective was to end the oppression of the working class, while its immediate targets were the cutbacks caused by the war, price differences within the industry, the system of work distribution, and the shoemakers' working conditions. It founded a newspaper, *El Sindicalista,* and in May and June 1915, together with Callao's shoemakers who had formed a syndicate of their own, tested its strength against that of the employers' society by staging a series of rotating strikes. They demanded a closed shop, better wages, and the right to belong to the syndicate without fear of losing their jobs. The authorities sided with the employers, harassing the strikers and arresting several anarchists, including Barba, but threats of an industry-wide strike secured Barba's release and many of the strikers managed to win their demands.[20]

The shoemakers' success convinced other sectors of the labor force to form their own syndicates. Lima's bricklayers and tailors hoped that through their new organizations they would win higher wages, a fixed minimum wage, better treatment, freedom to organize, more hygienic working conditions, paid vacations, social security, and the right to strike. For the tailors, the industry-wide unity of a syndicate also seemed to offer some protection against the competition of women workers who were being used as strikebreakers and accepting lower wages.

The success of the syndicates, however, was fleeting, and they soon lost their impetus and support. By July 1916 those of the bricklayers and shoemakers had temporarily suspended operations, with anarchist commentators charging that they had done little to further the spirit of association among their fellow workers or to educate their own members. The anarchist central organization, the FORP, also ceased operations, and by 1918 many other anarchist-influenced groups were nothing but empty names.[21]

Their failure may have been a result of internal divisions over philosophy and strategy. Other factors were the strong competition from the mutual aid societies and the overall conservatism of the workers at this time. Furthermore, the anarchists faced a hostile government that adopted repressive measures to control them and, in the process, greatly limited their influence.

Persecution began almost immediately. In September 1914 two members of the anarchist-led Sociedad de Resistencia de Oficios Varios (Divers Trades' Resistance Society), Daniel Antuñano and Rafael Montoya, were arrested in the Carabayllo Valley, near Lima, for possessing "socialist propaganda," urging local plantation workers to call a general strike, and attempting to organize an anarchist society in the area. They were held in jail for two weeks, and Antuñano, an Argentine, was deported on his release.[22] In November Delfín Lévano was arrested for publishing an antimilitary article in *La Protesta*. His long ties with the workers produced loud protests at his arrest and secured his early release. However, his books, pamphlets, and newspapers, which had been confiscated, were burned because of their "anarchist, socialist, and syndicalist content." In June 1917 he was arrested again along with Carlos Rivadeneyra for distributing pamphlets and protesting at the recent massacre of striking workers in Huacho.[23] The arrests set off a brief strike by Lima's bakery workers that lasted until the two anarchists were released. It resumed when Rivadeneyra charged he had been tortured by his jailers. However, only a portion of the bakery workers participated, so the strike had little impact and ended when the government ordered the bakeries to reopen or risk losing their licenses.

Carlos Barba was arrested twice in May 1916 as he tried to form a new organization, the Comité Pro-Abaratamiento de las Subsistencias (Committee for Cheaper Essentials). Its aim was to reduce food prices by establishing discount shops and limiting the export of essential goods. It enjoyed little success as police disrupted its meetings and arrested its leaders while *La Protesta* charged that it was too moderate, supporting discussions and memorials instead of more militant action. Over the following months other foreign anarchists were arrested for fomenting unrest, urging strikes, criticising the government, and pressing for price reductions, and all were eventually deported.[24]

In an attempt to curb anarchist activity further, the government reintroduced Leguía's project for an aliens' law. Some workers supported the idea, claiming that such a law would protect the "tranquil and docile" workers of Peru from the "evil influences of disruptive foreign elements." In his address to Congress on July 28, 1917, Pardo urged the passage of the law as well as one regulating strikes, claiming that recent strikes had been the work of "foreign agitators, fugitives from the justice of other countries who, protected by the excessive tolerance of our laws, have taken refuge here." Adequate laws would safeguard society and permit the authorities to expel those who came to "sow false doctrines" and induce violence among the workers. Both legislative chambers approved projects allowing the president to prohibit entry by and expel suspect foreigners, but no law was passed.[25]

The anarchists still insisted that contrary to the government's belief local anarchist support owed little to foreign agitators and pointed to the various anarchist newspapers that had appeared over the years, founded and sustained only by Peruvians.[26] However, they failed to convince the authorities, who continued to arrest suspected agitators, disrupt meetings and, despite the lack of legal backing, deport foreigners. The government also turned its attention to what had been a fruitful area for the anarchists in the past; they paid much closer attention to strikes, intervening more openly on the side of employers. As the number of strikes in Lima and Callao declined, so too did the anarchists' area of influence.

The attitude of the authorities to labor agitation became apparent at an early date during the most serious strike of this period in the urban sector. It involved the Vitarte workers who, together with the rest of the textile workers, had been particularly affected by the outbreak of the war. The mills responded to the crisis by cutting their work force, wages, and hours of work. El Inca reduced its wages by 35 percent in August and then by a further 20 percent in November.[27] At Vitarte the work week was cut by two days in August, which reduced wages by one-third. In December, following an additional 30 percent reduction, the workers went on strike. Their employers adamantly refused to negotiate or even to accept arbitration and on December 11 declared a month-long lockout. The mill should have remained closed for the full month, according to Billinghurst's strike decree, but on January 9, 1915, the owners loaded a boxcar of sheetings for shipment to Lima. Five hundred men, women, and children tried to stop the train in Vitarte, but were met by a detachment of police who had orders to assist the owners, by force if necessary. They opened fire on the crowd, killing one person, Andrés Vilela, and wounding six others. Nonetheless, the workers managed to take over the train, which they drove to Lima, only to be arrested on their arrival.

The violence threw Lima's societies behind the strikers. They asked President Benavides to intervene and demanded the release of those who had been arrested, as well as the indictment of the police responsible for the shootings. The government complied, freeing all the prisoners except one who was accused of distributing pamphlets and arresting the officers in charge of the police detachment. The company now showed some willingness to negotiate. On January 28 it agreed to a fifty-six-hour work week and cancellation of the rents for the period of the strike on the accommodation of all those strikers who returned to work by February 1.

One result of the strike was to win support for the anarchists at Vitarte. Describing the killing of Vilela as a "massacre," they urged the workers to make further demands. Their appeals were echoed by workers in Callao who called on their colleagues to "wash the streets with blood" if this was necessary to protect their rights. "To die defending the cause of the proletariat," they wrote, "is preferable to dying on the dungheaps of hunger and misery." In April the Vitarte workers elected Adalberto Fonkén, an anarchist, president of their union.[28]

This militancy was short lived. In December 1915 some members called for the union's reorganization after accusing the anarchists of trying to ruin it. The following month, when the spinners at El Inca went on strike to protest their working conditions, one instigator, an anarchist, was suspended for a month while the rest were allowed back without penalty. The workers were willing to contribute to the anarchist's lost wages, but nothing more. In January 1917 a proposed march in Vilela's memory threatened to lead to a confrontation between the Vitarte union and management. The anarchists' plans for a militant display of solidarity by the workers were prevented by Víctor Herrera y Vera, who intervened and convinced the marchers to avoid any display of violence. In fact, only forty workers participated and of these only eight, including Fonkén, were members of the Vitarte union. When the latter were subsequently fired, the workers showed little concern, and the union soon ceased operations.[29]

Despite government intervention, labor agitation did not disappear entirely. The increase in the cost of living as the war progressed, plus the low wage rates, ensured continuing discontent. In January 1916 Lima's bakery workers threatened a strike to obtain the implementation of wage rates promised in 1913, only to be prevented by the government, which invoked the strike law. More successful were Callao's bakery workers who won two wage increases in 1917 following strikes.[30] Demands for a return to prewar wage rates also led to strikes by the telegraph operators in October 1916 and the workers at El Inca in May 1917. The latter were successful, winning higher wages, better working conditions, the reinstatement of some workers who had been fired, and censure of some English managers who were accused of seducing women workers. The El Inca success moved Vitarte, San Jacinto, La Victoria, and the Santa Rosa flour mill to raise their workers' wages to avoid similar problems. On the other hand, the telegraph operators were unsuccessful owing to a lack of unity and the arrest of their leaders; when President Pardo asked them to return to work and released their colleagues, they complied.[31]

Similar weaknesses undermined strikes by Lima's tram workers and Callao's harbor workers. The tram workers went on strike in June 1917 for a 40 percent wage increase, better overtime pay, a shorter work day, better quality uniforms, cheaper food, and other improvements. They turned to President Pardo for assistance in the belief that he might support them because their employer's brother, Jorge Prado, led the congressional opposition to him. The workers undermined their position by allowing some reduced tram services, and after nine days they agreed to conciliation. The board refused any wage increase, but raised the monthly award paid for good service, provided for cheaper food, a shorter work day, and sick pay, made uniforms no longer mandatory, ended worker responsibility for unintentional damage to the trams, and assured the workers that there would be no reprisals for the strike.

The agreement proved worthless. The company failed to increase the monthly award and fired a number of workers and their leaders. The workers again sought Pardo's help, but he refused to intercede, claiming that he was too busy at this time even to see them.[32]

The Callao harbor workers were relatively passive during the war in contrast to their earlier activism. The decline in shipping at the outset seriously affected them, and the presence of large numbers of unemployed workers subsequently left them in a vulnerable position. As a result, they were involved in only a few disputes. In July 1916 they refused to work overtime when the companies failed to increase overtime pay. In August 1917 they went on strike for better wages and some other improvements, although they had already received one increase three months earlier. Their employers claimed they had to wait six months before negotiating another, in accordance with the strike decree, while the strikers felt that recent increases in the cost of living justified a further increase at that time. The companies received support from the authorities who sent in soldiers, sailors, and civilians to unload the ships, while the strikers received only limited backing, possibly because they were already earning more than most other workers. After twenty-three days the strikers returned to work with only the release of a number of workers who had been arrested to show for their efforts.[33]

This period of relative calm in Lima and Callao came to an end as the war entered its final stages. By June 1918 the situation of the workers was critical. *La Prensa* noted:

> We are all aware that as a consequence of the world war the volume of public wealth has grown dramatically, but only for the benefit of the fortunate few; the people as a whole have not been able to take advantage of the good fortune that has smiled on the capitalists.
>
> Rents are as high as ever; the lack of hygiene in the workers' homes gets worse each day and the municipal ordinances in this regard have had little effect since no landlord has complied with them; the [prices of] popular necessities are found in the clouds despite the great efforts taken by the government to lower them; and, meanwhile, wages have been and continue to be reduced wherever possible.[34]

As a result, dissatisfaction with the government grew, the workers felt that the time had come for more direct action, and strikes began to occur with greater frequency. Callao's harbor workers, the Vitarte workers, the employees of the Otero mill, Lima's bakery workers, the Central Railway linemen, and the workers in one of Lima's tanneries all went on strike between April and October 1918, demanding in each case some improvement in their pay system that would increase their wages. In most instances they won at least a small increase. Elsewhere, firms were raising wages voluntarily to prevent confrontations.[35]

The resumption of labor agitation in 1918 was accompanied by renewed anarchist activity. The anarchists lost their founder, intellectual leader, and most influential adherent in July with the death of González Prada. More deportations also occurred at this time. Nevertheless, a more aggressive tone was apparent. The Gremio Liberal de Empleados reappeared; the Vitarte union readopted a syndicalist orientation; new unions and study groups were formed; contacts were established with the American anarchosyndicalist group, the International Workers of the World; and the anarchist press was prospering, often attacking the now ineffective mutual aid societies and their leaders.[36] With the war about to end, the anarchists were making renewed efforts to assume leadership of the local labor movement. The fact that the workers once again seemed willing to engage in industrial action indicated that they might have some success.

A postwar resurgence in labor agitation seemed inevitable unless the government acted quickly to appease the workers. And it was not only the urban workers who were forcing the government to reconsider its labor policies. Workers in the rural areas, particularly on the coastal estates, in the sierra mines, and in the northern petroleum fields had engaged in violent strikes during the war. Their agitation added a new dimension to the labor movement. By the end of the war the number of workers capable of applying pressure had grown dramatically, and a united movement, incorporating both the revitalized urban workers and the emergent rural workers, now seemed possible.

8 Rural Workers in the Labor Movement

While the main stimulus for the Peruvian labor movement came from workers in Lima and Callao, rural workers also played a role in its development. They comprised a much larger proportion of the total labor force and were employed in more vital sectors of the economy than the urban workers. Peru's dependence on the export of raw materials such as sugar, cotton, copper, and petroleum meant that the workers employed in these areas effectively controlled national economic development. However, they seemed unaware of their importance and began to mobilize gradually in response to a decline in their standard of living and working conditions and the growing influence of the urban movement. One obstacle to rural mobilization was the workers' importance to the economy. Determined to maintain the flow of raw materials, the authorities were prepared to use whatever means necessary to keep the workers on the job. It was an attitude that the employers fully supported as they attempted to control all aspects of the workers' lives and labor. And while the government and employers were united in a common goal, the workers were divided into a variety of distinct groups. The coastal plantations, the sierra mines, and the northern petroleum fields employed a combination of permanent, short-term, contracted, sharecropping, and other forms of labor. Each had its own interests that often conflicted with those of another group, so that bringing them together was a far greater challenge than uniting the urban workers.

Many of the difficulties in organizing the rural workers were evident in the principal form of labor recruitment used during this period, the *enganche* system. Enganche was introduced originally to contract sierra Indians for work in the mines, and its success resulted in its adoption by other rural employers in the sierra as well as on the coast and in the selva.[1] The workers or *enganchados* were not a true proletariat: most were sierra peasants who accepted jobs on a short-term basis, but who continued to hold small plots of land in the sierra to which they returned on completing their contracts. Thus, organizing them was difficult because they remained only a short time, and they had very little commitment to their jobs.

The enganche system itself was a dual contractual arrangement that utilized the skills of a labor contractor or *enganchador*. The enganchador signed a contract with the employer to supply a certain number of workers at a fixed wage for a definite period of time. The employer supplied money that the enganchador distributed among the potential workers in the form of advances. The second part of the arrangement was completed in the sierra with the *serranos* (sierra inhabitants). The enganchador drew up contracts specifying the period of the contract, the wage, the number of hours of work or the daily output (tarea), and the daily ration. For his services the enganchador received a commission for every worker recruited and, in some instances, on every tarea completed. On some estates he also had the right to operate shops selling goods to the workers, usually at greatly inflated prices. Under the system he was directly responsible for the enganchados. The employer assigned and directed the work, but the enganchador paid the laborers and supplied their rations. Frequently, he or his agent acted as a kind of foreman, and if any workers fled before completing their contracts, he was expected to pursue the fugitives and bring them back, by force if necessary.

The system was successful in obtaining workers because there were always some serranos who needed money. Debts had to be paid, fiestas financed, local officials bribed, land and supplies bought, and religious obligations met. Moreover, the peasants were willing to foresake their small sierra plots for a time if offered good wages or an attractive advance. Overly large advances were not popular since they required too much time and work to pay off and could lead to discontent. Yet, advances did vary and seem to have increased as the demand for labor and the returns on agricultural and mining production grew.[2]

The system very quickly became the principal means of obtaining workers, and contracting serranos became an important local business. According to the subprefect of the province of Chota, which was supplying Indians to sugar estates in Lambayeque and La Libertad, contracting workers was one of the province's "principal industries," providing monthly commerce in 1897 worth 6,000 soles. With this as an incentive, a steady stream of workers flowed to all parts of the country. In 1892, five hundred were being hired monthly for the sugar estates in Lambayeque alone, while in 1910 one company hiring mine workers had almost six thousand under contract.[3]

The system, however, had one major drawback: it could not guarantee a constant supply of workers. Replacements had to be hired continuously, but they were not always available, especially during the serranos' sowing and harvesting seasons. To attract enganchados for longer periods, higher wages might have been offered, but the attraction of the system to employers was the low wages that could be paid. Wage rates, therefore, remained notoriously low, so low that the workers had no incentive to produce more than the bare mimimum. In addition, the work was hard and conditions were poor, so that few workers had any desire to stay beyond the contracted period. Indeed, many broke their contracts and fled back to their homes. The threat of flight and the competition for scarce labor may have pushed up wages and improved conditions to some extent over the years, but not enough to provide all the workers that were needed by the rural employers.[4]

The employers sought to surmount this problem by transforming temporary laborers into permanent ones. They manipulated the enganche system in various ways to achieve this result. Enganchadores attended Indian fiestas, got potential workers drunk, and then helped them to spend all their money so that they were receptive to the offer of an advance. A few coins left in a serrano's hut or pressed into his hand constituted a legal advance. Once the worker was indebted, he was obligated by law to work until the debt was repaid, and the employer made this as difficult as possible. He took advantage of the serrano's illiteracy and altered the terms of the written contract from the original verbal agreement by extending the period of work or the size of the advance. He maintained and increased the debt by adding purchases made at the enganchador's store, charging interest rates of up to 50 percent for loans, and imposing fines. If these were not successful, he made "mistakes" in his books to show that the advance still had to be repaid. Debts were handed down from father to son, and indebted Indians were exchanged between haciendas. In these instances the system was more akin to slavery or Mexican debt peonage than free wage labor.[5]

Reports of these abuses began causing widespread concern in the early twentieth century. It was claimed that because of the excessive work demanded of the enganchados, 10 percent of the workers were dying on the coastal estates or shortly after returning to their sierra homes. Low wages were preventing them from obtaining medical assistance, and the result of the system was a weak and spiritless labor force, exactly the opposite of what the country needed. Demands for reforms grew, and beginning in 1909 the government issued a number of laws that attempted to regulate the system and end the abuse. However, they failed to have much effect, largely because many local officials had a vested interest in the system, receiving kickbacks either for helping the enganchador fill his quota or for preventing the enganchados from breaking their contracts.[6]

While there is no question that abuses of the system occurred, the instances may have been less than critics charged. In many areas workers returned year after year to the same estate or mine, apparently satisfied with the arrangement.[7] The system may, in fact, have become more attractive as the serranos' need for cash grew in response to their increasing absorption into a money economy. Whatever the reason, enganche managed to survive the criticism and continued operating well into the twentieth century.

To fill the labor gap left by enganche, employers turned to a number of other schemes. The cotton planters, while depending upon short-term enganche labor for help during harvesting, employed a sharecropping system known as *yanaconaje* for their permanent work force. It varied according to local conditions, but in general involved the planter giving the worker or *yanacona* a piece of property to work, as well as water, seed, and oxen. In some instances the worker could cultivate what he wished, cotton or vegetables or both, but more often he had to plant what the owner demanded. Usually he paid a small rent for his land. He worked the owner's fields, repaired roads, cleaned ditches, and fulfilled other duties on the estate for which he was paid little or nothing. He gave half his crop to the owner and sold the remaining cotton to the owner at a price lower than the market rate. The attraction of the system to the Indian was that it provided a piece of land that he could call his own.[8] For the landowner, it meant he could pay very low wages.[9]

Planters also turned to immigrant workers to meet their labor needs. Chinese coolies had been imported between 1849 and 1874, mainly to work on the coastal plantations and the guano islands. Until the trade was suspended in 1874 following reports of harsh treatment by the Peruvian employers, some 90,000 coolies arrived.[10] They were not a self-generating group since few women were included in the shipments, nor did they form a permanent labor force since most left the estates once they had completed their contracts. Following the War of the Pacific attempts were made to reopen the trade, as the planters who were short of funds saw the coolies as the cheapest labor available. However, it was not until the end of the century that the flow of contract labor resumed with workers from Japan as well as China. The Japanese were not cheap, costing an estimated thirty pounds sterling more per worker than local Peruvian labor, but the planters were now desperate and seemed confident that with increased exports of sugar their returns would justify the expense. In April 1899 the first shipload of 832 Japanese workers arrived in Callao, and by 1923 when the trade was suspended Japanese emigration companies had sent 17,764 free and contract laborers to work in Peru. The Chinese trade resumed later with the first load of 635 workers arriving in 1905. By 1920 Chinese immigrant workers also numbered around 15,000.[11]

The Asians comprised an important section of the work force on the coastal estates. Chinese coolies had constituted the majority of the plantation workers in the past, and in 1891 the British minister reported that the labor on the sugar plantations was still "exclusively Chinese." This was an exaggeration, but it indicated their continuing prominence and the paucity of native labor on the coast. In 1893 the majority of the workers on the estates in the Chicama Valley were Chinese. The proportion fell as contracts expired and serranos were contracted—in 1905 a survey estimated that of thirty-five thousand workers on the sugar estates, one thousand were Chinese—but it grew again as the flow of Asians increased. On the estates in the Cañete Valley, Japanese workers comprised between 28 and 38 percent of the total work force before 1920. Thus, while enganchados came to constitute the majority of plantation workers in the early twentieth century, Asians remained a vital component in some areas.[12]

The immigrants filled some of the country's labor needs, but their appearance created a new obstacle to working class unity in the rural sector. Because of their favored conditions, tension developed with the native elements of the population. Comparisons between the Japanese and the serranos revealed that the former did not have to pay for their passage to Peru; they were promised a bed in a room that they would share with only one other worker; they had the services of a doctor; they did not work on Sundays or holidays; they had good food; and they received one sol per day. The serranos, in contrast, had to find their own way to the coast; they earned fifty to eighty centavos, part of which went to the enganchador; they were poorly fed; and they were not paid when they were sick. The manager of estates in the Cañete Valley considered the Indians "infinitely better workers" than the Japanese, yet the latter received good housing, baths, schools, and other facilities, while "the serrano gets what is left over," earning no more than the Japanese women who did one-quarter the amount of work.[13]

These differences in material benefits aroused hostility fed by racial prejudice. The rural Peruvian workers shared the views of the Lima workers that the Asians communicated diseases to the local population, were morally degenerate, and monopolized some professions to the detriment of local workers and small commerce. One commonly held view was that the immigrants reduced wages on the coastal estates by forcing the native workers to accept lower pay; if the latter resisted, they were fired and had to look for work elsewhere, usually in the urban centers, thus driving down urban wages so that ultimately all Peruvian workers suffered.[14]

On occasion the hostility between the native workers and the immigrants exploded into violence. There were bloody clashes during the earlier period of the Chinese coolie trade, and in 1881 perhaps as many as one thousand Chinese were massacred by rebellious black workers in the Cañete Valley. With the renewed flow of Asians after 1899 there was a threat of further violence. Strikes involving Japanese on the estates of Huampaní in 1900, Casa Blanca in 1903, and San Jacinto in 1909 produced fears of racial confrontations. In fact, there was only one reported clash, on the Santa Clara estate in 1904, where a fight broke out between Japanese and black workers.[15]

The outbursts after 1900 were rare, but they indicated the depth of division between the two groups that hindered any type of organizing for better wages or working conditions. The Japanese formed mutual aid societies, but these were exclusive and did little to foment working class unity as a whole.[16] Also blocking unity was the fact that both immigrants and natives were isolated from their employers: the Asians through the emigration companies which were held responsible for their conduct, and the natives through the enganchadores. As a result, the target of their hostility was not always the person who was actually responsible for their situation.

The rural labor scene was further complicated by the existence of other distinct groups, like women workers and the descendants of black slaves. The former constituted a significant proportion of the labor force on the coastal estates (see table 6). Some of them were Japanese, as two thousand women were brought from Japan in the early twentieth century.[17] In the sierra, mining companies hired women and children for the lighter work. This potpourri of races and sexes, free and contract labor, yanaconas and enganchados, immigrants and natives, made organization and mobilization in the rural sector extremely difficult. It was only after several years that these differences were overcome and a movement began to develop.

The Coastal Plantations

The most politically active workers in the rural sector were those on the coastal plantations, particularly the sugar workers who were caught in an economically uncertain industry. The sugar industry had begun to expand during the nineteenth century, but it suffered a serious setback with the War of the Pacific. The plantations were an easy target for the Chilean invaders who looted estates, burned fields, and destroyed machinery. This occurred at a time of falling prices and scarce credit so that after the war Peru's planters faced the task of trying to restore their estates without capital or credit in order to sell to a depressed market. Many failed and went bankrupt. Others managed to survive by amalgamating their estates, while still others sold to foreign concerns. Regardless of their nationality, the planters had to keep their expenses to a minimum in the postwar period. This meant exploiting cheap labor, hence their use of the enganche system and the attempts to import Asian contract workers.[18]

The planters' determination to keep wages low may have been economically sound at the time, but eventually it led to worker discontent. Conditions were dismal: the workers lived in filthy, unhygienic housing that lacked sanitary facilities, water, and electricity. They were subject to disease and most of them were illiterate. At the turn of the century conditions deteriorated further as the buying power of the sol declined, in part because of the expansion of sugar cultivation at the expense of other crops. In the important sugar producing region around Trujillo, for example, small farms that had grown food crops were being absorbed into the sugar plantations. As a result, food production declined, prices were driven up, and strikes began to occur. In May 1894 a reduction in wages led to a strike by workers in the Sama Valley; in November 1906 workers on estates in the Huacho region went on strike for better pay, as did Paramonga workers in January 1908.[19]

The most serious labor agitation before 1912 involved Asian workers. Within weeks of the arrival of the first Japanese, a strike occurred on the San Nicolás estate in the Supe Valley when the owners insisted that the immigrants purchase their necessities from the estate store rather than the cheaper Chinese shops. Sending five ringleaders back to Callao ended this strike, but a new confrontation followed almost immediately, and eventually the estate sent all but twenty-odd of the immigrants back to the port. Similar disputes produced similar results on the other estates that had contracted Japanese. In addition, many workers were fleeing the estates, so that within six months of their arrival nearly 40 percent of the original group were back in Callao. Some were reassigned to new estates, others found urban jobs, but many remained without work and a visible target for discontented urban workers.

The source of the trouble between the Japanese and the planters was, in essence, a conflict in expectations. The former expected to make a certain amount of money and then return to Japan; the latter expected the immigrants to be at least as productive as the natives. The Japanese, however, were not accustomed to the work and so produced less than the lower paid locals. Moreover, they were susceptible to diseases such as malaria, typhoid, yellow fever, and dysentery. During the first year, 143 of the 943 Japanese died; many more were unable to work because of illness. At Casa Blanca in the Cañete Valley over 85 percent of the Japanese became ill. With their expensive workers incapacitated, the planters tried to minimize losses by reducing rations, cutting wages, and switching from paying wages to paying by tarea. Under this system, however, the unskilled Japanese had difficulty earning the amount promised in their contracts and discontent resulted. The Japanese accused the planters of violating their contracts, demanding excessive work, underpaying them, providing insufficient food, whipping them, and in general treating them like slaves. The planters charged that the Japanese were lazy, overly sensitive, and insubordinate and that they banded together to intimidate the better workers.[20]

Similar disputes followed subsequent arrivals. In September 1903, three hundred Japanese went on strike at Casa Blanca and robbed the estate store of 1,700 soles. In 1909 the Japanese at San Jacinto went on strike, attacked the estate house, and tried to assault the administrator.[21]

Among the native workers agitation was less common, but the pressures were growing. They shared many of the same grievances as the immigrants, and they now had their example to follow. Moreover, urban agitators were beginning to disseminate their ideas in the countryside, providing an ideological basis for action. In January 1906 an anarchist was arrested on the Lince estate near Lima for discussing the concept of the equal division of property and the need for labor agitation to achieve it. Urging the workers to strike he charged, "We have nothing; the rich have everything." The workers, however, preferred the advice of the estate administrator, who convinced them that their best interests lay in continuing to work. In the north, workers were incited by the Trujillo newspaper, *El Jornalero*. In 1906 it exhorted, "If all the workers . . . who live on a miserable wage united and refused to work under the conditions which they do today; if all those who groan under the cudgel of the hacendado protested like free men against these crimes and abuse, capitalism would have to retreat and give its victims some of what is theirs. Today it only crushes the dignity, rights, and lives of the workers." Five years later the newspaper forecast an inevitable revolution that would end the exploitation by the privileged class who lived off the sweat of the oppressed and transform the workers from slaves into free men.[22]

There seemed little basis for this prediction since the rural workers had shown only a limited willingness to resort to direct action. However, the situation was changing. In April 1912 a series of strikes erupted in the Chicama and Santa Catalina Valleys. They were the most violent demonstrations by plantation workers so far and produced widespread fears of an imminent social revolution.

The trouble began on the German-owned estate of Casa Grande, which had recently introduced changes into its operations. Germans had replaced Peruvian personnel, the enganchadores and their stores had been suppressed, and the workers' tarea had been increased. The workers, who were already suffering because of a low daily wage of sixty centavos and a fourteen-hour work day, supported the agitation of the disgruntled enganchadores by declaring a strike on April 8. Almost the entirety of the estate's five thousand workers participated, demanding a wage increase, a reduced workload, and removal of the German foremen. Armed with axes and machetes and shouting anti-German slogans, they occupied the sugar mill and attacked a shop. Police intervened, a fight ensued, and at least five workers were killed.

Similar disturbances followed on the neighboring estates where the workers were equally alienated. Here, however, the enganchadores seem to have been a target rather than the leaders of the workers. On April 11 workers on the estates of Chiquitoy and Sausal, a dependency of Casa Grande, attacked the stores and the haciendas. At Cartavio the workers demanded the suppression of the enganchadores and permission to open their own stores, plus wage increases. At Laredo the workers sacked the estate store and demanded better wages, an eleven-hour day, and removal of the local police commissioner. On each estate police and troops fired on the strikers and killed several. More and more troops were called in and gradually brought the strikes under control but, according to later estimates, between one hundred fifty and two hundred workers had been killed.

New strikes occurred at the end of the month at Casa Grande and Sausal after the administrator failed to implement promised reforms and fire a number of German employees who had antagonized the workers.

These strikes were peaceful and ended when the administrator agreed to remove the offending Germans, reopen schools, construct a hospital, and increase wages.

The violence in the north had widespread reverberations. In Lima the Asamblea de Sociedades Unidas issued a protest at the "bloody events" and named a special delegate to investigate the affair. The government also wanted more information and appointed the president of the superior tribunal of accounts, Felipe de Osma y Pardo, to undertake the enquiry. His investigation convinced him that the real source of the troubles was not some conflict between capital and labor nor the local working conditions, but rather the enganchadores and the enganche system which, he felt, should be reformed. The authorities in Trujillo disagreed. They saw anarchist agitation as the real cause and arrested Julio Reynaga and the other editors of *El Jornalero*. The journalists admitted that they had urged militant action—indeed, they said that they would continue to do so—but they denied that they had participated in the recent events, and they were shortly released. Seven Indians, however, who had also been accused of fomenting the strike were still in jail a year later.

The Chicama Valley workers gained little from their actions. The general conditions remained unchanged while the owners' attitude towards them hardened. Nonetheless, the strikes had given some indication of an emerging working-class consciousness, an ability to unite, and a readiness to strike. Osma failed to recognize this; he stated that unity among the rural workers was an impossibility because they were "not a social unit but rather a group of individuals who lack a link with the soil, stability of place, a spirit of communality for common ends, freedom to use individual energies and initiative, and an occasion to participate in and be responsible for a common and suitable goal." Yet, following the strikes, guilds were formed on the estates, and by January 1914 a more general organization, the Sociedad Artesanos y Braceros Valle de Chicama (Chicama Valley Artisans and Workers Society), had been formed.[23]

The immediate beneficiaries of the Chicama Valley strikes were workers on other plantations, as owners took steps to ensure that their workers were not contemplating similar action. At Cayaltí the estate administrator was instructed to visit the hospital daily, improve the quality of the workers' rations, and keep prices in the estate store at a reasonable level. The estate also built better and more sanitary housing for its workers. Following the January 1913 strikes in Callao, which secured the eight-hour day for the harbor workers and involved some plantation workers from the surrounding region, further instructions were given to ensure the satisfaction of the Cayaltí workers. At the same time the administrators took great care in selecting workers to eliminate the potentially disruptive ones.[24]

Despite remedies of this sort, greater militancy was becoming evident among the plantation workers, particularly those in the Lima region who came under the direct influence of the urban labor movement and anarchist agitators. Some of the plantation workers who participated in the January 1913 strikes were successful, and at least one estate, La Estrella, had an organization that represented the workers' interests. These workers even managed to overcome the divisions caused by race. In May 1914 the entire labor force, both Japanese and Peruvians, went on strike to protest the firing of eight workers and, with the assistance of Lima's resistance societies, they obtained a satisfactory solution.[25]

The result of this early agitation was that some rural mobilization preceded the outbreak of war in Europe. Organizations had been formed, strikes had occurred, and the forces dividing the workers had proved superable. The war gave added impetus to these developments. At first, however, the rural situation reflected the labor situation in Lima and Callao; with the closing of overseas markets and the paralysis of trade, planters reduced their labor force, cut production, lowered wages, and replaced cash with estate vouchers. In La Libertad, for example, almost three-quarters of the rural and urban labor force were out of work in early August, while in the Cañete Valley the wage per tarea was reduced from 2 to 1.50 soles. In both areas vouchers were introduced. The measures were accepted "without a murmur" because of the uncertain situation and, although some workers left their estates, they soon returned because of the lack of jobs elsewhere.

A period of economic expansion followed, and the export sector boomed as prices for both sugar and cotton recovered. Acreage under cultivation, workers' productivity, and investments in the primary sector all expanded. The change prompted the British minister to note in June 1917 that the planter class "just now, is enjoying a prosperity which three years ago would have seemed fantastic."[26]

The workers, however, received few benefits from the prosperity. The influx of capital resulted in increases in the cost of living that were not offset by commensurate increases in wages.[27] In addition, planters were demanding more work from their labor force to maximize their profits, so hours of work were increasing (see table 14). The effect was a general deterioration in the living standards of those whose labor made the boom possible, a contradiction that the workers increasingly realized. Discontent grew and from 1916 strikes, usually for better wages, began to occur on the plantations. These invariably led to violence as the government, also profiting from the boom, provided the planters with whatever assistance was needed to restore operations.

One area particularly affected by strikes was the Huaura Valley, north of Lima. Anarchist agitators had been active here organizing May Day rallies and assisting in the formation of the Sindicato de Oficios Varios (Syndicate of Divers Trades) of Huacho, the local port. The anarchists drew support from a rural population composed largely of yanaconas working on the surrounding sugar and cotton estates. They were an unorganized group, but their possession of land provided a kind of natural strike fund that allowed them to agitate. The sources of their discontent were common to workers everywhere in Peru at this time: rising prices and long hours of work. On August 31, 1916, the workers on three estates in the valley struck, demanding a 50 percent wage increase and a shorter work day. Other plantations and Huacho's harbor workers joined them, and there were soon two thousand workers on strike. Facing them were fifty soldiers commanded by the prefect of Lima, Edgardo Arenas, whom the government had sent to keep order. On September 2 the soldiers opened fire on a hostile crowd of strikers who had just been told their employers were prepared to offer only a 20 percent increase. Two workers were killed and six injured. Arenas, realizing his small force could not prevent further disorders, provisionally accepted the strikers' demands to

Table 14: Average Hours of Work and Wages in the Sugar Industry, 1912–1919

	Hours of Work		Wages (without rations)		
			Fields		Mill
	Fields	Mill	Men	Women	Men
1912	8.8	—	1.27	.87	—
1913	8.8	—	1.29	.82	—
1914	9.0	—	1.26	.79	—
1915	9.24	11.30	1.30	.78	1.55
1916	9.22	10.48	1.13	.85	1.49
1917	8.30	10.18	1.37	1.07	1.43
1918	8.14	10.00	1.60	1.02	1.83
1919	8.33	11.00	1.83	1.26	2.25

Sources: Ministerio de Hacienda y Comercio, *Extracto Estadístico del Perú 1926*, p. 106; Albert, *The Peruvian Sugar Industry,* tables 47–49, pp. 168a–170a.

get them back to work. A final agreement would be negotiated in Lima under the watchful eye of the government.

Other strikes followed in the area. On September 7 workers on the San Nicolás and Paramonga estates in the neighboring Supe Valley went on strike for the same improvements as the Huaura workers. These disputes were settled quickly for most of the workers were enganchados who had no land and, therefore, lacked the resources to remain on strike. Moreover, Japanese workers on the estates refused to participate, and troops armed with machine guns were brought in to keep order. Although the Huacho workers offered assistance, the strike ended after one day with the workers accepting a 10 percent increase and the establishment of reduced price shops.

The Huaura dispute, on the other hand, remained unresolved. The negotiators were unable to reach an agreement, and the dispute went to arbitration. The arbitrators agreed to most of the workers' demands for improvements in their working conditions, but could not agree on a wage settlement; Guillermo A. Seoane, an attorney, diplomat, and member of the Civilista party, was called in to end the deadlock. He had little sympathy for the workers as he awarded only a 10 percent increase, less than the employers had been offering. However, the workers had agreed to abide by his decision, and the dispute ended.

The attitude adopted by the hacendados and shared by Seoane revealed a lack of understanding of the real reasons behind the unrest. They, like employers elsewhere, believed that outside agitators were solely to blame. The planters' organization, the Sociedad Nacional Agraria (National Agrarian Society), urged the government to pass a law prohibiting foreign immigration, thereby eliminating this agitating element. Estate administrators, like those of Cayaltí, gave instructions that all strangers were to be apprehended and expelled immediately unless they had family working on the estate, in which case they could stay for twenty-four hours. They also asked the governor of Chiclayo to keep an eye open for known agitators. The prefect, Arenas, shared the belief of the planters and ordered the arrest of the president of the Huacho syndicate as well as two local syndicalists, one a Spaniard and the other a Chilean. The Lima anarchists Delfín Lévano and Carlos Barba were also ordered arrested as suspected instigators.[28]

The refusal of the owners to recognize the true source of the unrest ensured further trouble, especially as real wages were continuing to decline. Moreover, as the Huaura strikes had revealed, the workers were now more organized and willing to agitate. In the words of Ronald

Gordon, the administrator of estates in the Cañete Valley at this time, the workers "day by day are becoming more careful of their rights."[29]

In 1917 there were new confrontations in the Chicama and Huaura valleys. The Chicama area had been the scene of several strikes since the beginning of the war, with workers usually demanding higher wages. Their agitation culminated in a general strike in August 1916 that gained some improvements for the workers of Trujillo, but none for the local plantation workers who had participated. Suffering from long hours of work, the use of vouchers, poor rations, minimal medical services, and particularly rising prices—which the hacendados and local authorities insisted were not excessive—the rural workers began demanding reductions in the price of foodstuffs. When nothing happened, they once again went on strike on May 26, 1917.

The strike began among the field workers of the Sausal estate and then spread, first to the mill workers, then to the sister estate of Casa Grande, and finally to the other valley estates until it involved some two thousand workers. Their main demand was for higher wages to meet the rising prices. Some strikers tried to involve the people of Trujillo by setting up a camp in the city's Plaza de Toros. Others were reported to have returned to their sierra homes, giving rise to the story that homesickness and exploitation by the enganchadores were the real causes of the unrest. The Trujillo authorities believed that outside agitators were to blame and arrested four Chilean anarchists and three "agitators" from Callao. The strike lasted eleven days and won some improvements: mill workers obtained a nine-hour day, wages were increased slightly, and the Casa Grande workers were promised better accommodation. However, it also revealed the weaknesses continuing to hamper the rural movement; the strikers lacked organization and leadership, they failed to draw up a list of demands, the field and mill workers had acted independently, and the Japanese workers had refused to participate at all. In some ways these problems were unavoidable for the strike leaders had been arrested at the outbreak, troops armed with machine guns had been stationed on the estates, and the memories of the 1912 massacres were still fresh. But it meant that the strike achieved less than it might have, and the position of the workers remained unchanged.[30]

While the Chicama strike was being settled, a new dispute flared in the Huaura Valley. Anarchists from Lima had remained active in the area, winning support by assisting the workers and providing them with goals and leadership. In 1917 they helped the cotton workers compose a list of demands that included a general wage increase of 50 percent and an eight-hour workday. When the owners rejected the demands, the workers struck on June 6. The strike began on the Andahuasi estate, then spread to the neighboring plantations, and into Huacho. The wives of the strikers participated by refusing to bring produce to the local market, creating a food shortage. Violence accompanied the strikes. An attempt to arrest strikers on one estate led to a shooting incident in which one worker was killed. Soldiers under the command of Edgardo Arenas forced the Andahuasi strikers back to work and arrested strike leaders and other militants. The agitation culminated on June 14 in a march by the strikers and their wives through the streets of Huacho. It was led by sixty to one hundred fifty women who, as an anarchist commentator later wrote, possessed "no weapons other than their limbs, no defense other than their breasts." According to the authorities, the women had been drinking and when they approached a detail of soldiers, they hurled first abuse and then sticks and stones. The soldiers answered with a volley of shots. Casualties were high: as many as eighteen workers were killed, four of them women, and one hundred more were wounded. The violence seemed to dishearten the strikers, for they gradually returned to work with only a small wage increase to show for their pains.[31]

Hacendados and officials in the Huaura area continued to believe that outside agitators were responsible for the trouble and not hunger and low wages as the strike leaders charged. Elsewhere, however, some planters were beginning to realize the real cause of the discontent; although anarchist literature was discovered on a Lambayeque estate during a strike in July, the owner refused to hold it responsible. Attempts were being made to control prices. At Cayaltí the owners clamped down on speculators by taking over the distribution of goods and selling them at cost. They also tried to eliminate some of the abuses of the enganche system and to keep the work load within reason. Rumors of possible strikes led to the introduction of subsidies for rice, sugar, and bread at Cañete, while at Paramonga the owners raised the wages of their Japanese workers.[32]

Although some of the problems of the plantation workers were finally being recognized by the end of the war, others emerged. Urban and rural wages were rising, attracting workers to the better paying jobs and forcing the less generous estates to increase their rates, but this meant more work for the remaining workers on some of the estates. In Cañete, men worked thirty-six-hour shifts in the cotton and sugar mills because of the labor shortage. It raised the specter of further labor troubles, which the Cañete owners tried to circumvent by hiring more short-term workers who "would have no time to study matters properly" and more women and children who were cheap and had a reputation for less militancy. On the sugar estates the percentage of women rose during the war years from 3.3 to almost 6 percent of the field workers (see table 6). They helped meet some of the planters' labor needs, but they hindered the development of a united rural labor movement by creating a new group of rural workers with specific interests.[33]

Despite the divisiveness and lack of organization that were still characteristic of the agrarian labor force in 1918, they had achieved some successes, and the low wages, long hours of work, and other hardships they continued to endure provided more than sufficient cause for further agitation and organization. The agricultural workers remained a target for anarchist propaganda as men like Delfín Lévano and Adalberto Fonkén continued to travel into the countryside to meet the people and assist in the formation of local societies. The mutual aid societies were also helping to organize rural workers. In 1918 the Asamblea de Sociedades Unidas sent a representative to the Cañete Valley to meet with the locals and explain the importance of worker unity.[34]

Within the agrarian sector a working class consciousness was developing, and the agitation that had occurred during the war indicated a willingness to resort to violent means to obtain change. It was a warning to the government and planters, and it provided a stimulus for those who hoped to establish a nationwide labor movement.

The Sierra Mines

A second area of rural labor mobilization was the sierra mining region. The mine workers were not "rural" in the same sense as the plantation workers, being concentrated in towns close to the mines. However, most of them were enganchados with strong links to the countryside, and the development of a labor movement among them encountered similar obstacles as on the coast and for the same reasons. Declining real wages, harsh working conditions, and abuses of the enganche system gradually overcame these obstacles. Strikes began to occur, and during the First World War agitation intensified in response to increased exploitation by the mining companies and a growing sense of solidarity among the workers.

The principal mining region was the copper-producing area of Cerro de Pasco where the mines were owned by an American firm, the Cerro de Pasco Mining Corporation. The copper was smelted at the company town of Smelter, using coal from the neighboring mines at Goyllarisquizga. In the early twentieth century the output of the mines expanded substantially as copper prices began rising, and by 1905 copper exceeded silver in value of exports, reaching a prewar peak of $9 million U.S. in 1912. While the primary beneficiary of this expansion was the Cerro de Pasco Corporation, other copper companies in the area profited too, particularly the Backus and Johnston Company with mines at Morococha, and the Morococha Mining Company, a subsidiary of the Cerro de Pasco Corporation, with mines at Casapalca.[35]

Little of the companies' profits went towards improving the conditions of the increasing numbers of mine workers who often worked for thirty-six hours, followed by a twelve-hour rest and then another thirty-six hours, sustained only by coca (see table 6). Above ground the conditions were not much better. Smoke and dust were everywhere. In the Cerro de Pasco foundry, work was described as "a truly hellish labor. The great Koque furnaces and the boiling liquid metal produce a maddening and cruel sensation; the intolerable gases released by the metals and the coal have a murderous effect."[36]

There were frequent accidents, injuries, and deaths. Between 1898 and 1907, over 150 workers were reported killed in the mines at Cerro de Pasco; between 1908 and 1920 a further 627 were killed in these and the mines in Yauli. The inefficient mining methods, the widespread use of unfamiliar machinery, the imprudence of the workers, and the bosses' lack of interest in safety were blamed for the accidents. The difficult working conditions and the long hours of work that dulled reflexes to possible danger were also factors. Those who were injured had little hope of recovery. The workers at Morococha paid one to three soles per month for a hospital, which was a miserable little room where the most common treatment was amputation and where patients were reported to die of starvation. Those who were fortunate enough to survive rarely received compensation. Mining accidents were one of the main reasons for the law of professional risk, and even though labor leaders from Lima, like Víctor Herrera y Vera, occasionally interceded to obtain indemnities, they managed to assist only a very few miners.[37] Local papers blamed the authorities whose ignorance permitted the companies to treat their workers like "animals".[38]

The living conditions of the miners were not much better than the working conditions. Housing was primitive with two, three, or even four workers and their families sharing a single, dark damp room measuring sixteen meters square and two meters high. Sanitary facilities were almost nonexistent so that there was a constant danger of epidemics, especially among children. Child labor was heavily employed in the mines—in 1907 children comprised one-third of the labor force at Morococha—and many of them succumbed to bronchitis, bronchial pneumonia, measles, and whooping cough. The situation of the workers contrasted sharply with that of their American bosses who had for their leisure hours a club house comprising a library, bowling alley, billiards room, gymnasium, and pool.[39]

The level of wages did little to compensate for the working and living conditions. The average daily wage was one sol (see table 15). Since prices in the mining region were 30 to 40 percent higher than in Lima and even more in the company stores, the wage was barely sufficient to meet the workers' needs. Payment in vouchers was also common. At Cerro de Pasco the company was reported to use a complicated pay system that, in effect, robbed the workers of their pay. Every day they received a metal coin that had to be exchanged for a cardboard one. After earning several of these, the workers converted them into a bond that was good only at the company store. "Oftentimes the Indians fail to understand this arrangement at the beginning and keep the metal coins without exchanging them for the pieces of cardboard, thus losing their pay." The bond issued one week was not valid for the next, so that those who failed to spend it also lost their pay.[40]

Attempts were made to protect the native miners from this exploitation. In Lima concerned individuals like Manuel González Prada had long tried to help the Indians. In October 1909 a group led by Joaquín Capelo, Pedro Zulen, and Dora Mayer formed the Sociedad Pro-Indígena (Pro-Indian Society), an organization whose aims were to assist the Indians in any way possible, make them aware of their legal rights, and try to end the exploitation they suffered, particularly from the enganche system. The Sociedad wanted to set up committees throughout the country that would act as local pressure groups to protect the Indians,

Table 15: Mining Wages in the Department of Junín, 1908–1918 (in soles)

1908	.80–1.80	1915	.80–3.00
1912	1.00–2.50	1917	.80–5.00
1913	1.00–2.50	1918	.80–5.00

Sources: Jiménez, "Estadística Minera del Perú en 1908," p. 73, "Estadística Minera del Perú en 1912," p. 91, "Estadística Minera del Perú en 1913," p. 94, "Estadística Minera del Perú en 1915," p. 137, "Estadística Minera del Perú en 1917," p. 277, "Estadística Minera del Perú en 1918," p. 175.

and it established contacts with Lima's mutual aid societies to assist in "the redemption of the aboriginal race." Some societies, like the Asamblea de Sociedades Unidas, formed pro-Indian commissions that pressed for the abolition of enganche and assisted the mine workers to form their own organizations and obtain the benefits offered by the law of professional risk. The Sociedad Pro-Indígena and the workers societies also helped in securing a number of new laws designed to protect the mine workers.[41]

This outside pressure to protect the Indians occurred in part because of the common assumption that they were incapable of protecting themselves. Dora Mayer summed up the misconception by explaining the reason for the mining and agricultural workers' lack of militancy was because they were "submissive" and "accustomed to all kinds of privations."[42] Her explanation ignored the frequent uprisings, rebellions, and strikes that had involved the Indians throughout Peru's history and showed they were prepared to agitate.

The problem was that various obstacles hindered the mobilization of the mine workers. First, although the conditions undoubtedly left much to be desired, they may not have been as bad as most critics charged; the mine owners (although hardly an unbiased source) claimed they were an improvement over those in the Indian villages. Secondly and more importantly, there was a lack of worker unity, a result primarily of the enganche system. As members of a transitory work force, the mine workers sought to satisfy their contractual obligations and return home as quickly as possible. Finally, there was always the fear of repression. In June 1904 workers constructing the Cerro de Pasco railway were fired on by troops when they attacked their bosses because of exploitative treatment—twenty were killed or injured. In the few other confrontations of this sort the story was the same: the workers were arrested, fired, or faced other forms of intimidation.[43]

As the mining sector expanded the workers became more willing to risk the consequences of militant action. According to Dora Mayer, four strikes occurred in the Cerro de Pasco region in 1908–1909 following accidents in the mines, unsuccessful demands for better wages and shorter hours of work, and resentment at reductions in the wages of older workers. In 1912 there was a one-day strike to end payroll deductions for lighting materials and hospital. Mayer reports the owners agreed almost immediately, fearing that there might be some connection between this dispute and the recent Chicama Valley strikes.[44]

The most serious strike of the prewar period occurred at Morococha in

December 1913. As in the Chicama Valley strike of plantation workers the previous year, this strike seemed to involve enganchadores, for they began agitating after the Morococha and Backus and Johnston companies failed to pay them according to their contracts. They received support from the workers who were also dissatisfied because of payment in merchandise instead of cash and the deduction of two soles per month for use of a nonexistent hospital. On December 5, over three thousand Backus and Johnston workers went on strike. Their demands indicated some contact with or knowledge of the labor movement in the rest of the country, for they sought an eight-hour day, strict compliance with the law of professional risk, suspension of work at noon on Sundays, construction of a hospital, and fortnightly and better pay. Expecting trouble, the government sent a commissioner with a detachment of troops. He managed to get most of the strikers back to work within three days by explaining that the strike, because it failed to comply with President Billinghurst's strike decree, was illegal and offering to submit their claims to the president if they were drawn up in a legal fashion. Some strikers were not satisfied and hurled rocks at the soldiers and exploded dynamite bombs. The dispute continued into January 1914, and eventually two representatives of the workers traveled to Lima to present their case to Billinghurst. They protested that their leaders were being arrested, contracts violated, and demonstrators fired, while abuses continued. Billinghurst provided no solution, probably because his attention was focused on more serious problems closer to home.[45]

Although, as the strike indicated, the mine workers could be aroused, they were still not prone to militancy. On the outbreak of war in Europe in 1914, wages and work force were cut, Sunday work was eliminated, and the workers were put on a rota system. In September the industry was almost completely shut down. One commentator after visiting Cerro de Pasco remarked, "The huge chimneys which reach menacingly into the heavens only occasionally belch their enormous puffs of smoke into space." Yet the cutbacks produced little worker reaction. When the Backus and Johnston Company forced some of its workers at Casapalca to vacate the company houses, it aroused considerable ill will, since the permanent workers had nowhere else to live, but no violence occurred. At Morococha the workers quietly returned to their villages when wages were reduced by 20 percent.[46]

Even with the rise in the cost of living and the increased pressures on the workers that accompanied the wartime expansion of the copper industry, the movement in the mining region was slow to develop. When

Víctor Herrera y Vera visited the Cerro de Pasco region in 1917, he found the organization of the workers to be "in an embryonic state." He commented, "The majority of the popular mass is in a completely backward state. They know nothing of the social organization of workers, their duties and rights, and especially the law of professional risk." There were no resistance societies, syndicates, nor strike funds, and while May Day was celebrated at Cerro de Pasco and Morococha, only a small proportion of the mine workers participated.

Nevertheless, there were indications of a nascent movement. The miners had been forming societies, often under the direction of workers from the coast. The goals of the societies were to foment worker unity, secure protection from exploitation, press for more labor legislation, and win the eight-hour day. In December 1915 a group of workers in Junín considered forming a Confederación Departamental Obrera de Junín (Workers Departmental Confederation of Junín) to incorporate all the workers of the department.[47]

In addition, strikes were occurring. In September 1917 the workers at Morococha declared a strike to protest having to eat their meals in the mine where poor ventilation concentrated dynamite fumes. They may also have been influenced by several recent accidents in the area that had caused two deaths.[48]

Rising prices and low wages provided ample cause for further agitation.[49] In January 1917 the workers at Morococha demanded the reestablishment of their prewar wages. The employees of the Morococha Mining Company were successful, but the Backus and Johnston Company refused even to recognize the workers society that presented the claim. In May workers throughout the Cerro de Pasco region went on strike to back demands for better wages and working conditions. The agitation began on the twenty-fifth among the foundry workers of Smelter who demanded a 50 percent wage increase, a reduction in the work day from twelve to eight hours, and other improvements. After three days the company agreed to the eight-hour day, wage increases of 10 and 20 percent, the ending of deductions for the hospital, and free medical treatment. Other strikes followed at Goyllarisquizga and Morococha where the mine workers demanded the same improvements. The government, which was reported to be losing 10,000 soles per day in export taxes because of the strikes, sent troops to the area to try to force a solution and prevent disorders. At Goyllarisquizga police and company employees opened fire on three hundred Indians who, according to the subprefect, were drunk and had attacked the company offices and store. Three or four people, including one woman, were killed. Fearful of further violence, the companies acceded to most of the workers' demands while charging that outside agitators had been responsible for the trouble.[50]

Despite the success of these strikes, the workers' standard of living continued to deteriorate. In November 1917 it was reported that the cost of living in the mining areas had risen to such an extent that essential goods now cost more than the poor could afford. Locally grown products like wheat were being shipped to Lima, creating local shortages and inflated prices.[51]

Trouble followed. In November 1917 a strike began among the workers at Smelter for better wages and then spread to the Casapalca foundry and to the mines. This time the workers failed, as the authorities invoked the strike decree and used police and soldiers to crush the strike. The workers at Goyllarisquizga were equally unsuccessful when they went on strike the following July. They wanted a 20 percent wage increase, cheaper food, more carbide for their lamps, and two Italian foremen reprimanded for interfering with their pay. The prefect, backed by eighty soldiers, and a representative of one of Cerro de Pasco's workers societies, convinced them to return to work, explaining that their actions were subverting the progress of the country and did not comply with the strike decree. The prefect added that all their demands, except for the wage increase, would be considered by the company.[52]

During this period strikes were also occurring in Peru's other mining areas, particularly the Ticapampa region. But as at Cerro de Pasco, few were successful, and the workers' conditions remained largely unchanged. The owners, like many coastal planters, continued to blame outside agitators for their troubles. They refused to accept the workers' contention that it was the harsh treatment, unhygienic and hazardous working conditions, long hours, inadequate medical services, unsatisfactory indemnities, and low wages—despite the high price of copper—that were the real causes of the strikes.[53]

The labor movement in the mining region remained weak and divided, but some progress had been made, including the formation of several new societies in the Cerro de Pasco area in 1918. One of the most notable was the Comité Pro-Abaratamiento de Subsistencias (Committee for Cheaper Essentials), apparently modeled on the anarchist-influenced society in Lima of the same name. The new society sought to obtain lower prices for necessities and charged that speculation and monopolization by local officials caused local increases.[54] Like the plantation workers, the mine workers now had a clearer idea of their rights and capabilities. They had challenged their employers and drawn the government into many of their disputes; they had indicated their willingness to strike, and as prices continued to rise and real wages fall, the area seemed ripe for more mobilization and agitation.

The Northern Petroleum Fields

The third rural area that experienced significant labor agitation during this period was the northern petroleum fields. Three main companies were involved in the production of oil in the area: Faustino Piaggio of Callao, with fields at Zorritos, the London and Pacific Petroleum Company, with installations at Negritos (also known as La Brea y Pariñas) and Talara, and the Lobitos Oilfields Limited, another British firm, with fields at Lobitos. American capital came to dominate the industry in 1913 when the International Petroleum Company, a subsidiary of Standard Oil of New Jersey, took over the London and Pacific Company and three years later added the small Lagunitas Oil Company, which had installations at Lagunitas.

Production of oil increased rapidly during the early twentieth century (see tables 1, 2, and 3). Simultaneously, the size of the labor force was growing, from 844 workers in 1905 to 2,678 in 1919. Many of them were smallholders who labored in the petroleum fields only part of the year. Attempts were made to transform them into a permanent labor force by offering grants of land in the area and high wages and, except for Lobitos with its lower rates, the companies seem to have had some success.[55]

Agitation in the petroleum fields was rare before the First World War, a result of the good pay as well as the concentration of the workers in a small number of camps, which gave the companies considerable control over the lives of their employees. The few instances of trouble included a disturbance at Negritos in September 1910 when the workers caused 1,200 soles in damage during an an attack on their English foremen and the company store, and a strike in January 1913 by Zorritos workers who won a 20 percent increase on their wage of one sol.[56] The oil companies, like employers elsewhere, blamed outside agitators for any local problems.

The oil companies had some justification, for anarchists from Lima and Callao were in the area and admitted involvement in a series of strikes that occurred in May 1913. The trouble began at Negritos on the eleventh after the company fired a worker who had opened a shop charging lower prices than the company store. The workers went on strike when his reinstatement was denied. They also demanded better pay and the eight-hour work day—an indication that they had had some contact with the movement elsewhere. After four days they accepted an offer of a general wage increase of twenty centavos, free medical treatment, full pay for injured workers, permission to open their own shop, and the reinstatement of their colleague. The Talara workers, who had joined the strike, won many of the same improvements, and on May 22 the workers at Lobitos and Lagunitas followed with their own strikes. The Lobitos manager tried to break the strike by offering any dissatisfied worker free passage from Lobitos. This provoked all the petroleum workers to threaten a general strike if a better offer was not forthcoming, and the company gave in by the end of the month.

One concession made by the companies was not to release any of their workers for six months. However, in June following a visit by a special government commission, several Negritos workers were fired. This set off a new strike and the July 1913 boycott of the Duncan Fox Company ships by the FORP and the Callao harbor workers. The fired workers were eventually offered reinstatement, but most had found other jobs and received instead a lump sum for their back pay.[57]

With the outbreak of war in Europe, agitation in the petroleum fields increased, declining real wages being the main cause. At Lobitos, prices tripled between 1914 and 1918, while wages remained the same. Payment in vouchers also produced discontent; the Zorritos workers went on strike in March 1915 to get them withdrawn.[58] More serious disputes occurred as the full impact of the price rise was felt.

The workers at Negritos declared a strike in May 1916 for a 60 percent wage increase as well as an imaginative list of other improvements in their living and working conditions, including the eight-hour day, full pay for sick and injured workers, free medical assistance, six months' notice and 500 soles severance pay for released workers, and one month's paid leave after a year's employment. When the company accepted only a few of the demands, the strike spread to Talara. President Pardo appealed for calm, but oil mains were broken, and clashes between strikers and troops left at least three workers dead at Talara and four injured at Negritos on May 31. Pardo once more appealed to the strikers and this time got them back to work by inviting a delegation to Lima to negotiate a settlement. Before arriving the workers condensed their demands to a 20-centavo increase, an eight-hour day, the appointment of a Peruvian doctor, compensation for the families of those workers killed, freedom to form mutual aid societies, and construction of schools. The company representatives were willing to concede only the last two. However, the continuing pressure of the workers, the support of Lima societies like the Asamblea de Sociedades Unidas (which in an unusual display of militancy threatened a general strike), and threats of a renewed walk-out at Talara convinced the company to change its position. On August 8 it accepted the arbitrator's decision, granting all the workers' demands except for the reduction in hours, which was to be discussed further.

The settlement was followed by a new strike in September at Lobitos after the company fired a group who had urged common action with the Negritos strikers. The strike ended quickly, but six of the strike leaders failed to regain their jobs.[59]

At Talara, the company tried to fulfill at least some of its promises. It built 400 rent-free houses described as "neat and comfortable" and "far superior to [those] of any labourers either in Paita or in any part of this district." Water was free and supplies were provided at cost price; work began on lighting and sewer services; a mixed school and a club were completed; and the company offered to construct a new church and a municipal building. Yet, not everyone was satisfied. A workers' center and a boys' school had not been built, nor had the Peruvian doctor been appointed, and it was uncertain whether the company would recognize the workers' representatives and negotiate with them. Relations between the company and its employees were also deteriorating because of the growing number of unemployed in the area. These were workers who had been hired for various construction projects in Talara, now completed, who remained in the area, building a community on company land between the town and the workers' accommodation. They were accused of having "time to foment trouble [and] get up demonstrations, not only against the Company but also against the local authorities."[60] A principal cause of the unrest was the rise in prices, which was also affecting those with jobs.

In late March 1917 a new strike occurred at Talara. It centered on a demand for better wages, although the workers also wanted the appointment of a Peruvian doctor, a workers' center, a boys' school, public lighting and sewers, better treatment and recognition of the workers' representative. The local manager, J. J. Polan, was willing to consider all of the demands except that for a wage increase, which had to be approved by the head office in Toronto, Canada, and his telegram for advice had not yet received a reply. The local prefect, the British vice-consul at Paita who apparently did not realize that the installations were now owned by a U.S. company, and the commander of the cruiser, "Almirante Grau," which had transported troops to the area to keep order, unsuccessfully intervened to try to end the strike. Polan then decided to suspend operations in the field indefinitely, but resumed negotiations when the strikers sought the support of the Negritos workers. On April 4 the strike ended as Toronto approved a 20-centavo increase for all the workers of Talara, Negritos, and Lagunitas. The workers, for their part, promised to avoid further agitation and, if they were dissatisfied, to meet with the manager and the prefect before undertaking any industrial action. They also forfeited their pay for the period of the strike.

While opinions differed as to who was really responsible for the strike, whether it was the strike leaders, the inexperienced Polan, or the community of unemployed, the company was now determined to assert its control over the workers. It immediately ordered the removal of the unemployed and a few months later tried to force the workers into signing a petition supporting its claim to water rights in the area, voting for its choice for senator, and renouncing further demands and agitation. When the workers refused, the president and secretary of their society and other leaders were arrested, their families were expelled, and the society was dissolved. The workers at Negritos retaliated by declaring a strike and demanding the prisoners' release. A delegation traveled to Lima in September, but despite the support of the Confederación de Artesanos and José Carlos Bernales, president of the Senate, they managed to obtain only an indemnity of 1,500 soles for their troubles.[61]

With the company less conciliatory and the cost of living continuing to rise, there was a very real likelihood of more trouble. The workers did not feel bound by their promise to avoid further industrial action since the company had not lived up to its promise to appoint a Peruvian doctor and construct a workers' center. They were now displaying greater militancy than ever before and had opened a strike fund. On November 14 the workers at Talara and Negritos went on strike after their demand for a 50 percent wage increase was refused. Although backed by workers societies from as far away as Lima, they were faced by a hostile prefect who had three hundred troops to carry out his wishes. He urged the strikers to return to work, began arresting their leaders, and, together with the company, opened a register at Talara for those who wanted jobs. He offered them his protection, while the rest would be released and given free passage to Paita. Some workers had already signed and returned to work when reports arrived of a shooting incident at Lobitos.

The Lobitos workers had gone on strike on November 25 for the same improvements as the Talara workers. Three days later, while they were collecting their back pay, they saw their leaders marching down to the docks, apparently under arrest. In fact, they were on their way to Talara to meet with the prefect and were merely being escorted. The crowd attacked the soldiers who opened fire, killing between nine and fourteen workers and injuring more than twenty. Another thirty were arrested.

The shooting ended the Lobitos strike, but the majority of the workers chose to return to their homes rather than risk their lives in the oil fields again. At Negritos there was a new shutdown. In Trujillo the workers issued a public protest, while in Lima the Confederación de Artesanos demanded the punishment of those responsible. The anarchists predicted that the killings marked the end of peaceful agitation. "Today," they wrote, "the worker who goes on strike does so not to protect what he already has, but to secure new rights and better conditions. And the right to liberty and equality is not won with pages of humiliating claims and trust in the goodness of the exploiting enemy; now . . . rights are won with the blade of the machete in open struggle." The prediction, however, proved inaccurate. By December 4 the oil fields had returned to normal and the workers had received nothing. A number of agitators were arrested and deported, and strike leaders were imprisoned. An amnesty freed them in November of the following year.[62]

During the war years the petroleum workers had won less than other sectors of the rural labor force. Although they formed societies, chose leaders, established contacts with workers elsewhere, and engaged in strikes, their situation did not change significantly. Following the 1917 strikes they avoided militant action for the rest of the war. The imprisonment of their leaders and the exodus of a portion of the labor force lessened the possibility of further agitation. So, too, did the failure of the most recent strikes and the brutality of the repression. In addition, the companies began to increase wages slightly (see table 16), which helped reduce militancy.

Table 16: Petroleum Workers' Wages, 1917–1919 (in soles)

Location	1917			1919		
	Max.	Min.	Av.	Max.	Min.	Av.
Lobitos	1.90	.90	—	2.40	.70	2.18
Lagunitas	2.70	1.20	1.95	6.25	1.20	3.72
Talara/Negritos	2.43	1.00	1.79	3.00	1.45	2.55

Sources: Jiménez, "Estadística Minera del Perú en 1917," pp. 118, 120, 121, "Estadística Minera del Perú en 1919," pp. 77, 79, 83.

Nevertheless, events in the petroleum fields had produced concern among officials and employers and had revealed that agitation could occur here as elsewhere.[63] The petroleum workers, like the plantation workers and the mine workers, had participated in strikes, and there was no guarantee that they would not participate in others.

Taken together, these various sectors of the rural labor force seemed to have been in a continuous state of agitation during the war years. It appeared that while the government had managed to keep the situation in Lima and Callao more or less under control, the economically more important rural sector was threatening to get completely out of hand. Even with the intervention of the army, which had frequently used force to try to prevent them, strikes had continued to occur. Moreover, the violence that had accompanied the rural strikes had discredited the government of President Pardo, assisted his enemies, and provided the more militant sectors of the labor force with ammunition to attack his government, in particular, and the capitalist system, in general.

It was in response to this situation and the prospect of renewed agitation among the workers of Lima and Callao, now in alliance with mobilized sectors of the rural labor force, that Pardo was compelled to admit at the end of the war that a new approach to labor problems was essential if even more serious disputes were to be avoided in the future. Repression was possible, but it seemed to be of only limited value. Some other solution was necessary and it was needed quickly, for prices were still rising and affecting the workers. If a solution was not found, Pardo faced the very real possibility of pressure from the revitalized urban workers acting in concert with the rural workers who had revealed that they were an active part of the working class and an increasingly important sector of Peru's labor movement.

9 The Eight-Hour Day, January 1919

With the signing of the armistice in November 1918, more than four years of warfare came to an end and the task of rebuilding began. Uncertainty prevailed as every nation, whether belligerent, nonparticipant, or neutral, adjusted to the changes wrought by the war. Those that had profited from the export of raw materials faced an especially uncertain future. Their wartime prosperity had rested to a great extent upon the disruption of traditional trading patterns that now seemed likely to be restored.

In the case of Peru, the end of the war found the country still struggling with the problems caused by inflation. The cost of living, which had risen steadily since 1914, increased even more rapidly between 1918 and 1919 (see table 12), while wages continued to lag far behind. One commentator calculated that between 1914 and 1919 the daily wage for a married country laborer had risen by 58 percent, while his expenses had risen by 86 percent; for an urban worker with four children, the difference was 27 percent against 32 percent; for a skilled laborer with four children, 28 percent against 57 percent.[1] Declining real wages had been the basic cause of the strikes occurring in both the urban and rural sectors during the war and now threatened further trouble unless the government took some initiative to satisfy the workers. It could not afford labor agitation of any kind since strikes might interrupt the flow of profitable exports and damage existing trade links that it wanted to protect. But something had to be done since it no longer had the war to blame for the increases.

The options open to President José Pardo were limited. Past experience had shown that repression was of questionable value and not really feasible if thousands of workers were involved. Legislation could force employers, especially those in the still booming primary sector, to raise wages, but controls of this sort ran counter to the free enterprise policies of the Civilistas, and it is unlikely that Pardo seriously considered them. Instead, he chose a solution that was designed to satisfy the workers without great cost to the government or employers: he decided to woo labor with some new labor laws.

Pressure for social legislation had grown throughout all of Latin America in recent years. It had been the focus of a 1916 international conference in Buenos Aires, which had recommended a common set of labor laws for all of South America.[2] Pardo had at his disposal the nine projects of José Matías Manzanilla that still had to be transformed into legislation and, with the prospect of new agitation propelling him forward, he introduced a number of bills to Congress. Not all were successful. A contract law that set out the obligations of employers and employees and created an office to oversee existing labor laws and introduce others failed to win support. But three other bills received congressional approval. On November 25 Pardo signed a law protecting women and child workers. A month later, on December 26, he instituted a mandatory day of rest on Sundays, civic holidays, and the first day of elections for workers in factories, shops, mines, construction sites, and for those who used mechanized equipment on estates. The following day he signed a third bill, compelling factories and firms situated more than one kilometer from the nearest urban center to provide houses, schools, and medical services for their workers.[3]

The most important of these laws was the first, which regulated working conditions for women and child laborers. Since its original recommendation by Manzanilla in 1905, support for such a law had grown with the increasing employment of both groups and their frequent job-related injuries. Women usually worked as long as men, but earned far less: in 1915 their wage seldom had averaged more than two soles per day. In Lima over one thousand women labored in the textile mills, garment centers, soap, candle, and biscuit factories, post office, and telephone exchange. In 1916 their plight drew the attention of the local mutual aid societies which convinced the government in August to increase wages for women employed in the state factories that produced soldiers' uniforms. Pressure for improvements also came from the women themselves, who had shown unexpected militancy. They had participated in strikes during the war and had begun organizing their own societies, like the Sociedad Labor Feminista (Feminist Labor Society) and the Sociedad "Progreso Feminista" (Society "Feminist Progress"). The latter, which was formed in 1916 as a federated society of the Confederación de Artesanos, comprised mainly seamstresses, but claimed to represent the interests of all women workers.[4]

Passage of the law was slow. Bills had been introduced during Billinghurst's presidency and again in 1916, but had failed to win support. Nevertheless, some employers felt that a law was inevitable and had begun releasing the women and children in their employ to avoid future problems. The bill finally came up for debate in the 1918 session and, because of the general interest, was quickly passed by Congress.

Except for those who were domestic servants and agricultural workers not using machinery, the law provided protection for all working women and for children between the ages of fourteen and eighteen who, it was felt, because of their "delicate physiological structure," needed more time than men to recover from the fatiguing effects of their work. Children between the ages of twelve and fourteen were prohibited from working unless they could read, write, and count and had a medical certificate confirming their ability to perform the work. Their hours were limited to six per day, thirty-three per week. Children between fourteen and eighteen and women could work only eight hours per day, forty-five per week. Neither group could be employed in the mines, nor could they work at night; their lunch break would last two hours; and they were to receive 25 percent more than men in compensation for injuries suffered on the job. Women were also to receive paid maternity leave, and factories that employed women of childbearing age had to furnish nurseries.[5]

Although ignored by some employers, the law, particularly the clause establishing the eight-hour work day for women and children, had a great impact on the workers. It especially touched the anarchists who had long been the primary force behind the struggle for the eight-hour day. They had been a key factor in the first success by a group of workers—Callao's harbor workers in 1913—and subsequently had seen a number of other workers, both urban and rural, win this major goal of the labor movement. Now, through the intervention of the government, a new group of workers—women and children—had been added to the list.

The law also had important implications for industry. In the textile industry, where the workers were already suffering because of the rising prices, the women's reduced work day meant less cloth was being prepared, production and wages of male workers fell because they had less to finish, and, thus, both men and women were earning less. Workers throughout the industry responded by pressing for the eight-hour day together with existing or better wages. On December 21 the El Inca workers went on strike for the eight-hour day and a 50 percent wage increase, marking the beginning of what was to be the most successful strike of this formative period of the Peruvian labor movement.

The lead taken by the El Inca workers was followed by the rest of the textile workers, so that by the end of December the entire industry was at a standstill. Although some strikers, those who were paid by tarea, were more interested in a wage increase than a reduction in the hours of work, the eight-hour day became the primary target. A wealth of data was used to back the demands, including claims that King George V of Great Britain had declared his support for the eight-hour day. Factory owners were not impressed; the war years had been profitable ones for them, but since the armistice orders had declined and all were presently overstocked.[6] As a result, the strike was, in the words of one commentator, "a blessing in disguise as far as the owners are concerned." They made no attempt to meet the workers' demands and considered closing their mills temporarily.

Other groups followed the textile workers. The bakery workers made their own demand for the eight-hour day, arguing that a reduction from the existing ten and twelve hours was vital to their health, which suffered from the heat, flour dust, lack of ventilation, and work at night. They also wanted the 1913 wage rates of 3.40 soles for day shifts and 3.70 soles for night shifts reestablished, a closed shop, and masters instead of owners in charge of work and pay. Only three bakeries accepted the principal demand of the eight-hour day, and on January 2 the workers in the other bakeries went on strike. They were followed by the tanners, the workers of the Ciurlizza y Maurer sawmill, and bakery workers in Huacho.

With the agitation spreading, there was growing interest in a general strike for the eight-hour day. A group calling itself the Comité Pro-Paro General (Pro-General Strike Committee) issued a handbill that urged, "Arise, compañeros! The day of proletarian reawakening has arrived and we must demonstrate to those who consider themselves powerful because of their capital that we, the workers, are not meek and submissive, that we deplore our miserable station as slaves of capital, and that as men, as human beings, we have a right to life. Join the struggle, not to ask but to fight for an ultimately human right—fewer hours of excessive work—so that we can devote more time to the cultivation of our minds in order to elevate our base, primordial spirit and develop like modern societies."[7]

As the tone of the handbill indicates, the militant elements had assumed leadership of the strike. Manuel Casabona and Fausto Nalvarte, two anarchists from Vitarte, had been chosen president of the textile workers' strike committee and head of the general strike committee, respectively. Other prominent anarchists, like Nicolás Gutarra, Héctor Merel, and Julio Portocarrero, were also playing an important role in the events. Their involvement was to be expected. Although still comprising only a minority of the labor force, the anarchists were the most active element in the Peruvian labor movement.[8] Their influence had grown in recent months in response to the general economic conditions and the resulting workers' militancy. Moreover, they had traditionally been influential in the textile and bakery industries; they had always encouraged industrial action, especially the general strike; and they had been the main proponents of the eight-hour day. Outside events, like a general strike that had paralyzed Buenos Aires and according to reports was led by radical elements, also stimulated the local anarchists with the vision of a much wider movement.[9] So, too, did the outbreak of strikes in early January among the Zorritos petroleum workers and the Casapalca foundry workers, which suggested that a nationwide attack on capitalism was about to occur.[10]

The petroleum workers wanted the eight-hour day and better pay, while the foundry workers wanted wage increases and reductions in the price of food. In a clash with police at least three Casapalca workers and one policeman were killed, others were injured, and several strikers were arrested. A delegation from Vitarte offered its services as arbitrators, while the government sent 200 troops to restore order. However, the strike lasted only a day, as the company offered a 20 percent wage increase, reduced prices for goods sold in the company store, and freedom of commerce. The Zorritos strike lasted two days, with the workers winning a nine-hour day.[11]

By themselves, these disturbances were not particularly important, but occurring as they did while support was gathering in Lima for a general strike, they gave the impression of a much wider movement that was further stimulating the strikers and greatly worried the government. In Lima and Callao the strikers' appeal for support had received a positive response from virtually every workers organization, and since the owners refused to satisfy their demands and the government refused to intervene on their behalf, the strike committee became convinced that a general strike was the only recourse left open to them.[12] On January 12 it announced that a forty-eight-hour general strike would begin the following day and invited all the workers of the nation to participate. It demanded the release of the workers who had been arrested at Casapalca and expressed support for the actions of the workers in Buenos Aires.

The next morning, groups of strikers posted themselves at the gates of the city's factories and invited the workers to join them. Almost all agreed, and by noon Lima was paralyzed. Markets closed and the tram service was withdrawn as the police could not guarantee its protection. The shutdown in Callao was less complete, but many factories closed. Strikes also occurred on the surrounding estates with the workers demanding the eight-hour day.

The strikers received offers of support from a variety of sources including the mutual aid societies. The latter had done little to regain leadership of the labor movement since the end of the war, possibly because they had not yet recovered from their financial difficulties, and they had played a negligible role in the events so far. It seemed unlikely that they would have much influence, since few of the participating groups belonged to their organizations and the strike leaders were anarchists. Also, they still favored the moderate approach to labor problems. The Confederación de Artesanos offered to put pressure on the government to find a solution to the strikes and to use its influence during the next session of Congress to ensure that a law granting the eight-hour day was passed. The strikers were unimpressed and, except for using the Confederación's "Ricardo Palma" library as a headquarters, they kept their distance from the societies.[13]

More welcome was an offer from the university students' Federación de Estudiantes del Perú (Federation of Peruvian Students). The students had become increasingly responsive to the problems of the popular classes in recent years as their social consciousness had grown.[14] At the outbreak of the textile workers' strike they had accepted an invitation to assist in finding a solution, and after the declaration of the general strike, the Federación named Bruno Bueno y de la Fuente, Valentín Quesada, and Víctor Raúl Haya de la Torre as delegates to aid the strikers. The students were accepted as one more group participating in the dispute, not arbitrators or leaders, and their offices, which were located next to the ministry of public works, were also taken over by the strike committee.

With support growing, passions were running high and occasional outbursts of violence marked the first day of the strike. Trams were damaged and, according to *El Comercio,* shots were fired, and the arsenal was attacked. Lima's electricity was cut, so that as night fell darkness blanketed the streets where police and soldiers patrolled, arresting suspects and preventing groups of strikers from gathering.

The authorities were willing to try anything to keep the strike under control in the belief that the same elements who had brought Buenos Aires to its knees were also present in Lima or that bolsheviks had entered South America and were fomenting strife. They had prohibited meetings and used police to break up those that had occurred. Workers' leaders and suspected agitators like Nicolás Gutarra, Delfín Lévano, and two French propagandists were arrested. A number of workers' headquarters, including those of the bakery workers and the Asamblea de Sociedades Unidas, were ordered closed, and the newspaper, *El Tiempo,* which had been supporting the workers, was shut down. The authorities even issued handbills that claimed those behind the strikes were unscrupulous people paid "by the enemies of Peru" who wished only to discredit the workers of Lima and Callao and their families. The handbills urged the strikers to return to work instead of serving the interests of Chile. There was also a report that Chileans were paying the anarchists to stir up the strike, which Delfín Lévano later refuted by pointing out that the anarchists were so poor they scarcely had enough to publish *La Protesta*.

On the second day of the strike the pressure of the strikers continued unabated. Their efforts were rewarded when several employers including the bakery owners gave in and agreed to the eight-hour day. The strike had aroused such a sense of solidarity that the victorious workers refused to return to work until the textile workers had also succeeded. This unity also managed to bridge a potential division later in the day when the student delegates proposed that the textile workers accept a nine-hour day with the extra hour paid at a higher rate of 20 percent during the day and 30 percent at night. The proposal provoked a heated debate that reached no decision except to reexamine the proposal the next day.[15] The debate had not weakened the strikers' commitment: they concluded the meeting by voting to extend the general strike indefinitely since the textile workers' demands had not been met.

The declaration of an indefinite strike came as a new strike broke out among the mining workers at Morococha. With the miners demanding the eight-hour day and wage increases and resorting to violence to back their demands, it seemed that the feared alliance between urban and rural workers was about to occur.[16] It placed increased pressure on the government to act. But what could Pardo do? Since virtually all the workers in Lima and Callao were on strike, violent repression was not really feasible. Furthermore, the alliance between the government and employers was disintegrating as employers were granting the eight-hour day. They, at least, seemed to feel that a reduction in the work day would not be economically disastrous, while a longer and wider strike might. There appeared to be only one option left open to the president.

On January 15 Pardo issued a supreme decree granting the eight-hour day. The decree declared that since certain industrial establishments had been unable to agree with their workers on the hours of work and new wage rates, and since it was the duty of the state to determine the most compatible conditions for workers in its own establishments and on public works projects, the executive had decided that the eight-hour day with existing wages would be the standard in the state's shops, railways, agricultural and industrial establishments, and public works programs. In privately owned establishments, the employers and workers could negotiate the hours of work, but if no agreement was reached, the eight-hour day would be the standard. If employers and workers were unable to agree on wages or duties, arbitrators would be named. To satisfy the workers completely, Pardo also ordered the release of all arrested strikers.

The general strike had been an outstanding success. Pardo's decree gave every wage earner in the country the right to demand the eight-hour day and to claim it as a matter of law if there was any dispute. The immediate effect of the decree was the end of the general strike. The interurban tram service was reestablished, shops reopened, and within the next few days the strikers began to return to work. Some delays occurred since most of the workers had been demanding wage increases in addition to the eight-hour day and their employers balked at granting both. Occasionally Pardo or some other official had to intervene before satisfactory solutions were reached, and the decree's arbitration arrangement was invoked in a few instances. In Callao the intransigence of some employers resulted in the threat of a new general strike before they cooperated. But by the end of the month all the workers from the factories, shops, plantations, and firms who had participated in the general strike were back at work.[17]

The effects of the strike and the decree were not limited to the capital. Throughout the country workers demanded the immediate implementation of the eight-hour day and frequently went on strike to back their demand. In Huacho, the railway and tram workers struck for the eight-hour day and better wages. The decree granted the former, but arbitrators had to be named before an agreement was reached on the latter. In Trujillo a dispute among the railway workers developed into a strike for the eight-hour day and better wages that involved most of the city's workers plus those of the neighboring port of Salaverry and the estates of Laredo and Cartavio. After a week the disputes went to arbitrators who decided in the workers' favor. However, the Peruvian Corporation representative, William Morkill, rejected the decision, provoking a riot in which the workers attacked the corporation's offices and set fire to the Trujillo station, ties, coal deposits, and freight and passenger cars, causing

700,000 soles in damage. The rioters seemed to have the sympathy of the police for no arrests were made until the following day.[18]

North of Trujillo, the harbor workers at Eten and the workers on the Tumán estate, a plantation owned principally by the Pardo family, received the eight-hour day without having to resort to industrial action. On the neighboring Cayaltí estate the decree was also enforced among the mill and the machinery workers. The field workers, however, who worked by tarea were not covered by the decree. Employers in the area continued to believe that foreign elements were behind the agitation, and the owners of Cayaltí issued instructions not to hire refugees from Chile because of their possible contacts with agitators in that country.[19]

South of Lima, in the Cañete area, the decree produced some agitation. At Pisco the railway workers obtained the eight-hour day without any problem, but the maritime guilds had to go on strike to secure it. At Cerro Azul, the valley's port, workers went on strike for better wages. The plantation workers in the area also agitated for fewer hours of work and better wages. On February 13 the field manager of the British Sugar Company's Cañete estates noted that every section of work in fields and factory had either been on strike or made demands. His workers succeeded in obtaining a shorter work day, but failed to get more pay. Introducing the eight-hour day even encountered some obstacles as the Japanese contract workers refused to accept it until it had been approved by the emigration company in Japan.[20]

While many workers were successful in winning the eight-hour day, either by the decree or agitation, not every wage earner in Peru was now working only eight hours. Many employers managed to ignore the decree: in the mining regions it was not implemented until 1925.[21] Employers also sought to circumvent it by maintaining the old work schedule and paying low overtime rates of 25 percent or less for the extra hours. Workers constructing the new presidential palace in Lima received only 10 percent more for an extra hour's work. As reports of this type of abuse began to appear, the Confederación de Artesanos compiled a list of the companies involved and offered assistance to their workers. A delegation of presidents of the federated societies toured the city's factories, firms, and construction sites to examine the effects of the decree and to ensure compliance. In April the Confederación was still receiving reports that the decree was being ignored and that owners were insisting on one or two extra hours of work with overtime rates rarely approaching the recommended 50 percent. It produced threats of new agitation.[22]

The attempts by the employers to undermine the decree resulted from the increased costs and reduced profits produced by the shorter work day. Studies made in October 1919 found that since the introduction of the decree factories had lost an average of six hours of work per week, per worker. In some firms such as the bakeries, smelters, and railways the amount of work had been reduced by four hours daily. Except where more workers were hired or overtime paid, the result was a decline in output. It was down by 32.9 percent at El Progreso, 18 percent at a cooking oil refinery, and 9 percent at a sawmill. Reduced output meant lower profits, with El Progreso, La Bellota, a leather goods firm, and the sawmill reporting substantial losses. Only those firms that had passed the increased costs on to the consumer had managed to maintain their old profit levels, although it is not certain that the others were really suffering. The decree was also blamed for promoting a lack of punctuality among the workers. One critic who accused the workers of being "lazy" claimed that before the decree they had worked only eight hours although hired for nine; now they worked only seven.[23]

The relative ease with which the employers could bypass the decree indicated the workers' continuing inability to ensure total compliance with their demands, as well as the weaknesses that still affected the movement. Decades of struggle seemed to have taught some workers very little. Many of them remained unaware of their real strength and capabilities, believing that the reason for their success had been the generosity and altruism of the government. Following the issuance of the decree, workers marched to the palace to thank President Pardo and groups outside Lima, who had made no attempt to join the strike or assist the strikers, sent him telegrams of thanks. Juan Goachet, the long-time labor leader, praised him as "the greatest benefactor of the proletariat anywhere." His name, Goachet added, "would be invoked across national frontiers by the most fervent socialists as an example to imitate, as a model government for democratic peoples."[24]

Pardo's record shows that he had long had some sympathy for the working class. On January 15 he declared, "The decree which you have just received is the fixed and emphatic proof that we, the men who serve the country, have but one aim, that of Justice, no matter to whom it may be due. I am happy to have signed a resolution which establishes for you, the men who toil, the principles of right and justice now enjoyed by other cultured peoples." In this case, however, the real reason behind his decision was the workers' actions. They allowed Pardo little room to maneuver and there was a constant undercurrent of potential violence. The bloody strike in Buenos Aires was the most recent and perhaps most frightening indication of where workers' agitation could lead. According to the anarchists, other recent events pointed in the same direction: the outbreak of war in Europe, the Russian Revolution, the revolutions in Germany and Austria-Hungary, the increase in prices in Peru that had produced agitation throughout the country, and the assassination of the women in Huacho that had reinvigorated socialist propaganda. Some workers believed Peru to be on the verge of a class struggle similar to the reported disturbances in Buenos Aires; Pardo was determined to prevent this, and he had succeeded in keeping the violence to a minimum. There were no fatalities during the general strike and, according to the president, the strikers' respect for order facilitated the employers' acceptance of the decree. Thus the workers, not Pardo, were ultimately responsible for the eight-hour day, yet many workers failed to recognize the fact.[25]

One of the general strike's most obvious effects on the Lima movement was the greater unity and militancy of the workers. A report in *La Prensa* described the strike as "a fine example of solidarity offered by the popular classes who without exception adhered enthusiastically to the general strike, perhaps against the particular interests of many of them, but moved by the very noble sentiment of ensuring that the just demand of a substantial number of workers was heard and satisfied."[26] This sense of unity and solidarity remained as the workers attempted to protect what they had won. The membership of existing societies grew and new organizations appeared. Of these the most important was the textile workers' Federación de Trabajadores en Tejidos del Perú (Federation of Textile Workers of Peru). It was formed on January 16 at a meeting chaired by Víctor Raúl Haya de la Torre, who had close contacts with many of the anarchist leaders and whose efforts on behalf of the workers during the strike were the roots of a long and fruitful relationship. The Federación was to be an industrial union incorporating all the textile workers of the country. It was dedicated to implementing the eight-hour day, defending its members, celebrating May Day, and assisting other groups in their struggle against "capitalist exploitation." Its goals included a further reduction in the hours of work, a minimum wage law, workmens compensation without state involvement, and improvements in the economic condition of all workers. The ultimate goal was a communist society. It professed no religious beliefs, adhered to no political party, and claimed to be federated to the Federación Obrera Regional del Perú which, although not functioning at this time, was regarded as the only representative entity of the Peruvian working class.[27]

The workers' new militancy was also evident from the acceptance of anarchists as their leaders. It placed members of the working class who were committed to revolutionary change in control of the movement for the first time. In addition, there was a greater sense of confidence among the workers. It seemed that the winning of the eight-hour day was not simply an end in itself, but rather the first step in a process that would lead to further improvements for the working class.

The success of Peru's workers in becoming one of the first groups in all of Latin America to have a government-decreed eight-hour day might be seen as simply a result of the particular circumstances of January 1919. But this ignores the decades of organization and struggle by the Peruvian workers that preceded it. Without that struggle there would have been no active labor movement to take advantage of the opportunity that presented itself that January. The events themselves had demonstrated once again that the Peruvian workers could be mobilized and could have an impact on national developments. It had been a long and at times bloody struggle, but the winning of the eight-hour day marked a coming-of-age for the Peruvian workers. The early stages of organization were over, the lines of confrontation had been drawn, leaders and goals had been chosen, and although the movement still had serious weaknesses, the workers seemed certain to play a more influential role in their nation's future: that is, if they could maintain the enthusiasm and solidarity that had won them the eight-hour day.

10 And After

Having won the eight-hour day, the Peruvian workers now seemed ready to demand a position in society more closely reflecting their numbers and their importance. As a result of their success, they were more confident, united, and militant than ever before and appeared willing to use their strength to challenge the old order. However, subsequent events clearly show that this challenge did not materialize. Further demands may have been made, strikes may have occurred, and organizations and political parties may have been formed, but the workers remained at the bottom of the social ladder, their impact on national developments minimal, and their claims to power successfully resisted by the elite. It has only been in recent years that the workers have come to play a more effective role in the country and to challenge the *status quo* once again.

Why did this occur? Why did the workers' position fail to improve as anticipated? The answer is complex and in many ways related to post-1919 developments both inside and outside Peru, which lie beyond the scope of this study. But there were also problems internal to the labor movement that had been evident for many years. They now destroyed the momentum created in January 1919 and subsequently limited the workers' influence and effectiveness. Internal divisiveness, reliance on bourgeois political leaders, and repression were the three major factors that continued to plague the movement; these had not been eliminated by winning the eight-hour day, as events quickly proved. Within months the movement suffered a new setback, and although it managed to survive the crisis, its inherent weaknesses were evident to all.

The event that brought the workers back to earth was a second general strike, this time over the cost of living. High prices had been a factor in the January strike, and they continued to rise. Beans, for example, which had been selling for thirty and thirty-six centavos per kilo in December, cost fifty and sixty centavos in March. Other necessities followed a similar path, with the result that the workers once again began to agitate.

Even before all the January strikes were settled, the Lima shoemakers struck to demand a 50 percent increase in shoe prices to offset the rising cost of foodstuffs and materials; they settled for 20 percent and a price freeze on some materials. In February the San Jacinto workers struck in support of colleagues who had been fired and replaced by lower-paid workers. They threatened an industry-wide strike that forced their employers to agree to pay equal wages and end unjustified firings. An increase in the price of tickets on the Central Railway in March produced attacks on the railway line and equipment by workers from the Vitarte mill and the Santa Clara estate. That same month, when Callao's coal handlers went on strike for better pay, the port was shut down completely as the rest of the workers joined in sympathy and protest against strike-breaking soldiers and sailors. After a week, the company agreed to a wage increase.[1]

The worsening economic situation was also marked by the formation of new workers organizations whose purpose was to fight the rise in prices. The most prominent of these was the Comité Pro-Abaratamiento de las Subsistencias. It had been formed originally in 1916 without much success, but its fortunes changed on its reappearance in April 1919, and it soon claimed to represent some thirty thousand workers from federations, guilds, societies, factories, plantations, and study centers in the Lima area. A similar organization was formed in Callao. Their popularity came from their attempts to combat the rising cost of living. They recommended various reforms including reducing food prices, rents, freight rates, and duties on essentials; abolishing tithes; prohibiting the export of essentials; compelling farmers to grow food crops; and setting maximum prices for meat, milk, cereals, coal, vegetables, and other necessities. The Lima Comité had links to the movement for the eight-hour day: its aims included ensuring strict compliance with Pardo's decree until a law was passed, and its leaders were some of the same anarchists who had led the strikers in January. The president was Nicolás Gutarra and the secretary-general Carlos Barba.[2]

The government, and Lima society in general, viewed the growth of the Comité with profound misgivings. They feared that the local workers were now led by individuals tied to European and Latin American revolutionaries. As proof, they pointed to the Comité's demonstrations, where participants shouted *"vivas"* to maximalism, the Russian Revolution, and the proletariat. The minister of government attempted a counterattack against anarchist influence by prohibiting "the cheering of nations unfriendly to Peru and the showing of red flags," and he resolved "to put down all manifestations which degenerated . . . into unlawful demonstrations of anarchy and social demolition." At the same time the government directed the police to prevent the Comité's meetings and refused to accept its recommendations for price reductions. Lima's mothers contributed to the growing hysteria by using the anarchists as bogeymen to frighten their children. The Comité's leaders were greeted in the streets by children who screamed, "Hide, here come Gutarra and Barba! They're going to eat us!"[3]

A second organization that appeared at this time was the Partido Obrero del Perú (Labor Party of Peru). It was the creation of many of the old, moderate labor leaders like Adrian Zubiaga, Víctor Herrera y Vera, José Cahuas, Alberto Montes, Fernando Vera, José Robles, and Horacio La Rosa, some of whom had been involved in the movement for over thirty years. Their condemnation of capitalist exploitation of the proletariat showed they finally had begun to accept some of the more progressive ideas, but unlike the anarchists they did not feel that an economic struggle alone was enough to resist the advances of capitalism. As the name of their organization indicates, they favored political participation. To attract support they called for reforms in the civil and penal codes, the constitution, and the electoral laws, universal suffrage, more labor legislation, and municipal autonomy. In response to the economic pressures of the time, they suggested eliminating taxes and duties to reduce the cost of living.[4]

The party became involved in the May presidential election, supporting the campaign of José Carlos Bernales. Bernales was president of the Senate and had supported the workers in the past, but his presidential chances were virtually nonexistent. Opposing him were ex-President Augusto Leguía and plantation owner Antero Aspíllaga. Leguía had the support of the students, the middle class, much of the army, and some popular elements, while Aspíllaga represented the old Civilista party and other enemies of Leguía, and the Partido Obrero could do very little to offset the electoral advantages of either candidate.[5]

In other areas the party was equally ineffective, largely because it had to contend with the more popular and militant Comité. The Comité's greater appeal was evident at the Partido Obrero's installation on May 1 when the organizers invited the president of the Comité, Gutarra, to speak since he was present. They soon realized their mistake, for the anarchist leader, who was "a genius as a speaker," used the opportunity to condemn the Partido Obrero and especially its adoption of the political route to change. He was so compelling that much of the audience accepted his invitation to a meeting then being held by the Comité, and insufficient numbers remained for the Partido Obrero to continue with its program.[6]

Gutarra's opposition to electoral participation and to political parties recalled the ideological split that had divided the Left in the past and would intensify in the future as socialists came to play a more active role in the labor movement. The first indication of this followed the formation of the third organization of this period, the Partido Socialista del Perú (Socialist Party of Peru), which was the culmination of a widespread interest in a socialist party.

Formed in the latter half of 1918 and installed on May 1, 1919, the party was headed by Luis Ulloa and included among its members Carlos del Barzo, Alberto Secada, and two young journalists, José Carlos Mariátegui and César Falcón. It was committed to the general principles of the class struggle, the need for organizations, unions, and cooperatives, and the use of industrial action as a weapon. At the same time, it supported political involvement, aiming to establish provincial parties and to seek recognition from the socialist central office in Brussels. With regard to the workers, it urged the passage of laws granting a mimimum wage, the right to strike, the eight-hour day, social security, and pensions, and it issued its own list of recommendations for reducing the cost of living.[7]

Having many of the same goals, the socialists and anarchists were initially prepared to cooperate. The two groups participated in the May Day celebrations together and Carlos Barba was elected to the executive of the Socialist party. They issued a joint demand for reductions in the cost of living and threatened a general strike if this demand was not met or if any of their members were arrested. On May 4 the socialists were present at another demonstration organized by the Comité when the two groups, before being dispersed by the police, issued a new list of demands for reducing the cost of living.

However, the ties soon frayed. The anarchists disagreed with the socialists' insistence upon political involvement, while the socialists disapproved of the Comité's radicalism, especially its support of maximalism and its commitment to a general strike. On May 5 the Comité published a letter stating it had no political coloring or doctrine and no ties with the Socialist party. Barba resigned from the socialist executive, and thereafter the two groups followed separate paths. Neither this particular Socialist party nor the Partido Obrero played a significant role in subsequent events.[8]

The formation of these organizations was accompanied by renewed labor agitation and the threat of a new general strike. On May 5 the Santa Catalina workers went on strike for a 20 percent wage increase; a week later all the textile workers declared a strike to back demands for the reinstatement of four La Unión workers who had been fired; and on May 20 the workers of the Empresas Eléctricas Asociadas went on strike for the eight-hour day and double time for overtime and holidays. They were successful after they received support from the Comité, which had been threatening a general strike if prices were not reduced and several workers who had been arrested as a result of the recent agitation were not released.[9]

The climax of the presidential election campaign added to the growing unrest. Initial returns from the voting on May 18 and 19 indicated that Leguía had won reelection. But Aspíllaga claimed that the rural vote was in his favor and until the Supreme Court examined the ballots and decided on the winner, there was a great deal of uncertainty. Nonetheless, it appeared that the more popular candidate had been elected and that the Civilistas had suffered a severe setback, which raised questions about their control over the electoral system and overall strength at this time.

While uncertainty reigned in the political sphere, workers' support for the long-threatened general strike was growing. The women's section of the Comité decided to hold a public demonstration on May 25 to protest against the rising prices that, they claimed, had pushed many families to the edge of starvation. Between two thousand and four thousand men and women participated, shouting as they marched from the Parque Neptuno to the Plaza de Armas: "Down with the bourgeoisie! We want bread! Down with the capitalists and the monopolists!" They hurled rocks at troops and police stationed along the route, who responded by charging the demonstrators, injuring five women and several men. In the Plaza de Armas the organizers described the march as the "baptism of blood" for the women of Peru in their defense of the rights of the proletariat, and once again they called for a general strike if their demands for reducing the cost of living continued to be ignored. That evening a review of the day's events produced an even stronger response. The Comité now insisted upon the removal of the officer in charge of the troops and threatened a general strike if the government did not comply within twenty-four hours. Later that evening they became even more hostile following the arrest of Gutarra and Barba, and when they learned that the Callao Comité had called a general strike for the next day in response to the arrest of some of its members, they immediately followed suit.

On the morning of May 27, commissions of workers toured Lima and Callao to win the support of the labor force. Despite police opposition they were successful almost everywhere, and the cities were soon paralyzed. In contrast to the January events, serious outbursts of violence accompanied the strike. Groups of looters attacked private homes, markets, and especially shops, since the latter were so closely linked in the workers' minds to their declining standard of living. Those operated by Asians received particular attention. The violence was a product of the deteriorating economic situation as well as the recent agitation, but the government seemed to view it as proof that revolution was imminent. Pardo called in the police and army, declared martial law, and gave the army full power to restore order. The commander prohibited groups from meeting in the streets and threatened to suppress with the utmost severity any act of aggression or demonstration against institutions, personal security, private property, or the army.

By late afternoon the two cities were under complete military control. Machine guns were set up in key positions and used to disperse groups of workers. Patrols shot looters on sight and as the day progressed the number of dead and wounded began to mount. That night the cities appeared to be under siege. A correspondent of *The West Coast Leader* provided a dramatic picture of Callao: "The streets in darkness, fusilades of shots breaking out here and there, the searchlights of the cruisers sweeping over the port and the sullen glare of a dozen *fondas* [cafés] burning in different parts of the town."[10]

The next day the strike continued. Shops and factories remained closed; streets were almost empty as most people were afraid to leave their homes; there were new attacks on grocery shops; demonstrators were arrested; and occasional volleys of firing could be heard. Ships' crews and plantation workers joined the strike in the capital, and further strikes were reported in Huancayo, Jauja, and Huacho.

The events seemed to be following the pattern set in January but, in fact, there were significant differences. The arrest of the Comité's leaders and the quick declaration of martial law had undermined the strike. The unanticipated violence had alienated large numbers of workers, so that there was less unity than in January; when the Confederación de Artesanos and the Asamblea de Sociedades Unidas met with government officials to find a solution to the strike, they received widespread worker support. On May 29 the strike began to collapse. Shops reopened, trams were running, a few automobiles could be seen in the streets, and there were fewer shooting incidents. The following day all the markets and banks were operating and, although they closed at the first sign of trouble, a degree of normalcy was returning to daily life.

The Comité had to capitulate. Recognizing that it could not carry out its pledge to remain on strike until its demands for price reductions were met and everyone who had been arrested was released, the Comité agreed on May 31 to end the strike within two days. It expressed regret at the looting, but satisfaction with the moral and material strength and solidarity displayed by the workers who, it concluded, had achieved all they could. It intended to continue agitating for reforms, but new methods would be tried. Moderate elements seemed to have replaced the imprisoned anarchist leaders, for the Comité's executive asked Antonio Miró Quesada and José Carlos Bernales to present the workers' case to the government. Some strikers demanded the release of their comrades before they returned to work, but by June 5 the two cities were back to normal.

The cost of the strike in terms of lives and property damage had been high. *The West Coast Leader* reported that at least one hundred people had been killed and several hundred injured.[11] Property damage exceeded 2 million soles, and two hundred small shops, owned mostly by Asians, had been destroyed.[12]

The violence and destruction drew universal condemnation, but opinions differed as to who was ultimately responsible. The mutual aid societies blamed the authorities for failing to meet the workers' demands. The socialists, after denying any personal responsibility since they had supported only a twenty-four-hour general strike, charged that provocateurs had been involved and that political clubs had played a part by arming their followers prior to the election. They also blamed the government because it had delayed reducing prices and had arrested the workers' leaders. Others felt that outside agitators, including expatriates from Chile, had been behind the trouble. Spokesmen for the business community, like *The West Coast Leader,* saw the anarchists as being the real culprits. The newspaper charged, "Ninety percent of the elements composing the mobs responsible for the looting and burning were irresponsible boys, ragamuffins, the hoodlum sediment at the bottom of the human melting pot. They were led by men who were either criminals or types of the extreme socialistic agitators whose brains have become parboiled through an over inhalation of the poisonous fumes issuing from the boiling cauldrons of Moscow and Petrograd and blown about the world by every wind of publicity."[13]

The authorities shared the view that anarchists and revolutionaries, both native and foreign, had been responsible. They charged that anarchist propaganda calling for the destruction of the government had been circulated during the strike and reported finding a printing press operated by foreigners who wanted to establish a bolshevik-style soviet. In addition to the repressive methods they used to crush the strike, the authorities ordered the arrest of anyone suspected of assisting or planning to assist the movement. The Callao police complied by arresting a reportedly dangerous propagandist named Michaelles and a foreigner whose only crime was to inquire about the situation. Peruvian anarchists like Adalberto Fonkén joined Gutarra and Barba in prison, and even liberal reformers, like Pedro Zulen of the Sociedad Pro-Indígena, were taken into custody.

Following the reestablishment of order, the government attempted to eliminate the radical influence altogether. The strike's failure had revealed that the anarchists were less strong than had been feared, and the disarray of the workers permitted a counterattack. Alleging that foreign anarchist agitators had been involved in the recent events, the government issued decrees on June 2 that compelled every foreigner arriving in Peru to hold a valid passport, created under the police a "Section of General Vigilance" to search out anarchist propaganda and superintend the movement of foreigners in the country, and prohibited meetings by groups who propagated anarchist doctrines. Only then was martial law lifted.[14]

At the same time Pardo attempted to satisfy some of the workers' demands, perhaps with the view of winning support away from the more radical elements. When he met with Miró Quesada and Bernales he expressed his willingness to consider some means of reducing prices. He claimed that unscrupulous middlemen were the real culprits, citing the example of meat being sold for forty-seven centavos per kilo in the slaughterhouse and two soles in the markets. His solution was to remove duties and taxes on necessities and open a weekly market where goods would be sold at cost price. He claimed that the government had been considering these measures since before the strike.[15]

The proposals provoked anarchist charges that the government had been the real culprit behind the violence. According to Delfín Lévano, if the government had introduced these measures before May 26, no general strike would have occurred. He rejected the government's contention that the Comité had incited the people to violence and that it intended to overthrow the elected authorities and transform society. The Comité's actions, he claimed, were nonpolitical and in response to the wishes of the workers. He added, "The joint action of the workers was against Hunger, against that terrible affliction that weakens the anemic bodies of the proletariat." He also claimed that the general strike had been a success, not in having accomplished its stated goals, but in having achieved greater working class solidarity. This view was echoed by other labor leaders, and it appeared that some vestiges of the working class unity that had been evident in January had managed to survive despite the arrest of the strike leaders and the bloody repression.[16]

It was not only the working class leaders who felt this way. Augusto Leguía viewed the workers as an influential group whose favor should be curried in order to further his aims. He planned to reduce and, perhaps, destroy the power of the Civilistas when he returned to the presidency, and the workers could assist him in his plan. But was he to be allowed to occupy the presidential palace for a second time? The initial rulings of the Supreme Court on the many irregularities in the May election were in Aspíllaga's favor, and it appeared that the final decision might have to go to Congress, where Leguía had very few friends. To forestall this, he mobilized his forces and on July 4 deposed Pardo by means of a bloodless coup.[17]

The workers welcomed the news. Pardo's failure to reduce prices and his brutal suppression of the May strike had alienated many of them, and they no longer shared the views expressed in January. Their hostility spilled over into attacks on those whom they considered to be friends of the old regime. Following the coup, workers invaded the Confederación de Artesanos and declared that the Confederación, the Asamblea de Sociedades Unidas, and the other mutual aid societies did not represent the people, nor did they express the ideas and sentiments of the working class since they had served the deposed oligarchy and they were thus traitors to the cause of the proletariat. The only true proletarian organization representing the workers was the Comité Pro Abaratamiento.

The workers were also impressed with Leguía, whose efforts on their behalf reminded many of Billinghurst. Weakened by the previous government's repression, they were attracted by his offers of assistance. In a further attempt to win their support he offered to lift the controls imposed by Pardo following the strike and ordered the release of Gutarra, Barba, and Fonkén.

Their release placed the labor movement once more in the hands of recognized militants. On July 9 under their direction the Comité, which had outlived its usefulness, was transformed into the more identifiably working-class organization, the Federación Obrera Regional del Perú. The new FORP was a direct descendant of its predecessor, an anarchosyndicalist organization whose aims were "to do away with capitalism" and create a society of free producers through solidarity with the working class and collective union action. All political parties, whether working class or bourgeois, were repudiated as the FORP took over the Confederación de Artesanos for its headquarters, renaming it the "Casa del Pueblo" (House of the People), and converted the headquarters of the Asamblea into a workers library.[18]

* * *

The events that took place between January and July 1919 give some indication of the direction the labor movement would follow in later years. Still weak, as the suppression of the May strike had clearly shown, the movement continued to suffer from disunity, largely because many workers remained unaware of their class links. Regardless of geography, divisions seem inevitable in any labor force, composed as it is of men, women, and children, artisans and industrial workers, the skilled and unskilled, employed and unemployed, organized and unorganized, nationals and immigrants, radicals and moderates, each with its own specific motivations and interests. From the 1920s, divisions among Peru's workers were increasingly along ideological lines, as anarchists confronted socialists and, later, communist unions challenged the APRA-backed Confederación de Trabajadores del Perú (Workers' Confederation of Peru) for leadership of the nation's workers.

A potential source of conflict was removed with the decline of the old mutual aid societies. Some, like the Asamblea de Sociedades Unidas, managed to survive, but only as hollow shells of those organizations that had been in the forefront of the movement during its formative years, when their organizing efforts had been a key factor in bringing the workers together for the first time.

One area originally dominated by the mutual aid societies grew in importance despite their decline. Political involvement attracted more and more workers who saw it as a means of obtaining improvements. New political parties representing their views were formed, like the Partido Socialista Peruano (Peruvian Socialist Party) in 1928 and the Partido Comunista Peruano (Peruvian Communist Party) in 1930. The ineffectiveness of these parties and the movement in general also caused the workers to turn to more broadly based parties, especially the APRA party, and to populist politicians, as both offered proworker programs to win their support. Leguía's populism lasted for only a brief period after he returned to office; he then turned on the workers and destroyed their power. It was a foretaste of what was to happen under some of his successors, like General Manuel Odría (1948–1956) who was a right-wing populist along the lines of Argentina's Juan Domingo Perón. On assuming power, he brutally crushed the existing popular organizations and then replaced them with his own. His popular support came largely from the unorganized workers and rural migrants who began flooding into Lima during his presidency. These destitute shantytown dwellers also provided much of the support for the later, more reform-minded populist, General Juan Velasco Alvarado (1968–1975).

Ties with populist leaders could win improvements for the workers as the Billinghurst period had shown, but they produced new divisions among the workers and also prevented the development of an independent labor movement. The workers came to rely on the government, whose officials participated in labor negotiations and whose participation was indispensable to favorable results. In this way the government, which had been closely involved in the labor movement since the beginning, maintained some control, directing the movement along nationalistic rather than class lines and reducing the workers' independence.

Weak and divided, the workers could be controlled further by intimidation and repression, which became more common during the twentieth century as the labor movement developed and the country became an increasingly attractive area for foreign investment. Peru's political and business elites were determined to protect this investment as well as their own positions, and viewed a powerful working class as a major threat to both. They were willing, therefore, to support individuals or groups who could control the masses. Since 1919 there has been a succession of dictators and military governments ruling Peru, a sharp contrast to the period between 1895 and 1919 when a degree of political freedom was evident. This change was not entirely a response to the emergence of the labor movement and its perceived threat to the elite—since the 1930s military coups and the suppression of human rights frequently have been a reaction to the activities of the APRA party—but the result was the same: the position of the Peruvian working class and the *status quo* in general remained virtually unchanged, while political democracy remained a hope for the future.

Although divisiveness, political dependence, and repression continued to characterize the labor movement after 1919, there were some positive developments. The very fact that political leaders sought the workers' support and frequently resorted to violence to control them indicated that the movement was alive and a vibrant force that had to be considered. The size of the labor force was constantly growing, which by itself was a measure of the workers' real and potential strength. So, too, was their past agitation and accomplishments. Individuals like Víctor Raúl Haya de la Torre and José Carlos Mariátegui who were sympathetic or committed to the working class could look to these past accomplishments for inspiration as they directed the labor movement along new and productive paths. While unconvinced of the workers' ability to achieve change on their own and more confident in a multiclass party with middle-class leaders, Haya realized that the workers were now vital to any successful political movement. Mariátegui, whose close ties with the workers developed during the agitation of the First World War, was aware that the movement still had serious weaknesses, but its past successes convinced him the workers were capable of organizing unions and a class-based political party and of participating in nationwide struggles. His confidence led him to press for the formation of both the Socialist party and the industrial union, the Confederación General de Trabajadores del Perú (General Confederation of Peruvian Workers). His efforts on the workers' behalf are responsible for his position as spiritual leader of the existing movement.

These subsequent developments can be fully understood only by examining the new conditions, both internal and external, that affected the working class and the country as a whole after 1919. Among these were the eleven-year dictatorship of Leguía and the regimes of his successors, the rise of Aprismo and the spread of Marxism, the growth of American investment and the 1929 Depression, the Second World War and the Cold War, and the "revolution" that began in 1968. They drew the labor movement in a variety of directions, altering its appearance from what it had been in 1919.[19]

But while later developments produced new wrinkles, the past cannot be ignored. To a certain extent the later developments of the labor movement merely built upon the framework laid down during the formative years. The lines of conflict and the responses of the contending forces had already been established; subsequent accomplishments were largely outgrowths of earlier successes. During the first thirty-five years of the labor movement, the workers achieved a degree of class identity and solidarity through the formation of numerous organizations designed for mutual aid, industrial action, and political pressure; through industrial action like strikes, boycotts, and general strikes; and through political participation that secured the election of one president, a number of deputies, and several municipal councilors. As a result of their organizing and industrial pressure, sectors of the work force obtained wage improvements, better working conditions, a shorter work day, social security measures, improved sanitation and safety features, housing, schools, and free medical attention from their employers. In the field of legislation they obtained laws granting indemnities for injured workers, legislated holidays, protection for women and children, and the eight-hour day. In doing so they made Peru one of the most advanced countries in terms of social legislation in all of Latin America.

These achievements were not simply the result of pressure by a small group of activists in Lima. They were the product of agitation by workers throughout the country, both in the urban centers and the countryside, with one group benefiting from the successes of another and ultimately creating the possibility of a united movement. In the process, Peru's workers revealed that they could win improvements through their own efforts and could influence government decisions. They became an active sector of the population whose interests could not be ignored by those in power.

The development of an influential labor movement at the turn of the century was not unique to Peru. Elsewhere in Latin America the workers began to play an important role in national affairs at about the same time and in much the same way. The achievements of the various movements demonstrated that the working class in economically dependent countries could overcome serious obstacles and succeed in much the same way as workers in industrialized nations. The Latin American workers responded to the changes produced by modernization, industrialization, and the growth of a capitalist economy like workers elsewhere, and although they, like their fellow workers in North America and Europe, still had to struggle for a more equitable society, they had shown themselves an identifiable group with specific aims and aspirations and who were willing to struggle. It did not take populist leaders in the 1940s and 1950s to establish the Latin American workers as an important sector of society. They had been mobilizing for decades and had already left their mark on their nations' development.

In the case of Peru, what the workers accomplished before 1919 remained as their memorial. Although replete with disappointments, setbacks, and unfulfilled hopes, the period between 1883 and 1919 was one of progress and notable successes. It marked the beginning of the modern labor movement and is a period in Peruvian labor history that both the participants and their successors can regard with a justified sense of pride and satisfaction.

Notes

Bibliography

Index

Abbreviations

The Bibliography contains full citations for all works cited in short form in the notes. Other abbreviations used in the notes are:

ACD	Archivo de la H. Cámara de Diputados, Lima
AFA-C	Archivo del Fuero Agrario Lima: Cayaltí papers
BCIMP	*Boletín del Cuerpo de Ingenieros de Minas del Perú*
BN	Sala de Investigaciones, Biblioteca Nacional, Lima
Debates	*Diario de los Debates de la H. Cámara de Diputados*
FO	Foreign Office files, Public Record Office, London
PCP	Peruvian Corporation Papers, ENAFER-Perú, Lima
UCL-DMSW	University College London, D.M.S. Watson Library

The two influential Lima newspapers, *El Comercio* and *La Prensa*, during the period under discussion published two or more separate editions per day. They have been labeled a, b, c, d to differentiate among them.

The author is responsible for all translations from the Spanish.

Notes

Preface

1. Basadre, *Historia de la República del Perú 1822–1933*, 13:25; Davies, Jr., "Indian Integration in Peru, 1820–1948," p. 195.
2. For the general pattern of labor developments in Latin America during this period, see Spalding, Jr., *Organized Labor in Latin America*, especially chs. 1–2. His bibliography is valuable as it contains most of the works on the movements in the specific countries.
3. E. P. Thompson, *The Making of the English Working Class*, (Harmondsworth: Penguin, 1972), p. 939.

Chapter 1: The Setting, 1883–1919

1. For this early period of Peruvian national history, see Basadre, *Historia del Perú*, vols. 1-8; Vargas Ugarte, *Historia General del Perú*, vols. 7–10; Pike, *The Modern History of Peru*, chs. 2–5.
2. In 1899, 108,597 people voted in the presidential election; in 1904, the number rose to 146,990. For this and other information on the elite's domination of the electoral system, see Basadre, *Historia del Perú*, 4:225–26, 9:209–10, 10:167–73, 11:18, 159.
3. For ownership of the sugar estates and mines, see Albert, *The Peruvian Sugar Industry*, pp. 33a–64a; Gilbert, "The Oligarchy and the Old Regime in Peru," pp. 43–46.
4. For the industrial boom, see Thorp and Bertram, "Industrialization in an Open Economy;" idem, *Peru 1890–1977*, ch. 3, pp. 118–31; Rippy, "The Dawn of Manufacturing in Peru," p. 147. For the Grace Contract, see Basadre, *Historia del Perú*, 9: ch. 112; Miller, "The Making of the Grace Contract." The bulk of the bondholders were British, plus several who were French.
5. Rippy, "The Dawn of Manufacturing in Peru," p. 148; Thorp and Bertram, *Peru 1890–1977*, table A.4.3., pp. 349–50.
6. Capelo, *Sociología de Lima*, 1:128; Perú, H. Cámara de Diputados, *Accidentes del Trabajo*, pp. xlvii–xlviii; Jiménez, "Estadística Industrial del Perú," pp. xxviii–xxxiv.
7. Figures on artisan shops come from *El Comercio* (Lima), Feb. 18a, 1903.
8. Chaplin, *The Peruvian Industrial Labor Force*, pp. 96–100; Thorp and Bertram, "Industrialization in an Open Economy," pp. 78, 79, notes 20, 23; Worral, "Italian Immigration to Peru: 1860–1914," pp. 193–95, 198.
9. For example, W. R. Grace purchased the Cartavio sugar estate and later the Vitarte textile mill. See Miller, "The Making of the Grace Contract," p. 100.
10. For the elite, see Basadre, *Historia del Perú*, 16:295–302; Gilbert, "The Oligarchy and the Old Regime."

11. For the middle class, see Capelo, *Sociología de Lima*, 2:151; Basadre, *Historia del Perú*, 16:302–03; Astiz, *Pressure Groups and Power Elites in Peruvian Politics*, pp. 65–70; Bourricaud, *Power and Society in Contemporary Peru*, pp. 58–60.

12. Basadre, *Historia del Perú*, 16:237; Cisneros, *Reseña Económica del Perú*, p. 207; Enock, *Peru: Its Former and Present Civilisation, History, . . . Topography, . . . Commerce*, pp. 115–16; Sulmont, *El Movimiento Obrero en el Perú 1900–1956*, table I–1, p. 245.

13. Dobyns and Doughty, *Peru: A Cultural History*, table 1, p. 298; Boyer and Davies, *Urbanization in 19th Century Latin America;* Perú, Ministerio de Fomento, *Censo de la Provincia Constitucional del Callao, 1905*, pp. 93, 95; idem, *Resúmenes del Censo de las Provincias de Lima y Callao, 1920*, table 1, p. 3; Clairmont, *A Guide to Modern Peru*, pp. 27, 69, 71.

14. Perú, Ministerio de Fomento, *Censo de la Provincia de Lima, 1908*, 1:117; idem, *Resúmenes del Censo de Lima y Callao, 1920*, table 24, p. 49, table 66, p. 166; idem, *Censo del Callao, 1905*, p. 189.

15. Capelo, *Sociología de Lima*, 2:37, 38; Cámara de Diputados, *Accidentes del Trabajo*, pp. xlvii–xlviii; Perú, Ministerio de Hacienda, *Resumen del Censo Lima y Callao, 1920*, table 4, pp. 266–77, table 5, pp. 286–93, table 6, pp. 296–303.

Chapter 2: The Early Mobilization, 1858–1895

1. Basadre, *Historia del Perú*, 3:183–84; MacLean y Estenós, *Sociología del Perú*, p. 108.

2. *La Prensa* (Lima), Oct. 29b, 1918. Basadre claims that it was called the Sociedad Filantrópica Democrática (Philanthropic Democratic Society). See *Historia del Perú*, 7:68. According to *El Nacional* (Lima), Apr. 16, 1889, the Sociedad Fraternal de San José (Fraternal Society of St. Joseph) of Lima was formed in 1855, which would make it Peru's oldest mutual aid society.

3. Basadre, *Historia del Perú*, 7:68–72, 9:232; Barcelli, *Historia del Sindicalismo Peruano*, 1:32–33; *La Prensa*, Jan. 1, 1917.

4. Basadre, *Historia del Perú*, 7:66–67.

5. For examples of these benefits, see Miró Quesada, *Legislación del Trabajo*, p. 101.

6. For the effects of the war on Peru, see Basadre, *Historia del Perú*, 9:10–11; Bonilla, "The War of the Pacific and the National and Colonial Problem in Peru"; Dávalos y Lissón, *Por qué hice Fortuna*, 1:62–63.

7. Brent, "Peru," pp. 229–33.

8. For details of some of the organizations formed after the war, see *El Comercio*, May 19, 1885, Aug. 17, 1886; *La Opinión Nacional* (Lima), Dec. 16, 1887; Basadre, *Historia del Perú*, 9:233. For Arequipa, see *La Bolsa* (Arequipa), Mar. 11, 16, 21, 1896; *El Deber* (Arequipa), May 8, 1917, Mar. 22, 1918.

9. Zubiaga was the son of tailor Juan Antonio Zubiaga who had founded the Sociedad Artesanos de Auxilios Mutuos.

10. Basadre, *Historia del Perú*, 9:232–33; *El Nacional*, May 31, June 30, July 1, 1886; *Ilustración Obrera* (Lima), Sept. 8, 1917; *La Prensa*, June 24a, 1918.

11. *El Comercio*, Oct. 25, 1888, May 17, 1889; Confederación de Artesanos "Unión Universal," *Constitución de la Confederación de Artesanos "Unión Universal;"* idem, *Reglamento Interno de la Confederación de Artesanos "Unión Universal."*

Notes to Pages 19–29   177

12. *Agrupación de Artesanos y Obreros* (Lima), Aug. 9, 1917; *El Comercio,* Dec. 11, 1888; *La Opinión Nacional,* July 27, 1889.

13. *El Comercio,* July 26b, 1892, Jan. 26a, 1894; *La Opinión Nacional,* Oct. 27, 1890; *Agrupación de Artesanos y Obreros,* Aug. 9, 1917.

14. Administratively, Peru was divided into a number of departments that were subdivided into provinces. These were administered by government-appointed officials—prefects over the departments and subprefects over the provinces. Quote by subprefect to the mayor of Lima, Jan. 17, 1884, BN D4452.

15. Ferreyros, *Memoria que el Prefecto del Departamento,* p. 5; BN D8045.

16. Basadre, *Historia del Perú,* 4:357–59; idem, *La Multitud, la Ciudad y el Campo en la Historia del Perú,* p. 183.

17. *La Situación* (Lima), July 12, Nov. 19, 21, 23, 1881; *La Prensa,* Sept. 18a, 1908.

18. For the financial situation in Peru after the war, see Basadre, *Historia del Perú,* 9:141–48; *El Comercio,* Mar. 15, 1887; *Panama Star & Herald,* Mar. 26, 1887. The latter is located in a collection of newspaper clippings filed under Council of Foreign Bondholders, "Peru," 14, in the Guildhall Library, London.

19. *El Comercio,* Sept. 14, 1886, Mar. 2, 4, 7, Apr. 5, 20, July 19, Oct. 5, 1887; *La Opinión Nacional,* Sept. 7, 1886, Oct. 5, 1887.

20. *La Opinión Nacional,* Nov. 22, Dec. 15, 20, 1887; *El Comercio,* Dec. 14, 15, 20, 21, 29, 1887.

21. *El Comercio,* Dec. 9, 15, 16, 19, 28, 31, 1887, Jan. 7, 11, 24, 1888.

22. Ibid., June 20a, 21b, 1892; Basadre, *Historia del Perú,* 9:258.

23. *El Comercio,* Aug. 6b, 9b, 11b, 12b, 16b, Sept. 3a, 7b, 1892.

24. Ibid., Jan. 26, 1888, Jan. 26a, 1893; *El Nacional,* Jan. 23, 24, 1888; *La Opinión Nacional,* June 10, 12, 16, 21, 27, 1890.

25. *El Comercio,* May 16a, 25a, June 6b, 8b, 20a, July 27b, 1892, Sept. 3b, 1894.

26. Ibid., Jan. 19b, 24h, 26a, Feb. 9b, 10a, 1893.

27. Subprefect of Callao, Mar. 31, 1888, BN D3961.

28. *El Comercio,* May 5a–6b, 14b–19b, 1892.

29. Ibid., Feb. 13b, July 26a, 26b, 31a–Aug. 4a, 17a, Sept. 18b–22b, 29b, 1894; Prefect of Callao, Sept. 21, 1894, BN D7516; Basadre, *Historia del Perú,* 9:257–58.

30. *Política Peruana,* p. 47.

31. According to the constitution, a president could not succeed himself.

32. For details of the "revolution," see Basadre, *Historia del Perú,* 10:96–112.

33. Hobart Spalding sees a number of direct links between the two types of organizations, while Rodney Anderson argues, in the case of Mexico, that the militant working-class movement "was not the product of the mutualist experience." See Spalding, *Organized Labor in Latin America,* p. 15; Rodney D. Anderson, *Outcasts in their Own Land: Mexican Industrial Workers, 1906–1911* (DeKalb: Northern Illinois University Press, 1976), p. 86. James Payne has taken the opposite point of view to mine for the case of Peru; see his *Labor and Politics in Peru,* p. 41.

Chapter 3: Political Involvement, 1895–1912

1. For example, the Club Artesanos (Artisans Club) of Callao was part of the Constitutional party and assisted in Cáceres's 1886 election. The Callao maritime guilds were forced to participate in a political rally for Morales Bermúdez in 1890. See *El Comercio,* Mar. 29,

1886; *La Opinión Nacional*, Feb. 7, 1890. See also Basadre, *Historia del Perú*, 7:68–70; *La Verdad* (Lima), Aug. 19, 1916; Brent, p. 232.

2. *El Comercio*, May 25b, 1895.

3. Ibid., Apr. 22b, May 23, 1895. The electorate chose, in addition to their sitting representatives, an equal number of substitutes *(suplentes)* who filled the seat when it was vacated.

4. *El Comercio*, June 22b, 24a, 1895; *El País* (Lima), June 24, 27, 1895.

5. For details of the congress, see *El Comercio*, July 10a, 20b, 24a, 27b, Aug. 17a–19b, Oct. 13, 1896; *El País*, Dec. 4, 9, 1895, June 20, July 1, 3, 9, Aug. 11, 18, 20, 25, 29, 1896; *El Tiempo* (Lima), June 20, Aug. 18, Sept. 22, 29, Oct. 7, 13, Nov. 14, 1896; Barcelli, *Historia del Sindicalismo Peruano*, 1:59–60.

6. *Debates*, Congreso Ordinario de 1896, 1:621, de 1903, pp. 156–57; Cámara de Diputados, *Accidentes del Trabajo*, pp. ix–xii.

7. *El Comercio*, Oct. 21a, 1895, June 1a, Oct. 21a, 1896; *Debates*, Congreso Ordinario de 1895, 2:23–24, de 1899, pp. 542–44, de 1902, p. 813; "Expediente cediendo a la Sociedad de Artesanos un local del Estado," ACD, 1894, Legajo 4, No. 107; "Expediente sobre adjudicación de un local del Estado a la Sociedad 'Unión Universal'," ACD, 1895, Legajo 5, Cuaderno 1, No. 6.

8. *Debates*, Congreso Ordinario de 1895, 2:1203; *El Artesano* (Lima), Jan. 21, 1899; *El Comercio*, Apr. 26b, Oct. 6b, 1899, Sept. 26b, Oct. 22a, Nov. 16b, Dec. 4b, 7a, 9b, 10b, 12a, 1903; *El Tiempo*, Oct. 6, 1899; "Expediente sobre protección al gremio de cigarreros," ACD, 1903, Legajo 16, Cuaderno 3, No. 15. In 1910 the cigarette industry was nationalized and reduced to one factory. See Thorp and Bertram, "Industrialization in an Open Economy," p. 68.

9. *El Comercio*, Feb. 13a, May 4b, 1896, Aug. 23b, 1898, June 17a, 19a, 1899; *El País*, Apr. 20, 1896; *El Tiempo*, May 27, July 14, 1896.

10. *El Comercio*, Apr. 9b, July 26b, 1898; *La Prensa*, Aug. 8b, 1904, June 16a, 1906; *El Artesano*, June 17, 1898. *El Artesano* began publication in May 1898.

11. This only gives a general idea of the total number of workers in the mutual aid societies since many workers belonged to several. For a list of the memberships of two prominent Lima artisans, Manuel S. Valcarcel and Justo González, see *Ilustración Obrera*, Apr. 29, 1916; *Agrupación de Artesanos y Obreros*, Aug. 9, 1917.

12. *El Comercio*, Feb. 3, 1891; *La Prensa*, Nov. 12a, 1907; Laos, *Lima "La Ciudad de los Virreyes,"* p. 271.

13. *El Comercio*, Dec. 4a, 1900, Jan. 13, Apr. 2a, 1901; *La Idea Libre* (Lima), Feb. 9, Mar. 16, Apr. 6, 1901.

14. *La Protesta* (Lima), No. 8, Sept. 1911.

15. Basadre, *Historia del Perú*, 11:258–59; *Diario de los Debates del H. Senado*, Congreso Ordinario de 1902, pp. 372–73, 436; Manzanilla, *La Responsabilidad por los Accidentes del Trabajo*, pp. 50–53. For more on Capelo, see Morse, "The Lima of Joaquín Capelo."

16. The two workers representatives were Ramón Espinoza of the Asamblea and Juan Goachet.

17. *El Comercio*, Feb. 18a, June 7, 1903; *Diario de los Debates de las Sesiones de Congreso Pleno*, Congreso Ordinario de 1903, pp. 11–12; Miró Quesada, *Legislación del Trabajo*, pp. 104–05.

18. *Diario de los Debates de las Sesiones de Congreso*, Congreso Ordinario y Extraordinario de 1904, p. 14; Manzanilla, *La Responsabilidad*, p. 49; *El Comercio*, July 7a, 1904.

19. During the 1905 debate Manzanilla introduced a second project dealing with safety and sanitation in industrial areas, but the members had their hands full with the bill on indemnities, and this project did not reach the debating stage until 1921. Manzanilla, *Legislación del Trabajo*, pp. 6–7, 65–67, 101; idem, *La Responsabilidad*, pp. 63–64; *El Comercio*, Nov. 15b, 1905; *Debates*, Congreso Ordinario de 1907, pp. 20–21.

20. *El Comercio*, June 17b, 1903, Feb. 8a, 1904; *La Prensa*, Sept. 12, 13, Oct. 6, 14a, Nov. 10a, 1907.

21. Manzanilla, *Legislación*, pp. 103, 131, 144, 157, 284, 291; *La Prensa*, Aug. 11a–15a, 1908.

22. *La Prensa*, Oct. 13a, 1908, Mar. 9a, 1919; *El Comercio*, Nov. 30a, 1909; *Debates*, Congreso Ordinario de 1909, p. 313.

23. *El Comercio*, Jan. 25a, 1910; *La Prensa*, Aug. 16b, 20a, 30a, 1910; *Debates*, Congreso Ordinario de 1910, pp. 118–19; Basadre, *Historia del Perú*, 12:192–93.

24. Basadre, *Historia del Perú*, 12:177–79; Manzanilla, *La Responsabilidad*, pp. 291–311. For an English resumé of the law, see Martin, *Peru of the Twentieth Century*, pp. 330–32.

25. Manzanilla, *Legislación*, pp. 320–24; *La Prensa*, May 6a, 1911, Dec. 3b, 1912; Mayer, *The Conduct of the Cerro de Pasco Mining Company*, p. 35.

26. *La Prensa*, July 29, 1912; *Ilustración Obrera*, Sept. 30, 1916.

27. *El Comercio*, Sept. 6a, Oct. 1a, 1895; *El Tiempo*, Oct. 21, 17, 1895; Confederación de Artesanos "Unión Universal," *Constitución*, art. 38.

28. *El Comercio*, Nov. 5b, 8b, 16b, 28a, 1898, Mar. 6a, 20a, 30, Apr. 11a, 15b, 1899; *El Artesano*, Dec. 7, 1898.

29. *El Comercio*, Mar. 25, 27a, Apr. 29b, May 3a, 9, 1899. *El Artesano* closed by the end of 1899.

30. *El Comercio*, Aug. 1a, 6b, 1901.

31. Ibid., Apr. 5a, 1904; *La Prensa*, June 1a–2a, Oct. 16, 1904.

32. *La Prensa*, Nov. 26b, 29a, 1904.

33. Cáceres was a member of the Confederación and the newly formed Liberal party.

34. *La Prensa*, Dec. 23a–24a, 1904, Mar. 11a, 19, 24a, 27a, Apr. 9, 10a, May 11b, June 8b, 1905; *El Comercio*, Apr. 8a, 10a, 1905; *Debates*, 2º Congreso Extraordinario de 1903, p. 601; Dávalos y Lissón, *Diez Años de Historia Contemporanea del Perú, 1899–1908*, p. 127.

35. *La Prensa*, Dec. 10a, 1906, Jan. 2b, Feb. 1a, 4a, 7a, Mar. 3b, 4a, 11a, Apr. 26b, 28, 29a, May 18a, 24a, 1907. Elguera may also have lost party support because of rumors he was opposed to President Pardo and receiving Democratic backing.

36. *La Prensa*, Dec. 8, 13b–15a, 21a, 29, 1907, May 22a, 25a, Oct. 4, Nov. 24b, Dec. 1b, 1908, Apr. 6a, 8a, May 16, 1909.

37. *Agrupación de Artesanos y Obreros*, Aug. 9, 1917; Perú, *Presupuesto General para 1912*, p. 14. In an interview in Lima on Aug. 1, 1973, Dr. Basadre described these subsidies as "bribes" designed to buy off the Confederación.

Chapter 4: The Influence of Anarchism, 1895–1912

1. *El Artesano*, Aug. 29, 1898.

2. Chavarría, "The Intellectuals and the Crisis of Modern Peruvian Nationalism: 1870–1919," pp. 261–65; Sánchez, *Don Manuel*, pp. 31–35, 97–102, 108–26; idem, *Nuestras vidas son los ríos . . . (Historia y leyenda de los González Prada)*, pp. 86–88, 179, 388,

ch. 11; Podestá, *Pensamiento Político de González Prada*, pp. 25–27, 32; James Joll, *The Anarchists* (London: Eyre & Spotiswoode, 1964), pp. 149–50.

3. *El Artesano*, Aug. 29, Sept. 2, 1898; *El Comercio*, Sept. 2a, 8b, 1898; Sánchez, *Nuestras vidas*, pp. 205–07.

4. Alba, *Politics and the Labor Movement in Latin America*, pp. 37–38.

5. Great Britain, *Parliamentary Papers* (1910), vol. 101, "No. 4423, Annual Series, Diplomatic and Consular Reports, Peru: Report for the Years 1908–09 on the Trade, Commerce and Finance of Peru," p. 25. See also *El Comercio*, Sept. 30a, 1909; *La Prensa*, Mar. 1a, 11a, 1909.

6. *El Comercio*, May 1a, 1897, July 28b, 1908; *La Prensa*, Jan. 16b, 1908; Subprefect of Lima, Mar. 20, 1896, BN D8656; Ministerio de Fomento, *Censo de Lima, 1908*, 1:108; Jerome to Grey, enclosure with no. 146, Aug. 29, 1911, FO 371/1206; des Graz to Grey, no. 38, Mar. 15, 1912, FO 371/1459.

7. *El Comercio*, Nov. 3a, 1904; *Los Parias* (Lima), No. 3, June 1904.

8. *El Obrero Peruano* (Lima), Dec. 10, 17, 1902, Jan. 8, 1903. For further information on the working conditions, see Chapter 5. For an interesting reconstruction of working class life during these years, see Stein, "Maximo Carrasco—or Working Class Life in Lima, 1900–1930."

9. *El Artesano*, June 13, 1898; *El Comercio*, Nov. 24, 1901; *El Obrero Peruano*, Nov. 19, 1902.

10. *Los Parias*, no. 3, June 1904; González Prada, *Anarquía*, pp. 12, 23–24; Gilimón, *Para los que no son Anarquistas*; Carreño, *La Anarquía en el Perú*. Tassara was the son of Italian immigrants who had been anarchists. He had been director of the libertarian newspaper, *La Idea Libre*. See Sánchez, *Nuestras vidas*, pp. 202, 227.

11. Enock, *The Andes and the Amazon*, pp. 92–93; Rouillón, *La Creación Heroica de José Carlos Mariátegui*, p. 295; Barba, "Las luchas obreras en 1919," *Rikchay Perú*, no. 2, p. 27.

12. Vázquez, "Immigration and *mestizaje* in Nineteenth-Century Peru," pp. 79–80; Worral, "Italian Immigration," p. 1; César Lévano, "Quien era Delfín Lévano?" p. 20; *La Protesta*, May 18, 1918.

13. *El Comercio*, May 2b–20a, 1904; *La Prensa*, May 23a, 1904; Basadre, *Historia del Perú*, 11:260–68; *Los Parias*, no. 3, June 1904.

14. Aliaga was not the first worker to die in a labor dispute. Two men and a woman had been shot by troops in Arequipa in 1902 during a strike by the Southern Railway workers. However, these killings had no impact on the Lima movement. For more on the Arequipa strike, see Blanchard, "The Peruvian Working Class Movement: 1883–1919," pp. 122–26.

15. *Los Parias*, no. 4, July 1904; *El Comercio*, May 21a, 1904; *La Prensa*, May 24a, 1904.

16. In 1896 a group of Peruvians, Danes, Italians, Spaniards, Belgians, and Germans held a banquet in a Lima restaurant to mark May Day. Subsequently, other individuals held small celebrations, and a few firms gave their workers the day off. See *El Comercio*, May 2b, 1896; *El País*, May 2, 1896.

17. González Prada, *Anarquía*, p. 16; *El Comercio*, May 1b, 2a, 1905; *La Prensa*, May 1b–2b, 1905.

18. *El Hambriento* (Lima), no. 21, Feb. 1907, no. 32, Jan. 1908; *Los Parias*, no. 14, June 1905; *La Prensa*, Apr. 30a, 1906; César Lévano, *La Verdadera Historia de la Jornada de las Ocho Horas en el Perú*, pp. 17–18.

19. *El Hambriento*, no. 4, Sept. 1905; *Los Parias*, no. 21, Jan. 1906; *La Prensa*, Jan. 3a, 10b, 17a, 28, Oct. 22a, 1906; MacLean, *Sociología del Perú*, p. 112. See also González Prada, *Prosa Menuda*, pp. 133–36.
20. *Los Parias*, no. 6, Sept. 1904; González Prada, *Anarquía*, pp. 83–84; *El Hambriento*, no. 19, Dec. 1906.
21. *El Hambriento*, no. 4, Sept. 1905; *El Oprimido* (Lima), Sept. 12, 1908; *La Protesta*, Mar. 15, 1911.
22. For the 1906 and 1907 celebrations, see *El Hambriento*, no. 12, May 1906; *La Prensa*, May 1b, 2a, 1906, May 1b, 1907; *La Bolsa*, May 2, 1906, Apr. 30, 1907; *El Pueblo* (Arequipa), May 2, 1906.
23. Some writers have argued that the campaign opened on May 1, 1905, when Caracciolo Lévano included it in the declaration of the principles of the bakery workers. If he did, it produced no further comment until the following year. See Cesar Lévano, *La Verdadera Historia*, pp. 10–11; Kapsoli, *Luchas Obreras en el Perú por la Jornada de las 8 horas 1900–1919*, p. 12.
24. González Prada, *Anarquía*, pp. 64–65.
25. *La Prensa*, Nov. 9a, 1908.
26. *El Hambriento*, no. 22, Mar. 1907, no. 23, Apr. 1907, no. 45, Dec. 1908, no. 49, Apr. 1909; *La Prensa*, Mar. 18a, 18b, 1907, Sept. 22b, 1908; César Lévano, "La Fuga Increible." A coeditor of *El Hambriento*, Luis Olea Castillo, was another leader of the Iquique strike.
27. *El Comercio*, July 28b, 1910.
28. Daniel Guérin, *Anarchism: From Theory to Practice*, trans. Mary Klopper (New York: Monthly Review Press, 1970), p. 154; Hart, *Anarchism and the Mexican Working Class, 1860–1931*, chs. 6–7.
29. Like other intellectuals of his day, González Prada was a man of ideas, not action. See Chavarría, *José Carlos Mariátegui and the Rise of Modern Peru, 1890–1930*, ch. 2; Podestá, *Pensamiento Político*, p. 36.
30. *El Oprimido*, Jan. 23, 1909; *La Protesta*, Mar. 15, 1911, no. 9, Oct. 1911.
31. *El Hambriento*, no. 30, Nov. 1907, no. 47, Feb. 1909; *El Socialista* (Lima), Feb. 6, 1909.
32. *La Protesta*, no. 4, May 1911, no. 12, Jan. 1912, Oct. 3, 1914; Pareja Pflücker, " 'La Protesta' 1911–1926: Contribución al Estudio del Anarquismo en el Perú," pp. 19–22.

Chapter 5: The Intensification of Industrial Action, 1895–1912

1. See the worker newspaper, *El Obrero Peruano*, Dec. 31, 1902 for a criticism of strike action and an appeal for negotiated improvements. Opposition to strikes was not unique to the Peruvian working class at this time; Mexican workers were also critical. See Anderson, *Outcasts in their Own Land*, p. 81.
2. It was because the company prohibited this and cut their wages almost in half that they went on strike in October 1895. See *El Comercio*, Oct. 14b, 17a, 19a, 1895; *El Tiempo*, Oct. 14, 1895.
3. *La Prensa*, July 23b–27a, Sept. 5b, 10a–12a, 15a, 17b, 25a, 25b, 28a, 29b, Oct. 18b–20b, 24a, 1906; *Los Parias*, no. 27, Aug. 1906; *Humanidad* (Lima), no. 8, Oct. 1906.
4. *La Prensa*, July 16a, 18a–19a, 1907, Oct. 17b, 1908.
5. *El Comercio*, June 17b–20, 23b, 28b, July 3a, 10b, 16b–27a, Aug. 7a, 1909; *El*

Hambriento, no. 53, Aug. 1909; enclosure with des Graz to Grey, no. 55, July 31, 1909, FO 371/720; The Peruvian Corporation Ltd., *Representatives' Annual Reports 1909–1913*, "Report for the Year Ending 30th June 1909," p. 2, "Report for the Year Ending 30th June 1910," p. 2, PCP, Informe no. 22.

6. *El Comercio*, Dec. 12a–18b, 1900; *El Tiempo*, Dec. 11–19, 1900.

7. *El Comercio*, Nov. 16c, Dec. 1a, 2a, 1904, Jan. 5b, 1905; *La Prensa*, June 15b, 1904, Jan. 5b–8, 12a, 1905.

8. *La Prensa*, Nov. 15b–16b, 20b–23b, 26b, 29a, Dec. 10b, 1906.

9. Ibid., Apr. 20b–23b, 26b, 29a, May 7a, 10a–21a, 1907; Memoria of the prefect of Callao, June 8, 1907, BN E2; Lima. Cámara de Comercio, *Memoria presentada . . . el 11 de Agosto de 1908 siendo presidente el señor D. Felipe Barreda y Osma* (Lima, 1908), pp. 12–13; Basadre, *Historia del Perú*, 11:273.

10. *La Prensa*, June 4b, 6a, 18b, Oct. 20, 24, 1907, Feb. 1b–9, 1908. Arenas later claimed that his intervention in disputes had almost always resulted in "suitable solutions." See Arenas, *Algo de una vida*, p. 43.

11. *La Prensa*, Sept. 15b, 18a, Oct. 5a, 20a, 1908, Jan. 21b, Feb. 6a, Apr. 14b, 1909; Great Britain, "Report for the Years 1908–09," p. 41.

12. Giraldo later became a member of Cirilo Martín's Socialist party.

13. *El Comercio*, Apr. 13a–22b, 26b, 27a, 30a, 30b, 1901; *La Idea Libre*, Apr. 20, 27, May 11, 1901.

14. Memoria of the prefect of Lima, 1901, BN E1913.

15. *El Comercio*, Jan. 6–7b, 1904; *El Tiempo*, Jan. 7, 8, 1904; *La Prensa*, July 31, 1907.

16. *El Comercio*, Dec. 28b, 1892, Aug. 28b–31b, Sept. 2a, 5b, 1896, June 26, 1898; *El País*, Apr. 20, Aug. 25, 29, Sept. 6, 10, 1896; *Debates*, Congreso Ordinario de 1896, 1:421–23, 542, 614–21, de 1900, p. 531; Basadre, *Historia del Perú*, 10:303–04.

17. *El Oprimido*, no. 10, June, no. 11, July, Oct. 10, 24, Nov. 14, Dec. 5, 1908; *La Protesta*, Mar. 15, 1911.

18. *El Comercio*, Feb. 28, 29b, Mar. 3a, 4a, 10b, 1904; *Los Parias*, no. 1, Mar. 1904; *La Prensa*, Feb. 29b, Mar. 1a, 4a, 9b, 10b, 15a, 1904.

19. *El Hambriento*, no. 8, Jan. 1906; *La Prensa*, Dec. 28b–31, 1905, Jan. 12a, 1906.

20. *El Hambriento*, no. 19, Dec. 1906; *La Prensa*, Dec. 19b–23, 28a, 1906, Jan. 3a, 7a, 9a, 19a, 29a, Mar. 14a, Apr. 1a, 1b, 4a, 5b, 10a, 15a, 17a, 1907.

21. *El Oprimido*, no. 5, Nov. 1907, Dec. 5, 30, 1908, Jan. 16, 30, Feb. 6, 20, 1909; *La Prensa*, Oct. 13, 19a, 1907, Mar. 24a, 24b, Nov. 28a, Dec. 13, 17a, 23a, 1908; *El Comercio*, Dec. 22b, 24a, 1908.

22. Blanchard, "Asian Immigrants in Peru, 1899–1923," pp. 65–71; *La Prensa*, May 8a, 10a, 14b–17a, 1909; des Graz to Grey, no. 37, May 22, 1909, FO 371/720, no. 67, Sept. 15, 1909, FO 371/722, no. 15, Jan. 5, 1911, FO 371/1206; Ulloa y Sotomayor, *La organización social y legal del trabajo en el Perú*, pp. 47–48.

23. *La Prensa*, Nov. 18b, 19a, 23a–25b, 27, 28b, 1910, Jan. 12b, 1911.

24. Ibid., Apr. 10a, 1911.

25. For the formation of the Unificación Obrera Textil de Vitarte, see Flores Gonzáles, *Medio Siglo de Vida Sindical en Vitarte*, pp. 20–21.

26. *La Prensa*, Mar. 17b–19, 23a–Apr. 13a, 17b, 1910, Apr. 11a, 1911, Apr. 10a, 1912; *La Protesta*, Apr. 1911; enclosure with Jerome to Grey, no. 64, May 8, 1911, FO 371/1206; Barcelli, *Historia del Sindicalismo Peruano*, 1:70–73.

27. *La Prensa*, May 4b, 1911; *La Protesta*, No. 8, Sept. 1911.

Chapter 6: The Impact of Guillermo Billinghurst, 1912–1914

1. An earlier version of this chapter appeared as "A Populist Precursor: Guillermo Billinghurst."
2. For an interesting analysis of populism, see Paul W. Drake, *Socialism and Populism in Chile, 1932–52* (Urbana: University of Illinois Press, 1978), pp. 5–13.
3. Basadre, *Historia del Perú*, 12:221–22; Ulloa y Sotomayor, *Don Nicolás de Piérola*, p. 330; *La Opinión Nacional*, Aug. 17, 1891; *El Comercio*, Jan. 7b, May 26, Aug. 1a, 1910.
4. Enclosure with des Graz to Grey, no. 44, Mar. 24, 1912, FO 371/1458.
5. *La Prensa*, Feb. 13b, 17b, Mar. 4a, 9a, 12a, 16a, 26a, Apr. 1a–3a, 6a, 6b, 10a, 16b–20a, 23a, June 21b, 1912; *Agrupación de Artesanos y Obreros*, Sept. 8, 1917. Castañeda's ties with the Leguiístas continued. During the First World War he was one of a group of supporters who conspired to put Leguía back in the presidency, by force if necessary. Their letters to Leguía, who was then in England, were intercepted by the British censor and sent to the Foreign Office. See FO 371/2991.
6. *La Protesta*, no. 15, Apr. & May 1912; *La Prensa*, May 1b, 2a, 1912.
7. *La Prensa*, Apr. 30a, May 4b, 7a, 10a–13a, 19a–20a, 1912; *La Crónica* (Lima), May 4, 1912; Aspíllaga, *Programa de Gobierno presentado a la consideración del país*, pp. 12–15.
8. For details of the electoral campaign see *La Crónica*, May 4, 1912; *La Prensa*, May 9a, 19b–26b, Aug. 3a, 9a, 1912; des Graz to Grey, no. 74, June 1, 1912, enclosure with des Graz to Grey, no. 109, Aug. 26, 1912, FO 371/1459; Basadre, *Historia del Perú*, 12:214; Capuñay, *Leguía, Vida y Obra del Constructor del Gran Perú*, pp. 102–03.
9. *La Prensa*, July 27b, Sept. 25a, 1912.
10. For these strikes see ibid., Sept. 1–13b, 17a, 19a, 29, Oct. 7–11a, 14b, Nov. 26a–28b, Dec. 2b, 3a, 1912; *La Protesta*, no. 17, Sept. 1912, no. 18, Oct. 1912; *La Acción Popular* (Lima), Oct. 9, Nov. 28, 30, Dec. 3, 1912; "Zitor," "Historia de las Principales Huelgas y Paros Obreros Habidos en el Perú" (1946), typed manuscript, BN E1221, pp. 33–38, 43–44.
11. Spagnoli's propagandizing also took him to Mexico. In late 1914 he was one of the organizers of the anarchist Casa del Obrero in Monterrey. See Hart, *Anarchism & the Mexican Working Class*, p. 127.
12. *La Prensa*, Dec. 5b, 9a, 23b, 1912, Jan. 6a–11a, 1913; *La Protesta*, no. 29 [sic], Jan. 1913, no. 20, Apr. 1913; *La Acción Popular*, Dec. 6, 1912; Pedro Parra, *Bautismo de Fuego del proletariado peruano*, pp. 47–58.
13. In fact the same options were not open to him in the later strikes. The dock handlers' working conditions were set by the government, which had allowed Billinghurst to intervene, whereas the other strikers had to deal with their respective employers. See *El Callao* (Callao), Jan. 10, 1913.
14. *La Prensa*, Jan. 12–Feb. 1b, 8a–12a, 17b–20b, 26b, 28b, Mar. 1b, 11a, July 29, 1913; *La Protesta*, no. 20, Apr. 1913; Pedro Parra, *Bautismo de Fuego*, p. 59; "Zitor," "Historia de las Principales Huelgas," pp. 51–53.
15. *La Prensa*, Apr. 28b, 30b, May 2b, 6b, 31b, June 1, 5a, 6a, 8, 16b, 23a, 1913; "Zitor," "Historia de las Principales Huelgas," pp. 46–48.
16. Basadre, *Historia del Perú*, 12:55, 233–37; Herminio M. Parra, *Legislación del Trabajo*, pp. 52–80; *La Prensa*, July 29, Oct. 6a, Nov. 15a, 1913; *La Nación* (Lima), Jan. 8, 1914.

17. Basadre, *Historia del Perú*, 12:241–42; *La Prensa*, July 19a, 24b–26a, Aug. 4a, Sept. 7, 9b, Oct. 21b, 1913; Laos, *Lima*, pp. 271–72.
18. *La Prensa*, Nov. 2a, 18b, 1912, Jan. 11a, 20a, 25a, Mar. 15a, Apr. 27, May 6a, 11, 17a, 31a, 1913.
19. *La Acción Popular*, Oct. 19, 1912. Castañeda seemed to be constantly at odds with the workers. In August 1912 one assaulted him outside the Chamber. See *Debates*, Congreso Ordinario de 1912, p. 35.
20. *La Prensa*, Mar. 4a, 22a, Apr. 11a, Aug. 25a, 1913.
21. Ibid., June 11a, 1913; Laos, *Lima*, pp. 276–77; Ulloa y Sotomayor, *La organización social*, pp. 140–41.
22. *La Protesta*, no. 18, Oct. 1912, no. 29 [*sic*], Jan. 1913, May 1, 1913, no. 24, Aug. 1913, no. 27, Nov. 1913; *El Comercio*, Nov. 14b, 1913; *La Prensa*, Sept. 23b, Nov. 14b, 1913.
23. *La Prensa*, July 8a, 10b, 17b, 18a, 1913; Delfín Lévano, *Mi Palabra*, pp. 10–13. For more on this strike, see pp. 142–43.
24. *La Protesta*, no. 28, Feb. 1914.
25. Des Graz to Grey, no. 180, Dec. 30, 1912, FO 371/1734, no. 95, July 29, 1913, FO 371/1735, no. 8, Jan. 5, 1914, FO 371/2082; *La Prensa*, June 4a, Sept. 2b, 1913; Martín, *El Gobierno de Don Guillermo E. Billinghurst 1912–1914*, p. 29; United States, State Department, *Papers Relating to the Foreign Relations of the United States 1913* (Washington, 1920), pp. 1141–43.
26. State Department, *Foreign Relations of the United States 1913*, p. 1142.
27. Lima, Cámara de Comercio, *Memoria presentada . . . el 28 de Marzo 1914 siendo presidente el Sr. D. Pedro D. Gallagher* (Lima, 1914), pp. 38–39; *La Prensa*, Aug. 25b, 27a, Sept. 10b–12b, Oct. 11b, 1913; *El Comercio*, Sept. 10b–12b, 16a, 1913; Peruvian Corporation Ltd., *Representatives' Annual Reports 1909–1913*, "Report for the Year Ending 30th June, 1913," pp. 5–7, PCP, Informe no. 22.
28. Des Graz to Grey no. 136, Nov. 17, 1913, FO 371/1735.
29. Des Graz to Grey, no. 141, Nov. 29, 1913, FO 371/2081; *La Prensa*, Nov. 13a–28b, Dec. 4b, 5b, 1913; *El Comercio*, Nov. 12b–29b, 1913.
30. For the response of the business community, see Ramón to Antero Aspíllaga, Dec. 1, 1913, AFA–C, Cartas Reservadas, Lima-Cayaltí, Oct. 1913–Apr. 1914.
31. According to Basadre, the loan amounted to only 200,000 Peruvian pounds, not 500,000 pounds sterling. See *Historia del Perú*, 12:266–67.
32. Ulloa y Cisneros, *Escritos Históricos*, pp. 319–78; des Graz to Grey, no. 143, Dec. 1, 1913, FO 371/2081, no. 6, Jan. 3, 1914, no. 8, Jan. 5, 1914, FO 371/2082; *El Comercio*, Jan. 30a, Feb. 2b, 1914. The editor of *La Prensa*, Alberto Ulloa, was one of the original conspirators against Billinghurst.
33. *La Nación*, Jan. 7, 26–28, 31, 1914; *La Prensa*, Jan. 31a, 1914; *El Pueblo*, Jan. 25, 26, 30, Feb. 3, 1914.
34. *The West Coast Leader* (Lima), Jan. 29, 1914.
35. Ulloa y Cisneros, *Escritos Históricos*, pp. 329–31; Basadre, *Historia del Perú*, 12:283–95; *Peru To-day* (Lima), no. 10, Jan. 1914; *The West Coast Leader*, Feb. 5, 1914.
36. Basadre, *Historia del Perú*, 12:285; *La Prensa*, Feb. 4d, 7a, 1914; Billinghurst, *El Presidente Billinghurst a la Nación*, p. 3.
37. Ulloa y Cisneros' view of this period was that "the political past of Peru [was] on its way to liquidation." p. 318. See also Ramón to Antero Aspíllaga, Feb. 5, 9, 1914, AFA–C, Cartas Reservadas, Lima-Cayaltí, Oct. 1913–Apr. 1914; Gilbert, "The Oligarchy and the

Old Regime in Peru," p. 172; Astiz, *Pressure Groups and Power Elites*, pp. 136–37; Villanueva, *El Militarismo en el Perú*, p. 46.

38. Billinghurst, *El Presidente Billinghurst*, pp. 78, 90–91; des Graz to Grey, no. 8, Jan. 5, 1914, FO 371/2082; Belaunde, *Memorias*, 2:256–57.

39. Military spending rose from 7,482,318 soles in 1912, including both ordinary and extraordinary expenditures, to 9,215,349 soles in 1913. See Perú, *Presupuesto General para 1912* and *Presupuesto General 1913*. Billinghurst later claimed that his government was unequaled in its desire to obtain equipment for the armed forces. See *El Presidente Billinghurst*, p. 22.

40. *La Prensa*, Oct. 6a, 1913; Perú, *Presupuesto General para 1914*; Billinghurst, *El Presidente Billinghurst*, p. 11; Basadre, *Historia del Perú*, 12:237–41, 281; Ulloa y Cisneros, *Escritos Históricos*, pp. 337–38; Villanueva, *100 Años del Ejército Peruano*, pp. 70–71. Billinghurst resisted demands that the arms of the Santa Catalina garrison be distributed among his followers, which would have created a real workers' militia. All he allowed was the distribution of light weapons and blanks. See Billinghurst, *El Presidente Billinghurst*, pp. 83–84. His refusal to create a workers' militia indicated that he was not prepared to risk a violent confrontation that might lead to a situation similar to the events then taking place in Mexico. It was an action characteristic of Latin American populist leaders. See Spalding, *Organized Labor in Latin America*, ch. 4.

41. Wilson to Grey, no. 20, Feb. 9, 1914, FO 371/2081.

42. *La Prensa*, Feb. 4d, 5a, 9a, 9b, Mar. 13a, 13b, 1914; *La Verdad*, Feb. 26, 1916.

43. *La Prensa*, July 1a, 1915, Oct. 26b, 1916.

Chapter 7: The First World War

1. *La Prensa*, Apr. 2b, 3a, 25b, 27a, May 7b, Aug. 2, 1914; *La Protesta*, no. 30, May 1914; Peruvian Corporation Ltd., *Representative's Annual Reports 1914–1918*, "Report for the Year Ending 30th June, 1914," p. 7, PCP, Informe no. 23.

2. For details of the immediate effects of the war, see *La Prensa*, Aug. 3b–5b, 10a, 10b, 14a, 14b, 22a, 1914; Rennie to Grey, no. 7, Jan. 29, 1915, FO 371/2439; Rowe, *Early Effects of the War Upon the Finance, Commerce and Industry of Peru*; Basadre, *Historia del Perú*, 12:341-51; Basadre and Ferrero, *La Cámara de Comercio*, pp. 89–90; Lough, "Financial Developments in South American Countries," pp. 35–37.

3. De Lavalle, *La Gran Guerra*, p. 81; *La Prensa*, Apr. 10b, 1917; *La Verdad*, Dec. 15, 1917, May 4, 1918; Martínez de la Torre, *El Movimiento Obrero Peruano 1918–1919*, p. 12.

4. *La Prensa*, Aug. 4a–8b, 29a–Sept. 1a, 5b, 6a, 16a–20a, 27a–30a, Oct. 5b–9a, 13a, 1914; *La Protesta*, Oct. 17, 1914.

5. *La Prensa*, June 7a, Sept. 19a, 1917, Feb. 27a, 1918; Basadre and Ferrero, *La Cámara de Comercio*, p. 118; de Lavalle, *La Gran Guerra*, p. 86.

6. *La Prensa*, July 21b, Oct. 29b, 1915, June 14a, 1916, Mar. 28a, 1917, Oct. 26a, 1918.

7. *Ilustración Obrera*, Oct. 21, 1916; Manzanilla, *Legislación*, p. 360; idem, *La Responsabilidad*, pp. 334–37; *La Prensa*, July 14a, 1914, Sept. 8b, 1915, Sept. 24, 1916, Nov. 5a, 1918.

8. *La Prensa*, July 28b, Sept. 24, Oct. 25a, 28, Dec. 7a, 1918; *Ilustración Obrera*, Oct. 26, 1918.

9. *La Acción* (Chincha Alta), May 14, 1917; *Ilustración Obrera*, May 4, June 15, 1918; *La Prensa*, Mar. 14a, 1917, Aug. 27a, 28a, 1918; Rennie to Balfour, no. 92, Aug. 26, 1918, FO 371/3276.

10. *La Prensa*, Oct. 4a, 1914, May 21b, 1915, May 11, 1916, Sept. 11a, 1917; *La Verdad*, June 3, 1916.

11. "Expediente: Confederación de Artesanos 'Unión Universal' piden protección pecuniaria," ACD, 1916, Legajo 8, Cuaderno 1, No. 59; *La Prensa*, May 21b, Dec. 28a, 1915, Jan. 4a–5b, Feb. 1a, 1916, Jan. 13a, 1917, May 14a, 15a, 1918; *La Protesta*, no. 62, Feb. 1918. During the war urban industrial expansion was "slight." See Thorp and Bertram, *Peru*, p. 128.

12. *Ilustración Obrera*, Sept. 22, 1917, May 25, June 1, 1918; *La Prensa*, Dec. 21a–23a, 1916, Jan. 29a, 1917, Feb. 13b, 1918; *La Verdad*, May 27, Dec. 16, 1916, Feb. 23, 1918; Blanchard, "Asian Immigrants," pp. 67–68.

13. *La Prensa*, Dec. 6a, 1916, Dec. 30, 1917; *La Verdad*, Dec. 2, 1916, Oct. 6, 20, 1917, July 13, 1918.

14. Balbuena claimed to be a socialist. See *El Comercio*, Sept. 10, 1916.

15. For details of the societies' political involvement, see *La Prensa*, Aug. 26b, Nov. 9a, 1914, Jan. 13a, 23a, Feb. 8a, Mar. 5b, 10a, 11a, 20b, 29a–Apr. 2, 6a, 7a, 17a, 21a, May 3b, 12b, Aug. 16a, 19b, Oct. 16a, Nov. 10b, Dec. 19, 1915, Feb. 21a, 23a, Mar. 3b, Apr. 2, June 26a, Aug. 20, Sept. 11a, 18b, Dec. 22b, 23b, 31, 1916, Feb. 10b, Mar. 10a, Apr. 23a, 24a, May 12a, 14a, June 17, 1917; *La Verdad*, Jan. 8, Oct. 21, 1916, Mar. 31, May 19, July 7, 1917, Feb. 9, 1918; *La Sanción* (Callao), Dec. 1, 1916, Jan. 22, Mar. 19, Apr. 9, June 25, 1917; *Agrupación de Artesanos y Obreros*, June 1, 1917; *Ilustración Obrera*, May 5, 19, 1917; *El Comercio*, May 12a, 19a, 22a, 1917.

16. *La Prensa*, Aug. 12a, 1918, July 18a, 1919.

17. Ibid., June 7, 1914, May 1b, 1915, May 1b, 1916, Feb. 10, May 1b, Aug. 21a, Nov. 24, 1918; *Ilustración Obrera*, May 6, 1916; *La Verdad*, Nov. 24, 1917, Mar. 16, Apr. 6, May 4, 18, June 1, Aug. 31, Sept. 7, 1918.

18. *La Prensa*, Nov. 29a, 29b, Dec. 4a, 7c, 17a, 1918, Jan. 3a, 1919; *The Times* (London), Jan. 13, 23, 1919; *La Verdad*, Nov. 30, 1918; Scott to Stronge, Dec. 13, 1918, no. 3, Jan. 2, 1919, FO 177/445.

19. *La Verdad*, May 4, 1918.

20. Butman, "Shoe and Leather Trade in Argentina, Chile, Peru, and Uruguay," pp. 53–55; *La Prensa*, May 8a, 10b, 21a, 24a, 27b–June 5a, 13–15b, 19b, 20, 1915; *La Protesta*, Oct. 3, 1914; *El Sindicalista* (Lima), May 1, 1915; César Lévano, "Memorias de una gesta," p. 24, [Interview with Carlos Barba].

21. "Volantes, Hoyas Sueltas, etc., 1915–1919," BN; *La Protesta*, no. 48, July 1916, no. 54, Mar. 1917, no. 62, Feb. 1918.

22. Antuñano was killed the following year in an accident in Valparaíso.

23. See p. 134 for a description of the massacre in Huacho.

24. *El Comercio*, Sept. 18b, 19a, 1914; *La Prensa*, Sept. 18b, 21a, Oct. 3a, 4a, Nov. 25a, 26a, 1914, May 26a, 29a, 31a, June 3b, 5a, 7a, 9a, 1916, June 24–26a, 1917, Jan. 1, 1918; *La Protesta*, Oct. 3, 10, 1914, no. 48, July 1916, no. 49, Aug. 1916, May 30, 1917; *El Sindicalista*, May 1, 1915; *La Sanción*, June 25, 1917.

25. *La Protesta*, Nov. 30, 1916; *Ilustración Obrera*, Sept. 23, 1916; *La Prensa*, Sept. 25a, 1916, July 29, 1917; Basadre, *Historia del Perú*, 12:485–86.

26. *La Protesta*, no. 48, July 1916.

27. *La Prensa*, Oct. 5b, 23a, Nov. 19a–20b, Dec. 10a, 1914.

28. Ibid., Dec. 12a, 23b, 24a, 1914, Jan. 10–31, 1915; *Debates*, 2° Congreso Extraordinario de 1914, pp. 308–13; Basadre, *Historia del Perú*, 12:326–27; Flores Gonzáles, *Medio Siglo de Vida Sindical*, pp. 24–33.

29. *La Prensa*, Jan. 4b, 5a, 1916, Jan. 10a, 12a, 1917; *La Protesta*, no. 43, Jan. 1916, no. 53, Jan. 1917; *La Voz de Vitarte* (Vitarte), Dec. 18, 1915.

30. *La Prensa*, Jan. 14b, 16–17b, 21a, 22a, Feb. 18b, 19a, 1916, Sept. 3b, 7a, 11a, 14a, 1917.

31. Ibid., Oct. 2a–3b, 6b, 10b–12a, 17a, 1916, May 14b–16a, 19a, 24a–26a, 29a, June 5a, 1917; *Ilustración Obrera*, June 9, 1917; Basadre, *Historia del Perú*, 12:483–84.

32. *La Prensa*, May 19a, June 9a–19a, 25a, July 2a, Sept. 8a, 14a, 1917; *La Protesta*, no. 59, July 1917; *La Sanción*, June 25, 1917; *The West Coast Leader*, June 9, 16, 1917; "Zitor," "Historia de las Principales Huelgas," pp. 62–65.

33. *La Prensa*, July 6a, 20a, Aug. 3a, 12a, 1916, Aug. 11b, 21b, 23a, 26–Sept. 3b, 1917; *El Tiempo* (Lima), July 18, 20, Aug. 3, 1916; *Ilustración Obrera*, Sept. 1, 1917.

34. *La Prensa*, June 1a, 1918.

35. For the 1918 labor agitation, see ibid., Apr. 15a, 26a–29a, May 23b, 24b, June 13a–14, 30, Aug. 14a, 16b, 29a–30a, Sept. 16b, 23b, Oct. 8a, 12a, 1918, Jan. 3a, 1919; *La Protesta*, no. 66, June 1918; Peruvian Corporation Ltd., *Representative's Annual Reports 1914–1918*, "Report for the Year Ending 30th June 1918," p. 8, PCP, Informe no. 23; Flores Gonzáles, *Medio Siglo de Vida Sindical*, p. 42; "Zitor," "Historia de las Principales Huelgas," p. 66.

36. *La Prensa*, May 24b, 1918; *La Protesta*, May 1, 18, 1918, no. 68, Sept. 1918, no. 70, Oct. 1918, no. 73, Dec. 1918.

Chapter 8: Rural Workers in the Labor Movement

1. *Enganche* (from *enganchar*, "to entrap") has many similarities with the Inca system of labor recruitment known as *mita*. Whether there is a direct historical link is unknown since no one has yet traced the roots of enganche back through the colonial period to the Incas.

2. This, in general, was how the system operated. It should be noted, however, that the system was not uniform, there were many local variations, and it changed over time. For more details see *El Comercio*, Apr. 19a, 1894, June 14a, 1897; Albert, *The Peruvian Sugar Industry*, pp. 89a–96a; Klarén, *Modernization, Dislocation and Aprismo*, pp. 26–30; Osma, *Informe que sobre las Huelgas del Norte presenta al gobierno su comisionado*, pp. 6–7; M. G. Masias, "Estado actual de la industria minera de Morococha," pp. 62–66; Flores Galindo, *Los Mineros de la Cerro de Pasco*, pp. 41–43; DeWind, "From Peasants to Miners," pp. 51–54; Manzanilla, *Legislación*, pp. 234–36; Blanchard, "The Recruitment of Workers in the Peruvian Sierra at the Turn of the Century: the Enganche System," pp. 63–83; Gonzales, "Capitalist Agriculture and Labor Contracting in Northern Peru, 1880–1905," pp. 291–315.

3. Memoria of the subprefect of Chota, June 30, 1897, BN D4502; Memoria of the prefect of Ancash, July 18, 1901, BN E937; *El Comercio*, Feb. 11a, 1892; *La Prensa*, Oct. 7a, 1910.

4. *El Comercio*, July 24a, 1893; Memoria of the prefect of La Libertad, Feb. 12, 1894, BN D5439.

5. For abuses of the system see *El Comercio*, July 14b, 1898; *La Prensa*, Sept. 9b, 1911; Memoria of the subprefect of Ancash, BN E937; Ulloa y Sotomayor, *La organización social*, pp. 80–99; Interview with Mr. Ronald Gordon, Lima, July 31, 1973.

6. *El Comercio*, Aug. 28b, 1900, Nov. 24b, 1909; *La Prensa*, Oct. 12a, 1910, June 11, July 25a, 1911; *Los Parias*, no. 34, May 1907.

7. Henri Favre has concluded that enganche was not necessarily coercive or oppressive.

He notes that the enganche system used to obtain Indians from northern Huancavelica for the cotton estates in the Cañete Valley was "a simple means of locating, regulating, and channeling the work force" (p. 255). He has examined the reasons for the Indians' participation in the system and found that they wanted money to set up traditional communities in the high sierra free from the influence of the white population. See "The Dynamics of Indian Peasant Society." See also Arnold J. Bauer, "Rural Workers in Spanish America: Problems of Peonage and Oppression," *Hispanic American Historical Review* (1979), 49:34–63.

8. The passion of the Peruvian Indian for agriculture and land possession can be traced back to the Inca period. See Bertram, "New Thinking on the Peruvian Highland Peasantry," pp. 96–98.

9. On some estates the *yanaconas* had to hire the seasonal cotton pickers. For more on *yanaconaje*, see Albert, *The Peruvian Sugar Industry*, pp. 79–80, appendix 1; Matos Mar, *Yanaconaje y Reforma Agraria en el Perú*, chs. 1-2; *El Comercio*, Feb. 8b, 1893; Cisneros, *Reseña Económica del Perú*, p. 156. For an agreement between a *hacendado* and a *yanacona*, see Aspíllaga Hermanos to Tomas S. Acevedo, Jan. 27, 1903, AFA, Palto Papers, Lima-Palto, July 1902–July 1907.

10. For the best survey of the coolie trade, see Stewart, *Chinese Bondage in Peru*. Other works on this subject claim that the total number of coolies imported may have been as high as 150,000. See Vázquez, "Immigration and *mestizaje*," p. 82.

11. For information on the Asian migration to Peru during this period, see Irie, "History of Japanese migration to Peru," 31:437–52, 648–64; Gardiner, *The Japanese and Peru 1873–1973*, ch. 2; Great Britain, *Parliamentary Papers* (1898), 97, "No. 2117, Annual Series, Diplomatic and Consular Reports, Peru: Report for the Year 1897 on the Trade and Finances of Peru," pp. 18–19; *El Comercio*, Apr. 17b, 1899, June 6c, 1905.

12. Mansfield to Salisbury, Mar. 1, 1891, FO 61/388; "Expediente relativo a una visita practicada a asiáticos que prestan servicios en la hacienda Viñita del valle de Chicama," July 31, 1894, BN D4951; *La Prensa*, Dec. 4a, 1905; Albert, *The Peruvian Sugar Industry*, pp. 272, 273, 275. One problem in examining the role of the Japanese and Chinese is that the sources rarely differentiate between the two groups.

13. Albert, *The Peruvian Sugar Industry*, pp. 18, 46–48; *La Prensa*, Dec. 3, 1905; *El Jornalero* (Trujillo), Dec. 1, 8, 1906.

14. *La Prensa*, Dec. 4a, 1905.

15. For details of these clashes, see Stewart, *Chinese Bondage*, pp. 121–24, 218–21; Bonilla, "The War of the Pacific," pp. 106–10; Arona *La Inmigración en el Perú*, pp. 99–104; *La Actualidad* (Lima), Jan. 24, Feb. 23, Mar. 9, Apr. 8, 28, 1881; *La Situación*, June 17, July 2, 1881; *El Tiempo*, Dec. 27, 1900, Sept. 22, 1903; *El Comercio*, Feb. 15, 1904, Sept. 10a, 15b, 1909.

16. Matos Mar, *Yanaconaje*, pp. 84–85.

17. Irie, "History of Japanese migration," 31:651–52; Gardiner, *The Japanese and Peru*, p. 34.

18. For the best survey of the sugar industry during this period, see Albert, *The Peruvian Sugar Industry*, pp. 1a–111a. For the effects of the war on the industry, see also Klarén, *Modernization, Dislocation and Aprismo*, pp. 5–10; Levin, *The Export Economies*, p. 121.

19. Diaz Ahumada, "Las luchas sindicales en el Valle de Chicama" p. 9; Klarén, *Modernization, Dislocation and Aprismo*, ch. 3; *El Comercio*, May 21b, 1894; *La Prensa*, Nov. 16a, 1906, Jan. 22a, 1908; *El Jornalero*, Jan. 26, 1907; *El Eco Popular* (Chiclayo), June 23, 1907.

20. Irie, "History of Japanese migration," 31:446–49; Gardiner, *The Japanese and Peru*, pp. 25–26; *El Comercio*, Apr. 26a, May 9a, June 12, 17b, 1899.

21. For these and other strikes involving the Japanese, see *El Comercio*, Aug. 20a, 1900, Sept. 21b, 25b, 26b, 1903, Sept. 10a, 15b, 1909; *El Tiempo*, Jan. 27, Aug. 20, 1900, Sept. 22, 1903.

22. *La Prensa*, Jan. 24b, 1906; *El Jornalero*, Dec. 29, 1906, June 15, July 1, 1911.

23. Osma, *Las Huelgas del Norte;* Klarén, *Modernization, Dislocation and Aprismo*, pp. 33–37; Albert, *The Peruvian Sugar Industry*, pp. 106a–09a; *La Prensa*, Apr. 11a, 15a, 23a, 30a, May 3b, Oct. 10b, 1912; *La Industria* (Trujillo), Apr. 8–15, 30, May 3, 6, 7, 1912; *El Jornalero*, June 11, July 25, 1912, June 20, 1913; *La Nación*, Jan. 31, 1914; des Graz to Grey, no. 57, Apr. 20, 1912, FO 371/1459; Aspíllaga Hermanos to Víctor Aspíllaga, Apr. 16, 1912, AFA–C, Cartas Administrativas, Lima-Cayaltí, 1911–1912.

24. Aspíllaga Hermanos to Víctor Aspíllaga, Jan. 17, 23, 24, 1913; Antero to Baldomero Aspíllaga, Jan. 28, 1913, AFA–C, Cartas Reservadas, Lima-Cayaltí, Nov. 1912–May 1913.

25. *La Prensa*, July 11b, 1913, May 13a, 14b, 1914; *La Protesta*, no. 30, May 1914.

26. *El Jornalero*, Aug. 15, 1914; *La Prensa*, Dec. 4a, 1914; Albert, *The Peruvian Sugar Industry*, pp. 117a–40a, 1–2; Rennie to Balfour, no. 42, June 18, 1917, FO 371/2990.

27. For the decline in real wages see Albert, *The Peruvian Sugar Industry*, tables 52–53, pp. 173a–74a.

28. Ibid., p. 183a; *El Comercio*, Sept. 1a–16b, 21a, 1916; *La Prensa*, Sept. 1b–9b, 11b, 16a, 18b, 22a, 26a, Oct. 3a, 1916; Víctor Aspíllaga to Aspíllaga Hermanos, Sept. 13, 1916, AFA–C, Cartas Administrativas, Cayaltí-Lima, Jan.–Dec. 1916.

29. Albert, *The Peruvian Sugar Industry*, p. 47.

30. Ibid., pp. 185a–88a; *La Industria*, Aug. 31, 1916; *El Derecho Obrero* (Trújillo), Aug. 25, Sept. 23, 30, 1917; *La Protesta*, May 30, no. 59, July 1917; *El Comercio*, May 30b, 31a, June 4a–8a, 11a, 1917; *La Prensa*, June 1a, 1917; Parra, *Bautismo de Fuego*, pp. 72–78.

31. Parra, *Bautismo de Fuego*, pp. 64–71; *El Comercio*, June 9a, 13a–21a, 26a, 1917; *La Prensa*, June 15a–22a, 26a, July 10a, 17b, 1917; *La Protesta*, May 30, no. 60, Sept. 1917, Mar. 8, 1919.

32. *El Comercio*, July 11a, 12a, 1917; *El Derecho Obrero*, July 28, 1917; *La Prensa*, July 12a, 1917; Ramón to Antero Aspíllaga, June 14, 1917, AFA–C, Cartas Reservadas, Lima-Cayaltí, May 1917–July 1918; Albert, *The Peruvian Sugar Industry*, pp. 147, 158–59.

33. Albert, *The Peruvian Sugar Industry*, table 46, p. 167a, pp. 163–64, 209.

34. *La Protesta*, no. 66, June 1918; *La Linterna* (San Vicente de Cañete), Oct. 18, 21, 1918.

35. Thorp and Bertram, *Peru*, pp. 77–83; Purser, *Metal-Mining in Peru, Past and Present*, p. 101; Miller, "Railways and Economic Development in Central Peru, 1890–1930," pp. 32–35; Dunn, *Peru, A Commercial and Industrial Handbook*, p. 171.

36. Mayer, *The Conduct of the Cerro de Pasco*, p. 6; Garland, *Peru in 1906 and After*, p. 241; *La Verdad*, Oct. 20, 1917; *La Voz de Junín* (Lima), July 15, 1917.

37. For some of Herrera y Vera's accomplishments, see *La Verdad*, Oct. 20, 1917.

38. Velarde, "Reglamentaciones Mineras para el Cerro de Pasco," pp. 23–25; Gastelumendi, "Informe Anual de la Comisión Minera del Cerro de Pasco en 1908," pp. 19–25; Jiménez, "Estadística Minera del Perú en 1921," p. 158; *Los Parias*, no. 18, Oct. 1905; *La Prensa*, Jan. 18a, Feb. 19b, 1909; *El Correo de Morococha* (Morococha), Oct. 23, 1916; *La Verdad*, Apr. 15, 1916; *La Voz de Junín*, June 30, 1917.

39. *La Voz de Junín,* July 15, 1917; Masias, "Estado actual de la industria minera," pp. 62–66; Jochamowitz, "Estado actual de la industria minera en Morococha," pp. 65–67; Flores Galindo, *Los Mineros de la Cerro de Pasco,* pp. 50, 59; Great Britain, "Report for the Years 1908–09," p. 44.

40. Mayer, *The Conduct of the Cerro de Pasco,* p. 8; *El Correo de Morococha,* Nov. 18, 1916; *La Prensa,* May 22a, 1909.

41. *La Prensa,* Mar. 24a, 1909, Jan. 26b, 27a, Feb. 3b, 13, 1912; Basadre, *Historia del Perú,* 12:188–89; Pike, *The Modern History of Peru,* p. 164; Davies, Jr., *Indian Integration in Peru: A Half Century of Experience, 1900–1948,* pp. 54–56.

42. Mayer, *The Conduct of the Cerro de Pasco,* p. 40.

43. *La Prensa,* June 14a, 20a, 1904, Jan. 1, 2a, 1906, Apr. 6b, 1907, June 11, 1911; *El Comercio,* May 30b, 1892; *Germinal* (Lima), Jan. 6, 1906.

44. Mayer, *The Conduct of the Cerro de Pasco,* pp. 40–42; *La Prensa,* Apr. 15a, 1912.

45. *El Comercio,* Dec. 6a–10a, 1913; *La Crónica,* Jan. 12, 1914; *La Prensa,* Dec. 6a, 6b, 9a–11a, 1913.

46. *La Prensa,* Sept. 6a, 8b, Oct. 4b, Nov. 11a, 1914; Rowe, *Early Effects of the War,* p. 39.

47. *La Voz de Junín,* Oct. 31, 1914, May 31, June 30, Oct. 31, 1916; *Los Andes* (Cerro de Pasco), May 7, 1915, May 7, 18, July 16, 20, 1916; *El Correo de Morococha,* Jan. 17, 1917; *La Verdad,* Oct. 20, 1917.

48. *El Comercio,* Sept. 4b, 1916; *La Prensa,* Sept. 2b, 4a, 14b, 1916.

49. Shortly before the war the mining companies had agreed not to compete for labor and had set a scale of wages. See Rowe, *Early Effects of the War,* p. 40.

50. *El Correo de Morococha,* Jan. 17, Feb. 2, 1917; *Los Andes,* May 28, 31, June 4, 1917; *El Comercio,* May 28a–31b, June 2a, 5a, 1917; *El Minero* (Cerro de Pasco), May 30, June 6, 1917; *La Prensa,* May 27–June 4a, 1917; *La Verdad,* June 16, 1917; *La Voz de Junín,* June 15, 1917; *The West Coast Leader,* June 2, 9, 1917.

51. *La Voz de Junín,* Nov. 30, 1917; *El Huallaga* (Huánuco), July 17, 1918.

52. *Los Andes,* Dec. 3, 1917, July 4, 1918; *El Comercio,* Dec. 4a–7a, 1917; *La Prensa,* Dec. 3a–5a, 1917, July 8b, 1918; *La Verdad,* Dec. 8, 1917; *El Eco de Junín* (Cerro de Pasco), July 2, 3, 1918.

53. *El Eco de Junín,* Jan. 8, 1918.

54. *Los Andes,* June 13, Nov. 19, 1918; *La Prensa,* June 16, 1918. There is information on this organization also in a manuscript by Arturo Sabroso in the Centro de Documentación, Pontificia Universidad Católica del Perú, Lima.

55. Thorp and Bertram, *Peru,* pp. 95–100; Denegri, "Estadística Minera del Perú en 1905," p. 28; Jiménez, "Estadística Minera del Perú en 1917," pp. 118, 120–22; idem, "Estadístiea Minera del Perú en 1919," p. 76; Lobitos Oilfields Ltd., "Historical Notes on the Activities of the Company from Early Origins to the Present," pp. 14–15, manuscript, UCL–DMSW.

56. *El Comercio,* Sept. 21b, 1910, Jan. 31a, 1913; *La Prensa,* Sept. 22b, Oct. 7a, 8b, 1910; *La Unión* (Lima), Feb. 9, 1913.

57. *La Prensa,* May 15b, 19a, 19b, 23b–27b, June 29, July 8a, 17b, 1913; *La Protesta,* May 30, June 30, 1913; Delfín Lévano, *Mi Palabra,* pp. 10–13; Federación Anarquista del Perú, *El Anarcosindicalismo en el Perú,* pp. 8–10.

58. Lobitos Oilfields Ltd., "Short History of Lobitos Oilfields," p. 40, manuscript, UCL–DMSW; *La Prensa,* Mar. 23b, 1915.

59. *La Prensa,* May 29b–June 3a, 6a, July 24a, Aug. 7a–10a, 22b, Sept. 20b, 21a, 29a,

1916; *El Comercio,* May 27b–June 10a, Sept. 27b, 28a, 1916; *El Tiempo,* July 22, 23, 26, 1916; *La Verdad,* Aug. 12, 26, 1916; *The West Coast Leader,* June 8, 1916.

60. Dawson to Rennie, no. 1, Apr. 13, 1917, FO 177/424.

61. Ibid., no. 1, Apr. 13, no. 2, Apr. 26, 1917, FO 177/424; *El Artesano* (Paita), May 5, 1917; *El Comercio,* Mar. 31a, Apr. 3a, 1917; *El Comercio* (Paita), July 10, 12, 14, 1917; *La Prensa,* June 26b, Sept. 14a, 1917; Perú, Ministerio de Gobierno, *Memoria que el Ministro de Gobierno y Policía presenta al Congreso Ordinario de 1917,* pp. iv–v; Rivera, *Los sucesos de Talara: Relación verídica e imparcial de los acontecimientos, escrita sobre el terreno.* Despite its title, this account must be used with care. The book's bias is evident from its dedication: to the general manager of the London and Pacific Petroleum Co. Ltd.

62. *La Protesta,* no. 61, Dec. 1917; *El Comercio,* Nov. 21a, 21b, 26a, 30a–Dec. 3a, 10a, 1917; *El Federal* (Trujillo), Dec. 3, 1917; *La Prensa,* Nov. 20b, 26a–Dec. 2, 5a, 20b, 1917; *La Verdad,* Nov. 24, Dec. 1, 8, 22, 1917; *The West Coast Leader,* Dec. 1, 8, 1917; "Expediente sobre amnistía a los enjuiciados de Talara, Negritos y Lobitos," ACD, 1918, Legajo 2, Cuaderno 1, No. 471.

63. Rory Miller has pointed out in a private communication that the strikes in November 1917 seriously threatened the deliveries of oil to Lima with the result that the oil-burning factories, the tramways, and the Central Railway faced the possibility of having to suspend operations. In other words, the petroleum workers, or the petroleum companies, could bring Lima to a halt. See *The West Coast Leader,* Dec. 1, 1917.

Chapter 9: The Eight-Hour Day, January 1919

1. F. W. Manners, "A Report on the Finance, Industry and Trade of Peru at the Close of the Year, 1919" in Great Britain, *Parliamentary Papers* (1920), 43:21.

2. *La Verdad,* May 27, 1916.

3. *Ilustración Obrera,* Oct. 26, Nov. 3, 1918; Manzanilla, *Legislación,* pp. 547–68; Basadre, *Historia del Perú,* 12:477; "Expediente Establecimientos industriales—Garantías a los obreros en cuento a su instrucción i salubridad," ACD, 1918, Legajo 2, Cuaderno 1, No. 113; "Expediente sobre descanso dominical," ACD, 1918, Legajo 2, Cuaderno 1, No. 56.

4. *Ilustración Obrera,* May 25, 1918; *La Prensa,* Dec. 13b, 1915, July 4a, 7a, 1917, May 18a, 1918, Jan. 26, 1919; *La Verdad,* May 27, Aug. 26, 1916.

5. *Los Andes,* Jan. 7, 1919; *La Prensa,* Dec. 7a, 1917, Mar. 8b, Aug. 14a, Oct. 23a, 31a, Nov. 29a, 1918, Jan. 29, 1919; Manzanilla, *Legislación,* pp. 385–93, 399.

6. *La Protesta* claimed that the textile mills had made "millions of soles" during the war. See no. 74, Jan. 1919.

7. *La Prensa,* Jan. 9a, 1919.

8. Of Vitarte's six hundred workers, only twenty belonged to the anarchist "La Protesta" group. See César Lévano, "1919: La Tempestad Obrera," p. 47, [interview with Héctor Merel].

9. For details of the labor agitation in Argentina, see David Rock, *Politics in Argentina 1890–1930: The Rise and Fall of Radicalism* (Cambridge: Cambridge University Press, 1975), ch. 7.

10. Some writers point to the formation of the Federación Obrera Local de Lima (Workers' Local Federation of Lima) at a workers convention in early December 1918 as further proof of the anarchists' revitalization and leadership of the campaign for the eight-hour day. See Barrientos Casós, *Los tres sindicalismos,* p. 149; César Lévano, *La Verdadera His-*

toria, pp. 36–37; Sulmont, *El Movimiento Obrero*, pp. 84–85. I have failed to find any information on a convention or an organization of this name at this time.

11. *El Comercio*, Jan. 7b–9a, 1919; *La Prensa*, Jan. 7b, 8a, 11a, 15b, 1919; *El Progreso* (Tumbes), Jan. 10, 1919; *El Tiempo*, Jan. 8, 9, 1919.

12. One notable exception to the positive response was the recently reorganized Federación Maritima y Terrestre del Callao whose leaders, Fernando Vera and José Robles, opposed the general strike. See *El Tiempo*, Jan. 13, 1919.

13. One group of mutualist leaders, including Víctor Herrera y Vera, was ejected from a strike meeting because of their unacceptable ideas. See *La Crónica*, Jan. 15, 1919. The Confederation's library was conveniently located across from the ministry of public works, where negotiations were proceeding.

14. The students' growing social consciousness was a result of the university reform movement that had developed in Córdoba, Argentina, in 1918 and had now reached Peru. It also reflected the increased enrollment of members of the middle class in the Peruvian universities. See Chavarría, "The Intellectuals and the Crisis," p. 277; Klarén, *Modernization, Dislocation and Aprismo*, pp. 96–97.

15. The student proposal of January 14 has provoked a certain amount of controversy since it involved Haya de la Torre. In an interview on June 14, 1973, in Lima he denied categorically that he or the other student delegates made such a proposal and insisted that it came from either the owners or the government. See also an interview with Haya in *Caretas* (Mar. 22–31, 1971), no. 432, p. 20. Critics of APRA from the Left have tried to minimize the roles of Haya and the students in the January 1919 general strike and have pointed to the proposal as an early indication of his opportunism and lack of real commitment to the workers' cause. See César Lévano, "Memorias de una gesta," p. 26, "1919: La Tempestad Obrera," pp. 47–48, *La Verdadera Historia*, pp. 38–42; Barba, "Las luchas obreras en 1919," no. 3, p. 23. The newspaper reports of the events indicate that the students made the proposal, but many workers supported it, including Nicolás Gutarra. See *La Prensa*, Jan. 14c, 15a, 1919; Lévano, "1919: La Tempestad Obrera," p. 47. Despite worker opposition, the proposal did not affect the standing of Haya and the students among the strikers. They were asked to intercede with the minister of government on behalf of those workers who had been arrested.

16. For details of the Morococha strike, which ended with the companies closing the mines and hundreds of workers returning home, see *El Comercio*, Jan. 22b, 1919; *La Prensa*, Jan. 22a–24a, 1919; *El Tiempo*, Jan. 25, 1919; *The West Coast Leader*, Jan. 25, 1919.

17. For details of the general strike, see *La Prensa*, Dec. 22, 1918–Jan. 31b, 1919; *La Protesta*, no. 73, Dec. 1918–no. 75, Jan. 1919; *El Comercio*, Jan. 14a–16a, 1919; *La Crónica*, Jan. 15, 1919; *El Tiempo*, Jan. 6, 1919; *The West Coast Leader*, Jan. 11, 18, 1919; Rennie to Balfour, no. 12, Jan. 20, 1919, FO 371/3893; Martínez de la Torre, *El Movimiento Obrero Peruano*, pp. 66–101; Flores Gonzáles, *Medio Siglo de Vida Sindical*, pp. 42–47; César Lévano, "1919: La Tempestad Obrera," pp. 47–48; Rouillon, *La Creación Heroica*, pp. 233–40. The aprista view of the strike is contained in Cossío del Pomar, *Víctor Raúl, Biografía de Haya de la Torre*, pp. 92–105. It greatly exaggerates the role of Haya.

18. *El Heraldo* (Huacho), Jan. 17, 22, Mar. 7, 1919; *El Comercio*, Jan. 29a, Feb. 1a, 7b, 10a, 17a, 21b, 22a, 25a, 25b, 1919; *La Prensa*, Jan. 29a, Feb. 5b, 17a, 17b, 21b, 22a, 26a, 1919; Robb to Wilson, no. 12, Feb. 21, 1919, FO 177/446.

19. *La Juventud* (Monsefú), Jan. 23, 1919; Víctor Aspíllaga to Aspíllaga Hermanos,

Jan. 24, Mar. 5, 1919, AFA-C, Cartas Administrativas, Cayaltí-Lima, Jan.–Dec. 1919. Refugees had begun arriving in Peru once again because of a renewed outburst of nationalistic fervor in Chile.

20. *El Comercio,* Jan. 29a, Feb. 1b–5b, 1919; *La Prensa,* Feb. 5a, 8a, 13b, 1919; Albert, *The Peruvian Sugar Industry,* pp. 217–24; interview with Ronald Gordon, Lima, July 31, 1973.

21. Flores Galindo, *Los Mineros de la Cerro de Pasco,* p. 58, note 1.

22. *La Prensa,* Jan. 28b, Feb. 5b, Apr. 2a, 1919; interview with Ronald Gordon, Lima, July 31, 1973; J. Roberto Gutiérrez, untitled ms. on the effects of the eight-hour day in Peru, Oct. 31, 1919, BN E1101.

23. Gutiérrez, untitled ms; José Vila, "La Jornada de Ocho Horas," Oct. 27, 1919, BN E1110.

24. *El Comercio,* Jan. 16a, 23a, 1919; *El Deber,* Jan. 17, 1919; *Ilustración Obrera,* Jan. 18, 1919.

25. *The West Coast Leader,* Jan. 18, 1919; *La Protesta,* Mar. 8, 1919; *Ilustración Obrera,* Jan. 18, 1919; Pardo y Barreda, *Perú: Cuatro Años de Gobierno Constitucional,* pp. 59–60.

26. *La Prensa,* Jan. 23a, 1919.

27. Ibid., Jan. 17a, 1919; Federación de Trabajadores en Tejidos del Perú, *Declaración de Principios y Reglamento*; Barrientos Casós, *Los tres sindicalismos,* pp. 156–57.

Chapter 10: And After

1. *La Prensa,* Jan. 23b, 29a, 30a, Feb. 3b–6a, Mar. 8b, 18b–21b, 25b–30, 1919; *La Protesta,* Feb. 22, 1919.

2. This and the following information on the activities of the Comité Pro Abaratamiento de las Subsistencias between April and July 1919 is taken largely from Martínez de la Torre, *El Movimiento Obrero Peruano,* pp. 14–39. See also *La Prensa,* Apr. 14a, 1919; Carlos Barba, "Las luchas obreras en 1919," no. 4, pp. 16–17; Simon, "Anarchism and Anarcho-syndicalism in South America," p. 5.

3. César Lévano, "Memorias de una gesta," p. 24; *La Prensa,* Apr. 21a, May 2a, 7a, 1919; *The West Coast Leader,* May 10, 1919.

4. Partido Obrero del Perú, *Declaración de Principios.*

5. *La Razón* (Lima), May 19, 1919; Basadre, *Historia del Perú,* 13:9–10.

6. Interview with Víctor Raúl Haya de la Torre, Lima, June 14, 1973; *El Comercio,* May 2a, 1919.

7. *La Prensa,* Mar. 21a, Apr. 20, May 2a, 8a, 11, 1919; Rouillón, *La Creación Heroica,* pp. 223–37.

8. One of the problems of the Socialist party was internal bickering between reformists and revolutionaries. See Rouillón, *La Creación Heroica*, pp. 246–54. See also *El Comercio,* May 6a, 1919; *La Prensa,* May 2a, 5a, 7a, 11, 12b, 1919.

9. *La Prensa,* May 5b–7a, 10a, 13b, 15b, 21b, 22a, 1919.

10. *The West Coast Leader,* May 31, 1919.

11. According to César Lévano, a secret official report exists that states that four hundred people were buried in Callao during the strike. See "Memorias de una gesta," p. 24.

12. *La Prensa,* May 15b, 26a–June 2a, 1919; *La Razón,* June 5, 1919; *The West Coast Leader,* May 31, 1919; Manners to Curzon, no. 62, June 16, 1919, FO 371/3893; Barba, "Las luchas obreras en 1919," no. 4, p. 18.

13. *The West Coast Leader,* June 7, 1919.
14. *El Heraldo,* June 16, 1919; *La Prensa,* June 2a–7a, 23a, 1919.
15. *El Comercio,* June 19a, 1919.
16. *La Protesta,* July 19, 1919; *La Razón,* June 4, 1919.
17. Enclosure with Manners to Curzon, no. 17, Feb. 6, 1920, FO 371/4545; *La Prensa,* July 5a, 1919; Chavarría, "La desaparición del Perú colonial (1870–1919)," pp. 151–52.
18. *La Prensa,* July 5a, 10a, 1919; *La Razón,* July 13, 1919; Simon, "Anarchism and Anarcho-syndicalism," p. 56; Federación Anarquista del Perú, *El Anarcosindicalismo en el Perú,* p. 17.
19. For details of the labor movement after July 1919, see Sulmont, *Historia del Movimiento Obrero Peruano (1890–1977);* idem, *El Movimiento Obrero,* chs. 3–7; Payne, *Labor and Politics in Peru.*

Bibliography

The documentary evidence for this work can be found in the Biblioteca Nacional, Archivo del Fuero Agrario, Archivo del Congreso, the ENAFER-Perú offices, and Pontificia Universidad Católica del Perú in Lima; and the Public Record Office and the University College London libraries in London.

Printed Government Reports

Two series of foreign government reports have been useful: the British consular reports published for several years between 1883 and 1919 in *Parliamentary Papers,* and the American consular reports published for the same period by the Department of State in *Foreign Relations of the United States.* The Peruvian government published the debates of Congress and the *Boletín del Cuerpo de Ingenieros de Minas del Perú (BCIMP).* The latter is invaluable for mining, petroleum, and industrial information. Other Peruvian government reports include:

Perú. *Presupuesto General para 1912.* Lima: Escuela Nacional de Artes y Oficios, 1912.
———. *Presupuesto General 1913.* Lima: "La Opinión Nacional," 1912.
———. *Presupuesto General para 1914.* Lima: Tip. y Encuadernación de la Penitenciaría, 1913.
Perú. H. Cámara de Diputados. *Accidentes del Trabajo.* Lima: "La Revista," 1907.
Perú. Ministerio de Fomento. *Censo de la Provincia Constitucional del Callao 20 de Junio de 1905.* Lima: Imp. y Librería de San Pedro, 1906.
———. *Resúmenes del Censo de las Provincias de Lima y Callao. Levantado el 17 de Diciembre de 1920.* Lima: Imp. Torres Aguirre, 1921.
Perú. Ministerio de Fomento. Dirección de Inmigración y Colonización. *Reseña Industrial del Perú.* Lima: Imp. del Estado, 1902.
Perú. Ministerio de Fomento. Dirección de Salubridad Pública. *Censo de la Provincia de Lima (26 de Junio de 1908),* 2 vols. Lima: "La Opinión Nacional," 1915.
Perú. Ministerio de Gobierno. *Memoria que el Ministro de Gobierno y Policía presenta al Congreso Ordinario de 1917.* Lima: Tip. El Progreso Editorial, 1917.
Perú. Ministerio de Hacienda. *Resumen del Censo de las Provincias de Lima y Callao levantado el 17 de diciembre de 1920.* Lima: Imp. Americana, 1927.
Perú. Ministerio de Hacienda y Comercio. *Extracto Estadístico del Perú 1926.* Lima: Casa Editora La Opinión Nacional, 1927.
The Lima Chamber of Commerce published reports in 1899, 1905, 1907, 1908, and 1914 which provide important information on the cost of living.

Other Primary Sources

Arenas, Germán. *Algo de una vida: para después de mi muerte*. Lima: n.p., n.d.

Aspíllaga, Antero. *Programa de Gobierno presentado a la consideración del país*. Lima: Tip. de "El Lucero," 1911.

Belaunde, Víctor Andrés. *Memorias*. 3 vols. Lima: Imp. Lumen, 1960-1962.

Billinghurst, Guillermo E. *El Presidente Billinghurst a la Nación, Primera Parte*. Santiago de Chile: La Imprenta Diener, 1915.

Bonafulla, Leopoldo. *Criterio Libertario*. Lima: Imp. "Americana," 1910.

Brent, H. M. "Peru" in *United States Consular Reports: Labor in America, Asia, Africa, Australasia and Polynesia*. Washington, D.C.: Government Printing Office, 1885.

Butman, Arthur B. "Shoe and Leather Trade in Argentina, Chile, Peru, and Uruguay" in U.S., Department of Commerce and Labor, Bureau of Manufactures, *Special Agents Series–No. 37*. Washington, D.C.: Government Printing Office, 1910.

Capelo, Joaquín. *Sociología de Lima*. 4 vols. Lima: Imp. Masias, 1895-1896, Imp. La Industria, 1902.

Carreño, Juan Manuel. *La Anarquía en el Perú*. Callao: Grupo Anárquico Luz y Amor, 1915.

Cisneros, Carlos B. *Provincia de Lima*. Lima: Carlos Fabbri, 1911.

———. *Reseña Económica del Perú*. Lima: Imp. La Industria, 1906.

Clairmont, A. de. *A Guide to Modern Peru: Its Great Advantages and Vast Opportunities*. Toledo, Ohio: Barkdull Printing House Co., 1908.

Clark, W. A. Graham. "Chile, Bolivia, Peru, Ecuador, Jamaica, and Porto Rico" in U.S., Department of Commerce and Labor, *Special Agents Series–No. 44. Cotton Goods in Latin America*. Washington, D.C.: Government Printing Office, 1911.

Confederación de Artesanos "Unión Universal." *Constitución de la Confederación de Artesanos "Unión Universal."* Lima: Imp. Comercial de H. La-Rosa y Cia., 1904.

———. *Reglamento Interno de la Confederación de Artesanos "Unión Universal."* Lima: Imp. Comercial de Horacio La-Rosa y Cia., 1912.

Dávalos y Lissón, Pedro. *Diez Años de Historia Contemporanea del Perú 1899-1908*. Lima: Librería e Imp. Gil, 1930.

———. *Por qué hice Fortuna*. 2 vols. Lima: Librería e Imp. Gil, 1941.

Denegri, M. A. "Estadística Minera del Perú en 1905." *BCIMP*, No. 41.

Dunn, W. E. *Peru, A Commercial and Industrial Handbook*. Washington, D.C.: Government Printing Office, 1925.

Enock, C. Reginald. *The Andes and the Amazon: Life and Travel in Peru*. London: T. Fisher Unwin, 1908.

Federación de Trabajadores en Tejidos del Perú. *Declaración de Principios y Reglamento*. Lima: Imp. Proletaria, 1921.

Ferreyros, Guillermo. *Memoria que el Prefecto del Departamento D. Guillermo Ferreyros eleva al Ministerio de Gobierno, Policía y Obras Públicas*. Lima: Imp. de Torres Aguirre, 1888.

Franck, Harry A. *Vagabonding Down the Andes: Being the Narrative of a Journey, Chiefly Afoot, from Panama to Buenos Aires*. Garden City: Garden City Publishing Co. Inc., 1917.

Garland, Alexander. *Peru in 1906 and After with a Brief Historical and Geographical Sketch*. Translated by George R. Gepp. Lima: "La Industria" Printing Office, 1908.

Bibliography 197

Gastelumendi, A.C. "Informe Anual de la Comisión Minera del Cerro de Pasco en 1908." *BCIMP*, No. 74.
Gilimón, Eduardo G. *Para los que no son Anarquistas*. Callao: Grupo Anárquico "Luz y Amor," 1913.
González Prada, Manuel. *Anarquía*. Santiago de Chile: Ediciones Ercilla, 1936.
———. *Bajo el Oprobio*. Paris: Tipografia de Louis Bellenand et Fils, 1938.
———. *Prosa Menuda*. Buenos Aires: Ediciones Iman, 1941.
Jiménez, Carlos P. "Estadística Industrial del Perú." *BCIMP*, No. 105.
———. "Estadística Minera del Perú en 1908." *BCIMP*, No. 76.
———. "Estadística Minera del Perú en 1912." *BCIMP*, No. 80.
———. "Estadística Minera del Perú en 1913." *BCIMP*, No. 81.
———. "Estadística Minera del Perú en 1915." *BCIMP*, No. 83.
———. "Estadística Minera del Perú en 1917." *BCIMP*, No. 95.
———. "Estadística Minera del Perú en 1918." *BCIMP*, No. 96.
———. "Estadística Minera del Perú en 1919." *BCIMP*, No. 100.
———. "Estadística Minera del Perú en 1921." *BCIMP*, No. 106.
Jochamowitz, Alberto. "Estado Actual de la Industria Minera en Morococha." *BCIMP*, No. 65.
Laos, Cipriano A. *Lima "La Ciudad de los Virreyes" (El Libro Peruano)*. [Lima]: "Editorial Perú," n.d.
Lavalle, Hernando de. *La Gran Guerra y el Organismo Económico Nacional*. Lima: Librería e Imp. Gil, 1919.
Lévano, Delfín. *Mi Palabra: La Jornada de Ocho Horas y El Boicot de la Casa Duncan Fox del Callao*. Lima: n.p., [1933].
Lough, William H. "Financial Developments in South American Countries" in U.S., Department of Commerce, Bureau of Foreign and Domestic Commerce, *Special Agents Series-No. 103*. Washington, D.C.: Government Printing Office, 1915.
Manzanilla, José M. *Legislación del Trabajo: Discursos Parlamentarios*. 2nd ed. Lima: Imp. Malatesta Rivas Berrio, n.d.
———. *La Responsabilidad por los Accidentes del Trabajo: Discursos Parlamentarios*. 4th ed. Lima: Imp. Gil, 1939.
Masias, M.G. "Estado actual de la industria minera de Morococha." *BCIMP*, No. 25.
Osma, Felipe de. *Informe que sobre las Huelgas del Norte presenta al gobierno su comisionado*. Lima: Imp. de la Casa Nacional de Moneda, 1912.
Pardo y Barreda, José. *Perú. Cuatro Años de Gobierno Constitucional*. New York: n.p., 1919.
Parra, Herminio M. *Legislación del Trabajo, Leyes, decretos y resoluciones supremas expedidas hasta la fecha: Recopilación*. Ica: Imp. La Industrial, 1923.
Partido Obrero del Perú. *Declaración de Principios del Partido Obrero del Perú*. Lima: Imp. "Artística," 1919.
Rivera, Arturo. *Los sucesos de Talara: Relación verídica e imparcial de los acontecimientos, escrita sobre el terreno*. Piura: Imp. y Tipografía "El Tiempo," n.d.
Velarde, Carlos E. "Reglamentaciones Mineras para el Cerro de Pasco." *BCIMP*, No. 30.

Newspapers (with years consulted)

La Acción (Chincha Alta), 1917.
La Acción Popular (Lima), 1912.

Bibliography

La Actualidad (Lima), 1881.
Agrupación de Artesanos y Obreros (Lima), 1917.
Los Andes (Cerro de Pasco), 1915–1919.
El Artesano (Lima), 1898–1899.
El Artesano (Paita), 1917.
La Bolsa (Arequipa), 1896, 1906–1907.
El Callao (Callao), 1913.
El Comercio (Lima), 1883–1919.
El Comercio (Paita), 1917.
El Correo de Morococha (Morococha), 1916–1917.
La Crónica (Lima), 1912, 1914, 1919.
El Deber (Arequipa), 1917–1919.
El Derecho Obrero (Trujillo), 1917.
El Eco de Junín (Cerro de Pasco), 1918.
El Eco Popular (Chiclayo), 1907.
El Federal (Trujillo), 1917.
Germinal (Lima), 1906.
El Hambriento (Lima), 1905–1909.
El Heraldo (Huacho), 1919.
El Huallaga (Huánuco), 1918.
Humanidad (Lima), 1906.
La Idea Libre (Lima), 1901.
Ilustración Obrera (Lima), 1916–1919.
La Industria (Trujillo), 1912, 1916.
El Jornalero (Trujillo), 1906–1907, 1911–1914.
La Juventud (Monsefú), 1919.
La Linterna (San Vicente de Cañete), 1918.
El Minero (Cerro de Pasco), 1917.
La Nación (Lima), 1914.
El Nacional (Lima), 1886–1889.
El Obrero Peruano (Lima), 1902–1903.
La Opinión Nacional (Lima), 1886–1891.
El Oprimido (Lima), 1907–1908.
El País (Lima), 1895–1896.
Los Parias (Lima), 1904–1907.
Peru To-day (Lima), 1914.
La Prensa (Lima), 1904–1919.
El Progreso (Tumbes), 1919.
La Protesta (Lima), 1911–1919.
El Pueblo (Arequipa), 1906, 1914.
La Razón (Lima), 1919.
La Sanción (Callao), 1916–1917.
El Sindicalista (Lima), 1915.
La Situación (Lima), 1881.
El Socialista (Lima), 1909.
South American Journal, 1890–1915.
El Tiempo (Lima), 1895–1904.
El Tiempo (Lima), 1916, 1919.

Bibliography 199

The Times (London), 1883–1919.
La Unión (Lima), 1913.
La Verdad (Lima), 1916–1918.
La Voz de Junín (Lima), 1914–1917.
La Voz de Vitarte (Vitarte), 1915.
The West Coast Leader (Lima), 1914–1919.

Secondary Sources

Alba, Victor. *Politics and the Labor Movement in Latin America*. Stanford: Stanford University Press, 1968.

Albert, Bill. *An Essay on the Peruvian Sugar Industry 1880–1920 and the Letters of Ronald Gordon, Administrator of the British Sugar Company in Cañete, 1914–1920*. Norwich: University of East Anglia, School of Social Studies, 1976.

Alexander, Robert J. *Organized Labor in Latin America*. New York: The Free Press, 1965.

Arona, Juan de [Pedro Paz Soldan y Unánue]. *La Inmigración en el Perú*. Lima: Academia Diplomática del Perú, 1971.

Arrús, Oscar F. *El Costo de la Vida en Lima y Causas de su Carestía*. Lima: Casa Editora La Opinión Nacional, 1925.

Astiz, Carlos A. *Pressure Groups and Power Elites in Peruvian Politics*. Ithaca: Cornell University Press, 1969.

Barba, Carlos. "Las luchas obreras en 1919." *Rikchay Perú*, No. 2 (Jan. 1971), No. 3 (Feb. 1971), No. 4 (Dec. 1972).

Barcelli S., Agustín. *Historia del Sindicalismo Peruano, Tomo I: 1886–1932*. Lima: Editorial Hatunruna, 1971.

Barrientos Casós, Luis Felipe. *Los tres sindicalismos: sindicalismo proletario, sindicalismo patronal, sindicalismo político*. Lima: Ediciones Continente, 1958.

Basadre, Jorge. *Historia de la República del Perú 1822–1933*. 6th ed. 16 vols. Lima: Editorial Universitaria, 1969–1970.

———. *La Multitud, la Ciudad y el Campo en la Historia del Perú*. 2nd ed. Lima: Editorial Huascarán S.A., 1947.

Basadre, Jorge, and Ferrero, Romulo A. *La Cámara de Comercio de Lima*. Lima: Santiago Valverde, S.A., 1963.

Bertram, I. G. "New thinking on the Peruvian Highland Peasantry." *Pacific Viewpoint* 15 (Sept. 1974): 89–110.

Blanchard, Peter. "Asian Immigrants in Peru, 1899–1923." *North/South: Canadian Journal of Latin American Studies* 4 (1979): 60–75.

———. "A Populist Precursor: Guillermo Billinghurst." *Journal of Latin American Studies* 9 (1977): 251–73.

———. "The Recruitment of Workers in the Peruvian Sierra at the Turn of the Century: The Enganche System." *Inter-American Economic Affairs* 33 (1979): 63–83.

Bonilla, Heraclio. "The War of the Pacific and the National and Colonial Problem in Peru." *Past & Present*, No. 81 (Nov. 1978), pp. 92–118.

Bourricaud, François. *Power and Society in Contemporary Peru*. Translated by Paul Stevenson. London: Faber & Faber, 1970.

Boyer, Richard E., and Davies, Keith H. *Urbanization in 19th Century Latin America: Statistics and Sources*. Los Angeles: Latin American Center, University of California, 1973.

200 Bibliography

Capuñay, Manuel A. *Leguía, Vida y Obra del Constructor del Gran Perú*. Lima: n.p., 1951.

Chaplin, David. *The Peruvian Industrial Labor Force*. Princeton: Princeton University Press, 1967.

Chavarría, Jésus. "La desaparición del Perú colonial (1870–1919)," *Aportes*, No. 23 (Jan. 1972), pp. 120–53.

──────. "The Intellectuals and the Crisis of Modern Peruvian Nationalism: 1870–1919." *Hispanic American Historical Review* 50 (1970): 257–78.

──────. *José Carlos Mariátegui and the Rise of Modern Peru, 1890–1930*. Albuquerque: University of New Mexico Press, 1979.

Cossío del Pomar, Felipe. *Víctor Raúl, Biografía de Haya de la Torre*. México: Editorial Cultura, T.G., S.A., 1961.

Davies, Thomas M., Jr. *Indian Integration in Peru: A Half Century of Experience, 1900–1948*. Lincoln: University of Nebraska Press, 1974.

──────. "Indian Integration in Peru, 1820–1948: An Overview." *The Americas* 30 (1973): 184–208.

DeWind, Adrian. "From Peasants to Miners: The Background to Strikes in the Mines of Peru." *Science and Society* 39 (1975–76): 44–72.

Diaz Ahumada, Joaquín. "Las luchas sindicales en el Valle de Chicama." In *Imperialismo y el agro peruano*, by J. Diaz Ahumada, Manuel Manrique, F. Chevalier. Lima: Publicaciones Universidad Ricardo Palma, n.d.

Dobyns, Henry F., and Doughty, Paul L. *Peru: A Cultural History*. New York: Oxford University Press, 1976.

Enock, C. Reginald. *Peru: Its Former and Present Civilisation, History and Existing Conditions, Topography and Natural Resources, Commerce and General Development*. London: T. Fisher Unwin, 1920.

Favre, Henri. "The Dynamics of Indian Peasant Society and Migration to Coastal Plantations in Central Peru." In *Land and Labour in Latin America: Essays on the Development of Agrarian Capitalism in the Nineteenth and Twentieth Centuries*, edited by Kenneth Duncan and Ian Rutledge. Cambridge: Cambridge University Press, 1977.

Federación Anarquista del Perú. *El Anarcosindicalismo en el Perú*. México: Ediciones tierra y libertad, n.d.

Flores Galindo, Alberto. *Los Mineros de la Cerro de Pasco 1900–1930*. Lima: Pontificia Universidad Católica del Perú, 1974.

Flores Gonzáles, Demetrio. *Medio Siglo de Vida Sindical en Vitarte*. Lima: Imp. EETSA, 1961.

Gardiner, C. Harvey. *The Japanese and Peru 1873–1973*. Albuquerque: University of New Mexico Press, 1975.

Gonzales, Michael J. "Capitalist Agriculture and Labour Contracting in Northern Peru, 1880–1905." *Journal of Latin American Studies* 12 (1980): 291–315.

Hart, John M. *Anarchism and the Mexican Working Class, 1860–1931*. Austin: University of Texas Press, 1978.

Irie, Toraji. "History of Japanese Migration to Peru." Translated by William Himel. *Hispanic American Historical Review* 31 (1951): 437–52, 648–64; 32 (1952): 73–82.

Kapsoli Escudero, Wilfredo. *Luchas Obreras en el Perú por la Jornada de las 8 horas*. Lima: Centro de Estudiantes de Historia de la Facultad de Letras, 1969.

Bibliography 201

Klaiber, Jeffrey L. *Religion and Revolution in Peru, 1824-1976*. Notre Dame: University of Notre Dame Press, 1977.
Klarén, Peter. *Modernization, Dislocation and Aprismo: Origins of the Peruvian Aprista Party, 1870-1932*. Austin: University of Texas Press, 1973.
Lévano, César. "La fuga increible." *Caretas*, no. 498 (Apr. 22–May 2, 1974).
———. "Memorias de una gesta." *Caretas*, no. 434 (Apr. 28–May 13, 1971).
———. "1919: La tempestad obrera." *Caretas*, no. 477 (May 21–June 7, 1973).
———. "Quien era Delfín Lévano?" *Caretas*, no. 395 (May 8–22, 1969).
———. *La Verdadera Historia de la Jornada de las Ocho Horas en el Perú*. Lima: n.p., 1967.
Levin, Jonathan V. *The Export Economies: Their Pattern of Development in Historical Perspective*. Cambridge: Harvard University Press, 1960.
MacLean y Estenos, Roberto. *Sociología del Perú*. México: Instituto de Investigaciones Sociales, 1959.
Marett, Robert. *Peru*. London: Ernest Benn Ltd., 1969.
Martín, José Carlos. *El Gobierno de Don Guillermo E. Billinghurst 1912-1914*. Lima: n.p., 1963.
Martin, Percy F. *Peru of the Twentieth Century*. London: Edward Arnold, 1911.
Martínez de la Torre, Ricardo. *El Movimiento Obrero Peruano 1918-1919*. Lima: Ediciones Cronos, n.d.
Matos Mar, José. *Yanaconaje y Reforma Agraria en el Perú*. Lima: Instituto de Estudios Peruanos, 1976.
Mayer, Dora. *The Conduct of the Cerro de Pasco Mining Company*. Lima: Imp. "El Progreso," 1913.
Miller, Rory. "The Making of the Grace Contract: British Bondholders and the Peruvian Government, 1885-1890." *Journal of Latin American Studies* 8 (1976): 73–100.
———. "Railways and Economic Development in Central Peru, 1890-1930." In *Social and Economic Change in Modern Peru*, edited by Rory Miller, Clifford T. Smith, and John Fisher. Liverpool: Centre for Latin American Studies, n.d.
Miró Quesada, Luis. *Legislación del Trabajo: Tesis para el doctorado en Jurisprudencia*. Lima: n.p., 1905.
Morse, Richard M. "The Lima of Joaquín Capelo: a Latin American Archetype." *Journal of Contemporary History* 4 (1969): 95–110.
Parra V., Pedro. *Bautismo de Fuego del proletariado peruano*. Lima: Editorial Horizante, 1969.
Payne, James L. *Labor and Politics in Peru: The System of Political Bargaining*. New Haven: Yale University Press, 1965.
Pike, Frederick B. *The Modern History of Peru*. London: Weidenfeld & Nicolson, 1967.
Pinelo, Adalberto J. *The Multinational Corporation as a Force in Latin American Politics: A Case Study of the International Petroleum Company in Peru*. New York: Praeger Publishers, 1973.
Podestá, Bruno. *Pensamiento Político de González Prada*. Lima: Instituto Nacional de Cultura, 1975.
Poblete Troncoso, Moisés, and Burnett, Ben G. *The Rise of the Latin American Labor Movement*. New York: Bookman Associates, 1960.
Política Peruana: Hombres i Cosas (Apuntes de Nuestro "Album—Memorial"): La Revolución de 1894-95, Reminiscencias i Revelaciones. Lima: Imp. de "El País," 1901.

202 Bibliography

Purser, W. F. C. *Metal-Mining in Peru, Past and Present*. New York: Praeger Publishers, 1971.

Rippy, J. Fred. "The Dawn of Manufacturing in Peru." *The Pacific Historical Review* 15 (1946): 147–57.

Rouillón D., Guillermo. *La Creación Heroica de José Carlos Mariátegui: La Edad de Piedra*. Lima: Editorial Arica S.A., 1975.

Rowe, L. S. *Early Effects of the War upon the Finance, Commerce and Industry of Peru*. New York: Oxford University Press, 1920.

Sánchez, Luis Alberto. *Don Manuel*. 4th ed. Lima: Populibros Peruanos, n.d.

———. *Nuestras vidas son los ríos . . . (Historia y leyenda de los González Prada)*. Lima: Universidad Nacional Mayor de San Marcos, 1977.

Simon, S. Fanny. "Anarchism and Anarcho-syndicalism in South America." *Hispanic American Historical Review* 26 (1946): 38–59.

Spalding, Hobart A., Jr. *Organized Labor in Latin America*. New York: Harper & Row, 1977.

Stein, Steve. "Maximo Carrasco–Or Working Class Life in Lima, 1900–1930." In *Historia Problema y Promesa: Homenaje a Jorge Basadre*, edited by F. Miró Quesada C., F. Pease G. Y., and D. Sobrevilla A. 2 vols. Lima: Pontificia Universidad Católica del Perú, 1978.

Stewart, Watt. *Chinese Bondage in Peru: A History of the Chinese Coolie in Peru, 1849–1874*. Westport: Greenwood Press, 1970.

Sulmont S., Denis. *Historia del Movimiento Obrero Peruano (1890–1977)*. Lima: Tarea, 1977.

———. *El Movimiento Obrero en el Perú/1900–1956*. Lima: Pontificia Universidad Católica del Perú, 1975.

Thorp, Rosemary, and Bertram, Geoffrey. "Industrialization in an Open Economy: A Case-Study of Peru, 1890–1940." In *Social and Economic Change in Modern Peru*, edited by Miller, Smith and Fisher. Liverpool: Centre for Latin American Studies. n.d.

———. *Peru 1890–1977: Growth and Policy in an Open Economy*. London: The Macmillan Press Ltd., 1978.

Ulloa y Cisneros, Alberto. *Escritos Históricos*. Buenos Aires: Espasa-Calpe Argentina, S.A., 1946.

Ulloa y Sotomayor, Alberto. *Don Nicolás de Piérola: Una Epoca de la Historia del Perú*. Lima: Imp. Santa María, 1949.

———. *La organización social y legal del trabajo en el Perú*. Lima: Tip. de "La Opinión Nacional," 1916.

Vargas Ugarte, Ruben. *Historia General del Perú*. 10 vols. Lima: Editor Carlos Milla Batres, 1971.

Vázquez, Mario C. "Immigration and *mestizaje* in Nineteenth-Century Peru." In *Race and Class in Latin America*, edited by Magnus Mörner. New York: Columbia University Press, 1970.

Villanueva, Víctor. *100 Años del Ejército Peruano: Frustraciones y Cambios*. Lima: Editorial Juan Mejía Baca, 1972.

———. *El Militarismo en el Perú*. Lima: Empresa Gráfica T. Scheuch, 1962.

Yepes del Castillo, Ernesto. *Perú 1820–1920: Un siglo de desarrollo capitalista*. Lima: Campodonicoediciones S.A., 1972.

Bibliography 203

Theses

Blanchard, Peter. "The Peruvian Working Class Movement: 1883–1919." Ph.D. dissertation, University of London, 1975.
Gilbert, Dennis L. "The Oligarchy and the Old Regime in Peru." Ph.D. dissertation, Cornell University, 1977.
Pareja Pflücker, Piedad. " 'La Protesta' 1911–1926: Contribución al Estudio del Anarquismo en el Perú." B.A. thesis, Pontificia Universidad Católica del Perú, 1973.
Worral, J. E. "Italian Immigration to Peru: 1860–1914." Ph.D. dissertation, Indiana University, 1972.

Interviews

Dr. Jorge Basadre, Lima, Aug. 1, 1973.
Ronald Gordon, Lima, July 31, 1973.
Víctor Raúl Haya de la Torre, Lima, Feb. 9, June 14, 1973.

Index

Aduvire, Manuel, 30
Aguila foundry, 55, 91
Aliaga, Florencio, 56–57, 60, 62, 70
Alianza Popular Revolucionaria Americana (APRA), xvi, 169, 170, 171, 192nn15,17
Anarchism, 47–64 *passim;* anarchosyndicalism, 47; attraction, 49–54 *passim*, 58; and strikes, 53–54; basis among immigrants, 54, 180n10; and striking workers, 55–57, 60, 65, 69, 79, 81–82, 89, 94, 116, 131, 133–34, 142, 151–54; and death of Florencio Aliaga, 56–57; and May Day celebrations, 57–58, 60; and political parties, 59, 163; and eight-hour day, 61, 89, 150–54, 158; and authorities, 61–62, 102, 114–15, 133, 167; decline, 62–63, 114–15; and socialists, 63, 163; recovery, 63–64, 119; and Billinghurst, 91, 93–94; and Asians, 109; during First World War, 113–15; and plantation workers, 127, 130, 131, 133–35; and petroleum workers, 142, 146; and leadership of the labor movement, 159; and May 1919 general strike, 161–69; mentioned, 33, 66, 76, 105, 132
Anarchist organizations: resistance societies, 58, 130, 140; syndicates, 113–14, 119, 132, 140. *See also* Comité Pro-Abaratamiento de las Subsistencias; "Estrella del Perú"; Federación Obrera Regional del Perú
Andahuasi estate, 134
Antuñano, Daniel, 114
Arenas, Edgardo, 131, 132, 134
Arenas, Germán, 71–72

Arequipa, xvi, 11, 13, 54, 58, 60, 95, 97, 180n14
Argentina, xvii, 24, 58, 170, 192n14
Arica, 31, 84, 85, 100, 112
Artesanos Billinghurst No. 1, 86
Artisans: numbers, 12; riots, 21, 22; and González Prada, 47–49; and anarchism, 49; mentioned, 8, 11, 15, 17, 18, 19, 25, 28, 30, 31, 33, 35, 42, 73, 113, 178n11. *See also* Asamblea de Sociedades Unidas; Confederación de Artesanos "Unión Universal"; Mutual aid societies
Asamblea de Sociedades Unidas: formation, 34–36; and Confederación de Artesanos "Unión Universal," 35–36, 43–46, 86, 110; and national workers congress, 35, 110; conservatism, 35; and law of professional risk, 38–39; involvement in politics, 43–46, 86, 110–11; and eight-hour day, 61; involvement in strikes, 69, 72, 78, 81; and textile workers, 78; and 1914 coup, 100; and Chicama Valley strikes, 129; and plantation workers, 135; and Sociedad Pro-Indígena, 138; and petroleum workers, 144; and May 1919 general strike, 165; attacked, 168, 169; survival, 169; mentioned, 57, 82, 154
Asamblea de Solidaridad Obrera, 105
Asians: hostility toward, 32, 34, 36, 80, 109, 124–25, 165, 166; immigration, 49, 51; workers, 124–25, 126. *See also* Chinese; Japanese
Aspíllaga, Antero: and 1912 election, 85–88; and 1919 election, 162, 164, 168
Austria-Hungary, 158

205

206 Index

Backus and Johnston brewery, 106
Backus and Johnston Mining Company, 136, 139, 140
Bakery workers, Callao, 73, 117
—Huacho, 151
—Lima: agitation, 23, 72–73, 76, 81, 114, 117, 118, 151–54; mentioned, 56, 157
Bakery workers organizations: Sociedad "Estrella del Perú," 21, 58–59, 72–73, 76; Federación de Obreros Panaderos "Estrella del Perú," 59, 63, 64, 69
Balbuena, Girardo, 110
Ballesteros, Samuel, 69
Barba, Carlos: and shoemakers, 113; arrested, 114, 164, 167; and Comité Pro-Abaratamiento de las Subsistencias, 114, 161; and Partido Socialista del Perú, 163; mentioned, 109, 132, 162, 168
Benavides, Oscar: and 1914 coup, 98; as provisional president, 99; and First World War, 103–04; and workers, 105, 116
Bernales, José Carlos, 145, 162, 166, 167
Billinghurst, Guillermo E.: background, 84–85; and Civilistas, 84–85; relationship with Piérola, 85; as mayor of Lima, 85; intervention in strikes, 85, 88–91, 96–97, 139; election, 86–88; as president, 88–98; and eight-hour day, 89–90; strike decree, 90–91, 103, 116, 139; working class support, 91–92, 94–95, 97; and Comité de Salud Pública, 95, 97; opposition to, 95–98; budget, 96–97, 99, 185n39; overthrown, 98–100; death, 101; mentioned, 83, 105, 106, 107, 108, 110, 149, 168, 170
Black workers, 125
Bolívar, Manuel, 18, 30
Bolshevism. See Communism
Brent, H. M., 17
Brewery workers, 90, 96, 106
Bricklayers, 113–14
Briggs, José, 62
British Sugar Company, 156

Buenos Aires, 62, 69, 149, 152, 153, 157, 158
Bueno y de la Fuente, Bruno, 153

Cáceres, Andrés A.: during War of the Pacific, 16; as president, 21, 22; coup and reelection, 27; overthrown, 28, 29, 30; and strikers, 55; mentioned, 5, 43, 177n1
Cáceres, Fidel P., 43–44, 61
Cahuas, José, 111, 162
Calderón, Serapio, 37
Canada, 39, 144
Candamo, Manuel, 55
Cañete Valley, 56, 124, 125, 127, 130, 133, 134, 135, 156, 188n7
Capelo, Joaquín: and indemnities law, 36; and Sociedad Pro-Indígena, 137; mentioned, 8, 10, 12
Carabayllo Valley, 114
Cartavio estate, 128, 155, 175n9
Carthy Caballero, Santiago, 79
Casa Blanca estate, 125, 127
Casabona, Manuel, 151
Casa del Obrero (Mexico), 183n11
"Casa del Pueblo," 169
Casa Grande estate, 128–29, 133
Casapalca, 136, 139, 152
Castañeda, Luis B., 44–45, 79, 80, 86, 93, 105, 184n19
Castilla, Ramón, 3
Castillo, Gustavo, 81, 82
Caudivilla estate, 22
Cayaltí estate, 129, 130, 132, 134, 156
Censuses, 11–12
Central Railway, 13, 25–26, 55, 66–67, 69, 90, 118, 161, 191n63. See also Guadalupe foundry; William Morkill
Centro de Estudios Sociales Primero de Mayo, 58
Centro Internacional Obrero de Solidaridad Latino-Americana del Perú: formation, 92; and May Day celebrations, 111; divisions, 111–12; hostility to Chile, 112
Centro Nacional de Obreros, 31
Centro Obrero Guillermo Billinghurst, 86

Index   207

Centro Socialista Primero de Mayo, 58
Cerro Azul, 156
Cerro de Pasco, 22, 39, 40, 135–41
Cerro de Pasco Mining Corporation, 40, 135, 136
Cerro de Pasco railway, 138
César, Julio, 18, 19, 30
Chamber of Commerce of Lima, 49
Chamber of Deputies: and workers' deputy, 30, 31, 33, 42–45, 59, 80, 93; and law of professional risk, 36–39, 60; mentioned, 4, 29, 184n19
Chicago General Strike of 1886, 57, 61
Chicama Valley, 124, 128–29, 133, 138, 139
Chiclayo, 58, 132
Children: law regulating labor, 32, 36, 149–50; in mining region, 125, 137; on plantations, 135
Chile: war with, 4, 5, 16, 21, 126; mentioned, xvii, 51, 58, 70, 84, 85, 92, 94, 96, 99, 100, 101, 111, 112, 154, 156, 166
Chinese: hostility toward, 22, 80, 125; coolies, 123, 124–25; mentioned, 85, 126
Chiquitoy estate, 128
Chosica, 66
Chota, 121
Church: and workers, 15; and mutual aid societies, 18
Cigarette factories: Cohen, 21, 23; Roldán, 23–24; Juan Duany, 23, 24; Oliva Hermanos, 23, 24
Cigarette industry: agitation, 21, 23–24; composition, 23; mechanization, 24–25, 33
Círculo de Obreros Católicos, 18
Círculo Literario, 48
Ciurlizza y Maurer sawmill, 79, 106, 151
Civilista party: formation, 4; return to power, 42–44; and workers' deputy, 41, 45, 46; and mutual aid societies, 46; and Billinghurst, 85, 86; and 1914 coup, 99, 102; and 1919 election, 162, 164, 168; mentioned, 10, 28, 37, 38, 48, 132, 148

Club Artesanos, 177n1
Club de Artesanos y Obreros Unidos, 30, 41, 43
Club "Motoristas y Conductores," 87
Coastal plantations, 126–35: workers, xvi, 13, 120–35, 156, 165; owners, 3, 10, 109, 132, 134; and Asians, 109, 123–25, 126–27; and *enganche*, 121–23; and *yanaconaje*, 123
Cohen factory. *See* Cigarette factories
Comité de Defensa Obrera, 105
Comité de Salud Pública, 95, 97
Comité Pro-Abaratamiento de las Subsistencias, Callao, 161, 164
—Cerro de Pasco, 141
—Lima: formed, 114–15; reappearance, 161; and anarchists, 161–62; and government, 161–62; and Partido Obrero del Perú, 162–63; and Partido Socialista del Perú, 163; support for strikers, 164; and May 1919 general strike, 164–68
Comité Pro-Paro General, 151
Communism: Partido Comunista Peruano, xvi, 169; bolshevism, 153, 167; maximalism, 161, 163; mentioned 77, 158
Confederación de Artesanos del Callao, 38
Confederación de Artesanos "Unión Universal": formation, 18; organization, 18–19; conservatism, 19; and bakery workers, 21, 59; and strikers, 23–24, 69, 70, 79 145, 146; apoliticism, 29, 30; and Vidaurre, 31, 33–34, 42; and Piérola, 33–34, 46; and *El Artesano*, 34, 42; and Asians, 34, 109; and Asamblea de Sociedades Unidas, 35–36, 43–46, 86, 110; and law of professional risk, 38, 109; political activities, 41–46, 86, 93, 110; and Civilistas, 46; and González Prada, 48; and Billinghurst, 97; and 1914 coup, 100; during First World War, 108-10; and women workers, 149; and eight-hour day, 153, 156; and May 1919 general strike, 165; attack upon, 168, 169; mentioned, 28, 54, 57, 92, 111, 179n33

208 Index

Confederación Departamental Obrera de Junín, 140
Confederación de Trabajadores del Perú, 169
Confederación General de Trabajadores del Perú (formed 1913), 93; and José Pardo, 107; political activity, 110; mentioned 108
Confederación General de Trabajadores del Perú (formed 1929), 171
Congress, 5, 30, 38, 88, 92, 95, 96, 97, 98, 99, 106, 108, 115, 149, 150, 153, 168
Constitutional party, 5, 43
Cooperatives, workers', 106
Cox foundry, 55
Cuzco, xvi, 11, 13, 97

Democratic party: attraction to workers, 4, 29, 48; and Vidaurre, 31, 41, 46; declining power, 42–43; loss of worker support, 44; and Billinghurst, 85, 98; mentioned, 27, 30, 179*n35*
Dock workers. *See* Harbor workers
Duncan Fox and Company: boycott of, 94, 96, 143; mentioned, 10
Durand, Augusto: and Liberal party, 4; and 1914 coup, 97, 99

Economy: exports, 3, 5, 6, 7, 104, 136; industrialization, 5, 7–9, 16, 25; investment, 7, 8, 170, 171; banking, 7, 16, 103; and War of the Pacific, 16–17; monetary depreciation, 17, 21, 22, 103, 105; cost of living, 21, 34, 49, 50, 103, 104, 105, 148, 160; 1908 trade depression, 49, 66, 72, 80; and First World War, 103–04
Ecuador, 19, 51
Eight-hour day: and anarchists, 61; and Asamblea de Sociedades Unidas, 61; strikes for, 89–91, 150–56; and mine workers, 139, 140; and petroleum workers, 143; and women workers, 150; decree granting, 154–55; avoidance of decree, 156–57; mentioned, 32, 112, 158, 159, 160, 161, 163, 172
El Artesano, 34, 42

El Comercio, 23, 55, 153
Elguera, Federico, 44–45
El Hambriento, 62
El Inca textile mill. *See* Textile mills
El Jornalero, 127–28, 129
El Minero Ilustrado, 40
El Oprimido, 58
El Pacífico woolen mill. *See* Textile mills
El Progreso textile mill. *See* Textile mills
El Sindicalista, 113
El Sol match factory, 91, 108
El Tiempo, 154
Empleados de Comercio, 58
Empresas Eléctricas Asociadas, 88, 164
Enganchado, 120–23, 125, 132, 135
Enganchador, 121–23, 128, 129, 133, 139
Enganche: system, 120–23; abuses, 122; government concern, 122–23; worker satisfaction, 123; mentioned, 126, 134–35, 137, 138
England, 183*n5*
Espinoza, Ramón, 178*n16*
"Estrella del Perú." *See* Bakery workers organizations
Eten, 156

Falcón, César, 163
Faustino, Piaggio, 142
Federación de Estudiantes del Perú; and 1919 strike for eight-hour day, 153–54
Federación de Obreros Panaderos "Estrella del Perú." *See* Bakery workers organizations
Federación de Trabajadores en Tejidos del Perú. *See* Textile workers organizations
Federación Obrera Local de Lima, 191*n10*
Federación Obrera Maritima y Terrestre del Callao, 94, 96, 97, 192*n12*
Federación Obrera Regional Argentina, 89
Federación Obrera Regional del Perú: formation, 64, 93–94; and Duncan Fox boycott, 94, 143; decline, 114; reappearance, 158, 169
Fernández Martínez, Arturo, 44
First World War: and urban workers, 102–19; initial economic effects, 103–

04, 139; and plantation workers, 130–35; and mine workers, 139–41; and petroleum workers, 143–46; mentioned, 5, 101, 149, 158, 171, 183n5
Fonkén, Adalberto, 116, 135, 167, 168

Gacitúa, Ismael, 54
García Calderón, Francisco: and mechanization of cigarette industry, 24–25
General strikes. *See* Strikes
George V of Great Britain, 151
Germany, 108, 128, 129, 158
Giraldo, Santiago, 73
Goachet, Juan, 93, 178n16
Gomez, Manuel, 18
González, Justo, 178n11
González Prada, Manuel: attack on artisans, 47–49; background 48; view of anarchism, 53; and *Los Parias*, 55; and May Day 1905, 57; opposition to political parties, 59; and eight-hour day, 61; leadership qualities, 62–63; death, 119; and Indians, 137
Gordon, Ronald, 132–33
Goyllarisquizga, 39, 136, 140–41
Graham Rowe and Company, 10
Gremio de Fideleros y Molineros, 58
Gremio Liberal de Empleados, 64, 93, 119
Grieve, Juan, 18
Grillo, Luis F., 83
Grupo de Luchadores por la Verdad, 64
Guadalupe foundry, 26, 55, 67, 91, 96
Guano industry, 3, 4, 8, 16
Guevara, José M., 32
Guilds, 15, 18, 19, 20, 24, 29, 30, 31, 58, 59, 73, 109, 129, 156, 161, 177n1
Gustinelli, Antonio, 89
Gutarra, Nicolás: and Asians, 109; and strikes for eight-hour day, 151, 192n15; arrested, 154, 164, 167; and Comité Pro-Abaratemiento de las Subsistencias, 161; and Partido Obrero del Perú, 162–63; released, 168; mentioned, 162
Gutierrez, Félix, 30

Harbor workers, Callao: agitation, 26–27, 55–56, 69–72, 89–90, 96–97, 117–18,

161; register, 26, 27, 56, 69, 70, 71, 72, 89; and eight-hour day, 61, 89–90; as strikebreakers, 72; and Duncan Fox boycott, 94, 143; boycott of Chilean ships, 112. *See also* Federación Obrera Maritima y Terrestre del Callao
—Cerro Azul, 156
—Eten, 156
—Huacho, 131
—Pisco, 156
Haya de la Torre, Víctor Raúl: and strike for eight-hour day, 153, 192nn15,17; and Federación de Trabajadores en Tejidos del Perú, 158; and workers, 171; mentioned, xvi
Herrera y Vera, Víctor: and injured workers, 109, 136; and workers' march, 116; view of mining workers, 140; and Partido Obrero del Perú, 162; mentioned, 192n13
Huacho: "massacre," 114, 134, 158; agitation, 126, 131, 132, 134, 151, 155, 165; anarchists in, 131
Huampaní estate, 125
Huancavelica, 188n7
Huancayo, 13, 165
Huaura Valley, 131–32, 133–34
Humanidad, 58

Ica, 22, 95
Iglesias, Miguel, 16
Immigrants: and anarchism, 54, 180n10. *See also* Asians; Chinese; Japanese
Indians, xv, 17, 78, 120–23, 129, 137–38, 140, 188n7
International Petroleum Company, 142, 144
International Workers of the World, 119
Iquique: 1907 strike, 51, 62, 71, 85; mentioned, 71, 85
Iquitos, 34
Italy, 54

Japanese: textile workers, 78; contract laborers, 123–27, 134, 156; hostility toward, 124–25; women, 124, 125; agitation, 125–27, 130; mutual aid societies, 125; refusal to strike, 132, 133

210 Index

Jauja, 165
Juan Duany factory. *See* Cigarette factories
Juarés, Juan, 102
Junín, 137, 140

Kosmos Shipping Company, 72

La Acción Popular, 93
La Bellota textile mill. *See* Textile mills
Labor Sections, 90, 91
La Brea y Pariñas. *See* Negritos
La Estrella estate, 93, 130
La Estrella soap factory, 91
Lagunitas, 142, 143, 145
Lagunitas Oil Company, 142
La Idea Libre, 73, 180n10
La Libertad, 121, 130
La Luciernaga match factory, 51
Lambayeque, 121, 134
La Oroya, 13
La Prensa: and 1911 general strike, 83; and Billinghurst, 88, 97, 98; and injured workers, 107; and cost of living, 118; and eight-hour day, 158; mentioned, 5
La Protesta, 64, 102, 114, 115, 154
"La Protesta" study group, 93, 191n8
La Providencia textile mill. *See* Textile mills
Laredo, 22
Laredo estate, 128, 155
La Rosa, Horacio, 30, 162
La Unión textile mill. *See* Textile mills
La Verdad, 110
La Victoria textile mill. *See* Textile mills
Law of professional risk: passage, 36–39; contents, 39; implementation, 40; limitations, 40, 106; anarchist view, 60; amendment, 106–07, 109; mentioned, 32–33, 44, 45, 46, 63, 88, 92, 136, 139
Leguía, Augusto: dictatorship, xvi, 171; and law of professional risk, 38–40; aliens law, 62, 115; and 1911 general strike, 81–82; and 1912 election, 85–88; Leguiísta party, 85, 88, 96; deportation, 95; and 1919 election, 162, 164;
coup, 168; populism, 170; mentioned, 72, 183n5
Lévano, Delfín: and "Estrella del Perú," 58, 63; and *La Protesta,* 64, 154; arrested, 114, 132, 154; and Comité Pro-Abaratamiento de las Subsistencias, 167–68; mentioned, 113, 135
Lévano, Manuel Caracciolo: anarchism, 54; and May Day, 57, 86; and mutual aid societies, 57–58; and "Estrella del Perú," 58, 63; opposition to political parties, 59; and law of professional risk, 60; mentioned, 56, 181n23
Liberal party, 4–5, 97, 99, 100, 179n33
Lince estate, 127
Lobitos, 142–46
Lobitos Oilfields Limited, 142
London and Pacific Petroleum Company, 94, 142
Lora y Quiñones, Carlos: and law of professional risk, 38–39; and 1907 election, 44–45; mentioned, 93
Los Parias, 55, 56, 61
"Luz y Amor," 64, 93

Malpartida, Pedro, 79
Manzanilla, José Matías: labor projects, 37, 107, 149, 179n19; and law of professional risk, 37–38, 40, 60; election, 43–44
Mariátegui, José Carlos, 163, 171
Martín, Cirilo: arrested, 62; and Socialist party, 63, 182n12
Marxism, 54, 171
Maximalism. *See* Communism
May Day celebrations, 57–58, 60, 86, 102, 111, 131, 140, 163, 180n16
Mayer, Dora, 137, 138
Mazzi, Manuel, 82
Merel, Héctor, 151
Mexico, xvii, 102, 122, 177n33, 181n1, 183n11, 185n40
Military: and 1914 coup, 98–100; 1918 revolt, 107–08; mentioned 3, 4, 5, 15, 28, 29, 102, 162
Mining industry, 135–42; agitation, 22, 138–41, 152, 154; accidents, 39, 40,

136, 138, 140; *enganche* in, 120, 121, 135, 137–38; working conditions, 136; living conditions, 136–37, 138, 141; wages, 137; mentioned, 10
Miró Quesada, Antonio: and law of professional risk, 37; and May 1919 general strike, 166, 167
Miró Quesada, Luis, 37, 110–11
Mollendo, 13, 58
Montes, Alberto J., 111, 162
Montoya, Rafael, 114
Morales Bermúdez, Remigio, 26, 27, 48, 177*nl*
Morkill, William, 67, 69, 102, 155
Morococha, 136–40, 154
Morococha Mining Company, 107, 136, 139, 140
Mosquito, 95
Muelle y Dársena Companía, 25, 106
Mutual aid societies: formation, 15–16; benefits, 16; expansion, 16–18, 34; officials' view, 19–20; political activities, 29, 41–46, 92–93, 109–11; and anarchists, 59, 60; and eight-hour day, 61, 112; and strikes, 65; and Billinghurst, 92; during First World War, 106, 108–12; financial difficulties, 111; internal divisions, 112; and rural workers, 135, 138; in Talara, 143–45; and women workers, 149; and 1919 general strikes, 153, 166; decline, 169; mentioned, 22, 28, 64, 168

Nalvarte, Fausto, 151
National Labor party, 110
Negritos (La Brea y Pariñas), 142–46
Nitrate industry, 4, 5, 16

Odría, Manuel, 170
Oliva Hermanos factory. *See* Cigarette factories
Osma y Pardo, Felipe de, 129
Otazú, Eulogio, 64, 94
Otero mill, 118

Pacific Steam Navigation Company, 71, 72

Paita, 144, 145
Panama, 95
Panama Star & Herald, 21
Paramonga estate, 126, 132, 134
Pardo, Manuel, 4, 29
Pardo family, 8, 10, 156
Pardo y Barreda, José: and Confederación de Artesanos "Unión Universal," 34; sympathy for workers, 37, 157; and law of professional risk, 38; and strikes, 66, 70, 71; reelection, 104; and workers during First World War, 105–08, 110, 117, 143, 147; and Asians, 109; and anarchists, 115; labor legislation, 148–49; decree for eight-hour day, 154–55, 157–58, 161; and May 1919 general strike, 165, 167; overthrown, 168; mentioned, 179*n35*
Pardo y Barreda, Luis, 79, 80
Partido Comunista Peruano. *See* Communism
Partido Obrero del Perú, 162–63
Partido Obrero Independiente, 43, 44
Partido Socialista del Perú. *See* Socialism
Partido Socialista Peruano. *See* Socialism
Peña Costa, José María, 8
Perón, Juan Domingo, 170
Peruvian Corporation, 7, 25, 26, 67, 96, 155
Peruvian Cotton Manufacturing Company, 77
Peruvian Steamship Company, 91
Petroleum industry: agitation, 94, 142–46, 152; wages, 143, 146; mentioned, 10, 120
Piérola, Nicolás de: and workers, 4, 29, 30, 31, 33, 34, 44; and 1895 revolution, 27–28; and socialism, 34; and 1896 Vitarte strike, 77; and Billinghurst, 85; mentioned, 42, 48, 54
Pisco, 156
Plantation workers. *See* Coastal plantations
Polan, J. J., 144, 145
Populism, 84, 169–70, 185*n40*
Portocarrero, Julio, 151
Prado family, 10

212 Index

Prado y Ugarteche, Jorge, 110–11, 117
Prado y Ugarteche, Mariano Ignacio: and law of professional risk, 37–38; election 43–44; mentioned, 8
Pujazón, Víctor A., 92, 111
Puno, 13

Quesada, Valentín, 153

Railways, 3, 14, 155–56, 157. *See also* Central Railway; Cerro de Pasco railway; Southern Railway
Refugees, 51, 71, 95, 112, 156
Rent strikes. *See* Strikes
Reynaga, Julio, 129
Rios Castell, Luis, 79
Riots: Lima, 21, 22, 80; Trujillo, 22; Laredo, 22; Cerro de Pasco, 22, 138; Negritos, 142
Riva-Agüero, Enrique de la, 111
Rivadeneyra, Carlos, 114
Robles, José, 97, 162, 192*n12*
Roldán factory. *See* Cigarette factories
Romaña, Eduardo López de: and law of professional risk, 36–37; split with Piérola, 42; and strikers, 70; mentioned, 85
Romero, Leonidas, 30
Rural workers, 13, 120–47. *See also* Coastal plantations; Mining industry; Petroleum industry
Russian Revolution, 158, 161

Salaverry, 155
Salcedo, Pantaleón, 56
Sama Valley, 126
Sánchez, José Ramón, 30
San Jacinto estate, 125, 127
San Jacinto textile mill. *See* Textile mills
San Nicolás estate, 126, 132
Santa Catalina barracks, 78, 185*n40*
Santa Catalina Valley, 128
Santa Catalina woolen mill. *See* Textile mills
Santa Clara cloth factory, 17
Santa Clara estate, 125, 161
Santa Rosa flour mill, 55, 96, 117
Santiago (Chile), 94, 111

Sausal estate, 128, 133
Secada, Alberto, 163
Senate: and law of professional risk, 38–39; mentioned, 4, 33, 95, 145, 162
Seoane, Guillermo A., 132
Serranos, 121, 122, 124
Shoemakers: syndicates, 113–14; agitation, 113, 161
Sindicato de Obreros Zapateros y Anexos, 113
Sindicato de Oficios Varios, 131
Smelter, 136, 140, 141
Socialism: socialist party of Cirilo Martín, 63, 182*n12*; Partido Socialista del Perú, 163, 166; Partido Socialista Peruano, 169, 171; mentioned, 4, 33, 34, 61, 77, 86, 112
Social structure, 8–11 *passim*
Sociedad Artesanos de Auxilios Mutuos, 15, 176*n9*
Sociedad Artesanos y Braceros Valle de Chicama, 129
Sociedad de Artesanos de la "Unión Universal," 18. *See also* Confederación de Artesanos "Unión Universal"
Sociedad Democrática del Callao, 15
Sociedad de Resistencia de Oficios Varios, 114
Sociedad "Estrella del Perú." *See* Bakery workers organizations
Sociedad Filantrópica Democrática, 176*n2*
Sociedad Fraternal de San José, 176*n2*
Sociedad Labor Feminista, 149
Sociedad Nacional Agraria, 132
Sociedad Peruana de Socorros Mutuos, 85
Sociedad "Progreso Feminista," 149
Sociedad Pro-Indígena, 137–38, 167
Sociedad Republicana de la "Unión Universal" de Artesanos, 18. *See also* Confederación de Artesanos "Unión Universal"
Southern Railway, 13, 40, 180*n14*
Spain, 48, 54
Spagnoli, José, 89
Standard Oil of New Jersey, 142
Strikes: Lima, 21–22, 23–24, 72–83, 88–89, 90, 91, 114, 115–18, 161, 164; Callao, 21, 25–27, 55–56, 66–72,

Index   213

89–91, 96–97, 117–18, 129, 161; plantation workers, 22, 125–34, 156; mine workers, 22, 138–41, 152, 154; changing demands, 65; petroleum workers, 94, 142–46, 152; rent strikes, 105; Japanese, 125, 126–27, 130; Huacho, 131, 134, 151, 155; for eight-hour day, 1919, 150–59; Trujillo, 155–56; May 1919, 164–68; Arequipa, 180n14
Strikes, general: proposal, 79; Lima 1911, 81–83; May 1912, 87; October 1912, 88–89; Callao 1913, 96–97; January 1919, 150–59; May 1919, 165–68
Sugar industry, 3, 16, 126, 131
Supe Valley, 126, 132
Supreme Court, 20, 36, 95, 107, 164, 168
Syndicalism, 64, 119, 132. See also Anarchism

Tacna, 31, 85, 100, 112
Tailors, 113–14
Talara, 142–46
Tarapacá, 4, 16, 84, 95
Tarma, 58
Tassara, Glicerio, 53
Telegraph operators, 25–26, 117
Textile industry: conditions, 51, 77, 78, 79; agitation, 76–83, 88–91, 115–18, 150–54, 164; and outbreak of First World War, 115; and law regulating women workers, 150; mentioned, 8, 10, 12, 93
Textile mills: Vitarte, 8, 51, 64, 77–83, 115–19, 151, 152, 161, 175n9, 191n8; San Jacinto, 8, 51, 79, 80, 117, 161; La Victoria, 8, 10, 51, 78, 79, 106, 117; El Progreso, 8, 78–80, 83, 157; La Providencia (El Inca), 8, 44, 78, 80, 91, 115–17, 150; La Bellota, 8, 157; La Unión, 8, 164; Santa Catalina, 8, 51, 64, 78, 88–89, 164; El Pacífico, 8
Textile workers organizations: Unión Obreros de Tejidos "33 Amigos," 58, 78–79; Unificación Proletaria Textil de Santa Catalina, 64, 82; Unificación Obrera Textil de Vitarte, 64, 82, 116–17; Federación de Trabajadores en Tejidos del Perú, 158

Ticapampa, 141
Toronto, 144, 145
Tram workers, 55, 117, 155
Treaty of Ancón, xv, 4
Trujillo, xvi, 11, 22, 57, 58, 97, 126, 127, 129, 133, 146, 155–56
Tumán estate, 10, 156
Typographical workers, 20

Ulloa, Luis, 163
Ulloa y Cisneros, Alberto, 184nn32,37
Unemployment, 17, 20, 21, 49, 80, 103, 106, 108, 144
Unificación Obrera Textil de Vitarte. See Textile workers organizations
Unificación Proletaria Textil de Santa Catalina. See Textile workers organizations
Unión Cívica, 41
Unión Jornaleros, 58, 69, 72
Unión Obreros de Tejidos "33 Amigos." See Textile workers organizations
Unión Nacional, 48
United States: 1905 recession, 8, 49; mentioned, 58, 102
University students, 153, 154, 162
Urmachea, Leopoldo; and death of Aliaga, 56–57; and "Estrella del Perú," 58, 63

Valcarcel, Manuel J., 18, 41, 178n11
Valparaíso, 94, 186n22
Valasco Alvarado, Juan, 170
Vera, Fernando, 97, 100, 162, 192n12
Vidaurre, Rosendo: nomination, 30; background, 31; election, 31, 40; as workers' deputy, 31–34; and provincial workers congress, 31–32; and law of professional risk, 32, 36; and Confederación de Artesanos "Unión Universal," 33–34, 46; conservatism, 33, 44; reelection, 41–42; opposition to, 42–43, 59; defeat, 43–44; and González Prada, 48–49; and Vitarte strike, 77
Vilela, Andrés, 116
Vitarte, 77
Vitarte textile mill. See Textile mills

214 Index

War of the Pacific: and formation of mutual aid societies, 15; effects on Peru, 16–17, 126; mentioned, xv, xvi, 4, 10, 48, 84, 123
The West Coast Leader, 98, 165, 166
White foundry, 91
Wilson, Woodrow, 112
Wolls, Pedro, 31
Women workers: and War of the Pacific, 17; in textile industry, 78, 117, 149–50; as strikebreakers, 114; on coastal plantations, 124, 125, 135; described, 149; organizations, 149; law regulating labor, 149–50; and Comité Pro-Abaratamiento de las Subsistencias, 164
Workers congresses, 31–32, 35, 36, 73, 110

W. R. Grace and Company, 10, 72, 77, 96

Yanacona, 123, 131
Yanaconaje, 123
Yauli, 136

Zevallos Agüero, Carlos, 62
Zorritos, 142, 143, 152
Zubiaga, Adrian: and 1899 election, 41–42; and Partido Obrero Independiente, 43; and 1907 election, 44–45; and Partido Obrero del Perú, 162; mentioned, 18, 79
Zubiaga, Juan Antonio, 15, 176n9
Zulen, Pedro, 137, 167

PITT LATIN AMERICAN SERIES

Cole Blasier, Editor

Argentina in the Twentieth Century
David Rock, Editor

Army Politics in Cuba, 1898–1958
Louis A. Pérez, Jr.

Authoritarianism and Corporatism in Latin America
James M. Malloy, Editor

Barrios in Arms: Revolution in Santo Domingo
José A. Moreno

Beyond the Revolution: Bolivia Since 1952
James M. Malloy and Richard S. Thorn, Editors

Constructive Change in Latin America
Cole Blasier, Editor

Cuba, Castro, and the United States
Philip W. Bonsal

Cuba in the World
Cole Blasier and Carmelo Mesa-Lago, Editors

Essays on Mexican Kinship
Hugh G. Nutini, Pedro Carrasco, and James M. Taggart, Editors

Female and Male in Latin America: Essays
Ann Pescatello, Editor

Gaitán of Colombia: A Political Biography
Richard E. Sharpless

The Hovering Giant: U.S. Responses to Revolutionary Change in Latin America
Cole Blasier

Illusions of Conflict: Anglo-American Diplomacy Toward Latin America, 1865–1896
Joseph Smith

Intervention, Revolution, and Politics in Cuba, 1913–1921
Louis A. Pérez, Jr.

The Origins of the Peruvian Labor Movement, 1883–1919
Peter Blanchard

The Overthrow of Allende and the Politics of Chile, 1964–1976
Paul E. Sigmund

Panajachel: A Guatemalan Town in Thirty-Year Perspective
Robert E. Hinshaw

The Politics of Mexican Oil
George W. Grayson

The Politics of Social Security in Brazil
James M. Malloy

Puerto Rico and the United States, 1917–1933
Truman R. Clark

Revolutionary Change in Cuba
Carmelo Mesa-Lago, Editor

Selected Latin American One-Act Plays
Francesca Colecchia and Julio Matas, Editors and Translators

Social Security in Latin America: Pressure Groups, Stratification, and Inequality
Carmelo Mesa-Lago

The United States and Cuba: Hegemony and Dependent Development, 1880–1934
Jules Robert Benjamin

Urban Politics in Brazil: The Rise of Populism, 1925–1945
Michael L. Conniff

DATE DUE

MAR 1 3 1991